D0897908

Cornelius
VAN TIL

AMERICAN REFORMED BIOGRAPHIES

D. G. HART AND SEAN MICHAEL LUCAS
Series Editors

Robert Lewis Dabney: A Southern Presbyterian Life
John Williamson Nevin: High Church Calvinist
Cornelius Van Til: Reformed Apologist and Churchman

Cornelius
VAN TIL
Reformed Apologist and Churchman

JOHN R. MUETHER

P U B L I S H I N G
P.O. BOX 817 • PHILLIPSBURG • NEW JERSEY 08865-0817

Page design by Lakeside Design Plus

Printed in the United States of America

Library of Congress Cataloging-in-Publication Data

Muether, John R.
  Cornelius Van Til : Reformed apologist and churchman / John R. Muether.
      p. cm. — (American Reformed biographies)
  Includes bibliographical references and index.
  ISBN-13: 978-0-87552-665-2 (cloth)
  1. Van Til, Cornelius, 1895– 2. Theologians—United States—Biography. I. Title.
  BX9225.V37M84 2008
  230'.51092—dc22
                                                                        2007018475

To Kathy

Steadfast, Unmovable, and Abounding

Contents

Series Preface   9
Acknowledgments   11
Introduction: Apologist and Churchman   15

1. A Child of the *Afscheiding*   21
2. "Fit Modesty and Unreserved Conviction"   41
3. From Dutch Reformed to American Presbyterian   65
4. Reformed or Evangelical?   91
5. The New Machen against the New Modernism   119
6. Through the Fires of Criticism   149
7. Presbyterian Patriarch   179
8. Steadfast, Unmovable, and Abounding   207

Conclusion: Against the World, for the Church   229
Notes   241
Bibliographic Essay   265
Index   279

Series Preface

"All history is biography," Ralph Waldo Emerson once remarked. Emerson's aphorism still contains a good deal of truth. History is the memory and record of past human lives, thus making biography the most basic form of historical knowledge. To understand any event, period, or text from the past, some acquaintance with specific persons is crucial.

The popularity of biography among contemporary book buyers in America supports this insight. Recent biographies of John Adams and Ben Franklin have encouraged many—who fear for America's historical amnesia—to believe that a keen and formidable interest in history still exists among the nation's reading public. To be sure, the source of this interest could be the stature and influence of the subjects themselves—the founding fathers of the United States. Still, the accessibility of biography—its concrete subject matter, intimate scope, and obvious relevance—suggests that the reason for the recent success of these biographies is in the genre of writing itself.

American Reformed Biographies, coedited by D. G. Hart and Sean Michael Lucas, seeks to nurture this general interest in biography as a way of learning about and from the past. The titles in this series feature American Reformed leaders who were important representatives or interpreters of Reformed Christianity in the United States and who continue to be influential through writings and arguments still pertinent to the self-understanding of Presbyterian and Reformed theologians, pastors, and church members. The aim is to provide learned treatments of men and women that will be accessible to readers from a wide variety of backgrounds—biography that is both sufficiently scholarly to be of service to academics and those with proficiency in American church history and adequately accessible to engage the nonspecialist. Consequently, these books are more introductory than definitive, with the aim of giving an overview of a figure's thought and contribution, along with suggestions for further study.

The editors have sought authors who are sympathetic to Reformed Christianity and to their subjects, who regard biography not merely as a celebration of past accomplishments but also as a chance to ask difficult questions of both the past and the present in order to gain greater insight into Christian faith and practice. As such, American Reformed Biographies is designed to make available the best kind of historical writing—one that yields both knowledge and wisdom.

Acknowledgments

When Cornelius Van Til delivered a lecture on Boston Personalism before the faculty of the Boston University School of Theology, on March 6, 1956, he began with characteristic modesty. "I would have indeed been happier," he said, "if you had invited me to listen to you instead of to speak to you. But, in a sense, I have already listened to you a good deal. I have listened to you by reading the great books of your truly great men."[1]

It is a daunting task to expect readers to listen to me on the life of Cornelius Van Til, and so I too must begin on Van Til's note of gratitude. It has been my privilege over the past several years to study the life and teachings of this truly great man. I met Cornelius Van Til on only a handful of occasions, but it seems that I have lived with him for all my life. As a baptized member of Franklin Square Orthodox Presbyterian Church (New York), I sat under the ministry of Van Til's students. My first pastor, Elmer Dortzbach (who earned his BD from Westminster Seminary in 1959), claimed that Van Til brought him "kicking and screaming" into the "delightful rigors" of the Reformed faith. He remembered being "devastated before the Scriptures as [they were] so beautifully and consistently proclaimed" in Van Til's classroom.[2] Likewise, my second pastor, John C. Hills (ThB, Westminster, 1941), who followed Dortzbach at Franklin Square, faithfully preached the self-attesting Christ of the Scripture for twenty-two years. Van Til continued to influence my life and thinking during my undergraduate studies with T. Grady Spires and at Westminster Seminary under John Frame, Richard Gaffin, Meredith Kline, Robert Strimple, and many others. I am grateful for the influence of these faithful pastors, teachers, and friends in my understanding of Van Til's work.

What emerges in this biography is a focus on Van Til the Orthodox Presbyterian, with the modifier in uppercase. Often neglected in the many evaluations of Van Til's thought is attention to his ecclesiastical life. A study of Van Til's Reformed apologetics apart from his Reformed ecclesiology risks a reduction of his work merely to the classroom. By tracing his labors as a minister in the Orthodox Presbyterian Church, this book is written with the hope of contributing to Van Til's legacy both to his denomination and to the universal church.

My debt to many friends is great. I am thankful to the trustees of Reformed Theological Seminary for granting me a sabbatical in the fall of 2004, when I conducted much of the research for this book (while distracted by a busy hurricane season). The editors of the series, Darryl Hart and Sean Lucas, were encouraging in their confidence that I could pull this off and patient when it appeared that I might not. Of course, I knew to rely on librarians, and many came through for me, including Harry Boonstra and Paul Fields at Calvin Seminary, Wayne Sparkman at the PCA Historical Center, Alan Strange at Mid-America Reformed Seminary, and especially Grace Mullen of Westminster Seminary in Philadelphia. Grace not only navigated me expertly through the Van Til archives at Westminster Seminary; she also fact-checked (often off the top of her head) so many details in this story that I was often left wondering why she hadn't written this book.

I am also eager to document my gratitude to my predecessor as historian of the OPC, Charles G. Dennison. Charlie's interviews with many Orthodox Presbyterian pastors turned up some wonderful episodes of Van Til's life and ministry. More importantly, Charlie modeled for me and many others the importance of history for the life and health of a Reformed denomination. His insight into Van Til's role in shaping the OPC's identity is echoed throughout this book.

My library colleagues at the Orlando campus of Reformed Theological Seminary, Michael Farrell, Keely Leim, and Karen Middlesworth, were gracious and efficient during my periodic absence and absentmindedness throughout the course of this project. Simon Kistemaker kindly translated for me several of Van Til's Dutch letters and articles.

Family and friends of Van Til's provided stories, letters, and hospitality during my visits, including Thelma Van Til (daughter-in-law), Case Van Til (nephew), Reinder Van Til (Henry Van Til's son and Cornelius's grand-nephew), and two children of John J. DeWaard, Leona DeWaard Klooster and John R. DeWaard. I must also express my thanks to Reinder Van Til for sharing his family's collection of letters between Uncle Kees and his nephews Henry and Nick Van Til. Often those letters found Van Til expressing himself in a most candid and intimate way.

Though not technically family, Bob den Dulk offered his memories of Oome Kees, and Robert Cara related his family connection to a grade-school teacher of Van Til's. Several friends and associates who are far more gifted in Reformed apologetics willingly served as conversation partners, including William Dennison, William Edgar, John Frame, Richard Gaffin, Scott Oliphint, and Lane Tipton. All of them encouraged me in fruitful directions and gently redirected me when I strayed. Thanks to readers of the manuscript who offered helpful suggestions: George Harinck, Stephen Oharek, Danny Olinger, Jack Sawyer, and David VanDrunen; and special thanks to my research assistant Laurence O'Donnell.

To paraphrase Abraham Kuyper, there was not one square inch of our home that this project did not claim as its own. My children and especially my wife patiently endured the domestic disorder that the book generated. I am glad to acknowledge Kathy's faithful encouragement in a small way by dedicating the book to her.

Introduction:
Apologist and Churchman

While he was alive, it was often observed that Cornelius Van Til's readers could be divided into those who did not agree with him and those who did not understand him. Little seems to have improved in the twenty years that have passed since his death in 1987. Debates over Van Til's teaching have divided his followers, who have created competing versions of the Reformed apologist. There are Van Tilians among mainline Protestants and fundamentalist Baptists; they are found both within his denomination, the Orthodox Presbyterian Church (OPC), and without. However, what his students often overlook is that to separate Van Til the apologist from Van Til the churchman is to eclipse the very heart and underlying simplicity of his thought and life. Thus, many of his followers are searching for Van Til's significance apart from the context in which he served.

Van Til's theological commitments cannot be understood apart from his ecclesiology. The faith that Van Til sought to defend was the faith of Reformed churches that found expression in Reformed creeds. His apologetic was self-consciously ecclesiastical as much as theological. "Van Til," Charles Dennison once wrote, "was nothing if he was not a faithful churchman."[1]

Failure to understand Van Til's thought in its ecclesial context is seen not only in his opponents, but also in his followers. Some of them have made extravagant claims about Van Til and his legacy that would have embarrassed him. Disciples have lauded him as the most creative mind since Immanuel Kant and the greatest Christian thinker since John Calvin. The allegedly innovative features of his apologetic approach have been applauded for their proto-postmodernism and either credited or blamed for distancing both Westminster Theological Seminary and the Orthodox Presbyterian Church from their American Presbyterian past. Yet, Van Til's ecclesiology is among the least explored features of his work, and for that reason many tend to overlook important episodes in his life and to misinterpret others.

Van Til's influence, to be sure, extends far beyond the church that he helped to establish and served for so long. Indeed, the universe of Van Tilians exceeds the modest membership of the OPC. Partly for this reason, interpreters tend to characterize Van Til's ecclesial interests as idiosyncratic, avocational, and even tangential to his supposedly more important apologetic insights. Absent an appreciation for Van Til's passion for the church, for example, some have struggled to understand how such an avowed evidentialist like J. Gresham Machen could hire a presuppositionalist like Van Til for Westminster Seminary. And a disregard for church politics during the early years of the OPC reduces Van Til's dispute with Gordon Clark to an embarrassing footnote in his career. These events, rather than being analyzed abstractly, ought to be understood within the context of Van Til's love for the church.

While not ignoring his teachings, this biography focuses on Van Til's ecclesiastical life more than on other interpretations or aspects of his career. This emphasis may appear surprising in an age of academic specialization where an ever-widening gap stands between the pulpit and the classroom. But Van Til's life demands that we reunite these generally unconnected worlds; for he is constantly found serving, teaching, and preaching from within this very gap.

Curiously, the failure to appreciate Van Til's churchmanship is often found among many who criticize him for the seemingly abstract character of his work. A common impression found in assessments of Van Til is that his focus in the ivory tower of apologetic methodology left him distant from the actual practice of apologetics. In truth, Reformed apologetics drove him to the pulpits of the Orthodox Presbyterian Church, to General Assembly study committees, to hospital beds, and even to New York City street corners. Critics who score Van Til for his alleged obsession with methodology may be most guilty of overlooking his passionate and practical churchmanship. Van Til's desire to strengthen the faithfulness of the people of God was no mere academic exercise, and his involvement in the church marked significant chapters in Orthodox Presbyterian history. Many who claim to be Van Til's heirs, as well as his critics, would do well to imitate his sensibilities as a Presbyterian churchman.

This book may also surprise readers who might have expected a deeper analysis of Van Til's apologetic approach. As useful as such studies may be,[2] I am persuaded that a proper assessment of Van Til's life and work yields an appreciation for the underlying simplicity of his teaching. This simplicity is found in his singular passion for proclaiming the glory of God from within the context of the Reformed faith.

In his own words, Van Til spent his lifetime attempting to raise the banner of the Reformed faith on the highest mountain. He referred to his system unpretentiously as "Reformed apologetics." Simply put, Van Til devoted himself to the insistence that only a Reformed apologetic could properly defend and propagate the Reformed faith. Anything less than a fully Reformed defense for the Reformed faith rendered the theology of the church unequally yoked.

This simple claim, of course, had profound consequences. It meant that a Reformed engagement with the world had to account for the epistemological self-consciousness of modern unbelief. It required a careful negotiation between guarding the antithesis and recognizing the elements of common grace in the expressions of unbelief. Unbelievers, Van Til was willing to concede, were capable of genuine good, but only to the extent that they were living on borrowed capital and thus without epistemological justification for their good accomplishments.

The Reformed character of Van Til's apologetics also shaped his understanding of the knowledge of the believer. The ontological gulf between God and humanity removed any epistemological equality between them. This Creator-creature distinction, foundational to all that Van Til wrote, protected the incomprehensibility of God. So the believer follows God's thoughts after him in a true, yet analogical fashion.

The close connection that Van Til maintained between apologetics and Reformed theology demands that the reader see his apologetic work in its ecclesial context. Van Til's commitment to the whole counsel of God as understood through the Reformed confessional hermeneutic provoked a relentless consistency in the way he went about his work. He desired to find the best defense of the faith, and that goal required the diligent and often polemical work of identifying inconsistency and exposing errors in both believing and unbelieving thought. Yet, what fueled his polemics was not a penchant for vain argumentation but a passion for the purity of the church.

Van Til's passion for the church also meant that Reformed apologetics served to shape the identity and direction of the church. Through his life and work Van Til directed the church into a deeper appreciation for the Reformed faith. Calvin's theocentricity, Vos's biblical insights, Kuyper's antithesis, Machen's confessional consciousness—all of these influences came to bear upon Van Til's Reformed apologetics. Specifically, the Reformed faith produced in the pen of Van Til a Reformed militance that characterized Westminster Seminary and the OPC during his nearly half-century teaching career.

Without the ecclesial context of Van Til's passion, his content becomes confused and even anemic. If Van Til considered it schizophrenic to establish Reformed theology on a non-Reformed apologetic, the situation today, twenty years after his passing, may be reversed. Van Tilian apologetics are often employed by apologists who are less than fully committed to what he would have regarded as a full-orbed Calvinism. In this way today's church is expressing another form of incoherence: a Reformed apologetic is servicing a theology that is more generically Protestant. This de-contextualization eclipses the Reformed distinctiveness at the heart of Van Til's system.

In a less than full-orbed Calvinism, the antithesis is not on display, the confession is not worn on the sleeves, and the banner of the Reformed faith is not raised as high as it should be. An apologetic system that does not reinforce a militantly Reformed ecclesiology will find only superficial similarities to Van Til's thought. A cut-and-paste approach to Van Til that promotes an "evangelical Van Tilianism" is an abstraction that fails to measure up to the deepest concerns of his work.

The present work is the second attempt to write a full-length biography of Cornelius Van Til. In 1979, Thomas Nelson published William White's warm personal memoir, *Van Til, Defender of the Faith*. In his review of White's biography, John Frame faulted the book for saying "very little about the main developments in Van Til's thought and life after 1945."[3] Frame is right, but his observation underscores the apparent dilemma for Van Til's biographer. By 1945, when Van Til turned fifty, much of his life was settled. His classroom syllabi were mostly written (at least in early editions). In that same decade he experienced his two major skirmishes with Karl Barth and Gordon Clark, episodes that have largely shaped the popular impression of his work. By this time his habits of work, church, and family life were firmly established, and the main contours of his theological system developed. Indeed, after Van Til joined the faculty of Westminster Seminary in 1929, he never switched vocations, nor did he serve another employer, and he did not change his mind. In short, the last few decades of his life may appear stagnant and uneventful.

Still, there is a story to tell that I trust will engage and challenge the reader. In the last thirty years of his life, Van Til was embroiled in plenty of controversies, which were not mere footnotes to his earlier energetic life. Moreover, the seemingly unremarkable steadiness of Van Til's later years is important for the light it sheds on other stories that engaged him intimately. For example, the schools and churches that he joined (Westminster Seminary and the OPC) and left (Princeton Seminary and the Christian Reformed Church) were shaped either from his influence or from the ways they fell under his critical scrutiny. Furthermore, his work bears on larger developments in Protestant theology, such as the American reception of Barthianism and the development of the evangelical movement.

More importantly, throughout all the years of his life's work Van Til modeled a way of being faithfully Reformed and fully American. Amid a culture of unbelief he embodied a distinctively Reformed spirituality that bears pondering for the church today. As Christians continue to confront the challenge of unbelief in our age, we would do well to examine the ways in which Van Til taught the church of his day to meet that challenge in the previous century. If Reformed apologetics required Van Til's entire life and complete devotion then, we cannot expect it to demand any less of us now.

1

A Child of the Afscheiding

All American Reformed biographies begin in the "old world," at least in a general sense. The lives of these fathers in the faith are part of the greater narrative of European Calvinism's transition into the new world. They are stories of continuity and change, of resistance and accommodation.

This is literally true for the life of Cornelius Van Til. The Netherlands was the land of his birth and his early youth. Many new-world pilgrims come ashore and never look back, so intent do they seem on establishing new habits of life and thought. Van Til, however, never forsook his homeland, and his story was an American life that constantly looked back. The old world was the source of his most powerful theological influences and even his fiercest antagonists.

Following the Protestant Reformation of the sixteenth century, Calvinism established its deepest roots in the Netherlands. The Belgic Confession (1561) gave early definition to the theology of the Dutch

Reformed Church. The Heidelberg Catechism, written two years later and quickly translated into Dutch, added warm autobiographical piety to the doctrinal standards. The Synod of Dort (1618–19) marked the victory of Calvinistic orthodoxy over the heresy of Arminianism, when Remonstrant pastors were expelled from the Dutch church. The Synod consolidated the Reformed movement in the Netherlands, and it confirmed the church in its theocentric, predestinarian Reformed orthodoxy. Together, these "Three Forms of Unity" became the foundation for the theology and polity of the Dutch Reformed Church. They also established Holland as a center of international Calvinism and its universities as the heart of Reformed learning. The Netherlands was also a powerful political force in Europe, and at the time the Synod of Dort was meeting, Dutch settlers had begun to establish the New Netherlands in the Hudson Valley in North America.

This Calvinistic golden age—if it could be called that—did not last in the Netherlands. Soon the Catholic counter-Reformation made inroads, especially in the southern provinces of the Netherlands. Nor was the country sheltered from the emerging spell of the Enlightenment. By the nineteenth century concern grew among the orthodox of the Dutch Reformed Church over the inroads of modernism in Dutch life, especially from the influence of the French Revolution. As Groen Van Prinsterer expressed it, the unbelief of the Enlightenment gave birth to the spirit of revolution that was undermining traditional patterns of authority in the home, the state, and the church. For traditional Dutch Calvinists there were many signs that the Nederlandse Hervormde Kerk (the Dutch Reformed Church) had spiritually degenerated.

Calvinistic decline took particular expression in a national Synod called in 1816 that modernized the church order of the Reformed Church and altered the ministerial subscription formulas. The Synod relaxed the polity established by the Synod of Dort, and its new polity decreed that traditional psalms be supplemented with man-made hymns in worship.

When these changes came with the sanction of the state, dissenting ministers regarded them as government intrusion on religious liberty. Traditionalists, led by Hendrik de Cock, a minister in the province of Groningen, organized an "Act of Secession and Return" in 1834. De

Cock and other Secessionists claimed that their movement was not establishing a new church but returning to the old church, moving back to the true faith and to the Reformed confessions that the state church had forsaken.

The Dutch government sought to put a quick end to the Secession, or *Afscheiding*. Persecution accompanied the growth of the Seceder congregations. Worship was severely restricted, and the military was deployed to disrupt illegal services. Ministers were disciplined and in some cases even fined and sentenced to jail. Businesses often dismissed Secession-sympathizers from their secular employment. Mobs damaged Seceder homes and barns and assaulted their members. Yet, in the midst of this opposition, the movement grew. De Cock, himself defrocked from the ministry by the state church, planted several churches in Groningen, and eventually the *Afscheiding* spread beyond the province and became a national movement.

The *Afscheiding* represented a coalition of diverse theological concerns. In the southern provinces, the Seceders articulated a broad-minded evangelical piety, similar in spirit to German Lutheran pietism, with an accent on individual conversion and an opposition to "dead orthodoxy." In contrast, northern Secessionists, especially in Groningen, placed greater stress on confessional orthodoxy. In the words of Robert P. Swierenga, "The northern party defended the doctrine, liturgy, and polity of Dort as biblically grounded; it was made up of strongly traditional Calvinists who stressed the need for Christian schools and catechetical instruction of youth to combat the 'godless influence' in the public schools."[1]

Numerically, the movement was small and marginalized, often lower class and rural, and largely comprised what Abraham Kuyper later described affectionately as the *kleine luyden* (little people). Though representing a fraction of the Dutch population, it would have greater significance in the new world, as the persecution of the Secessionists prompted their greater immigration to North America.

Dutch-American immigration took place in two phases. Dutch Reformed congregations in the mid-Atlantic colonies were established as early as 1628. These settlements gradually took on new-world values through their experience of American revivalism and the fight for

American independence. In 1792 these churches formed the Dutch Reformed Church, later (in 1867) changing their name to the Reformed Church in America.

A different set of dynamics shaped later immigration to the American Midwest. The rhetoric of nineteenth-century Dutch-American immigration was laced with the hope for religious liberty, and especially the prospect of founding Christian schools. However, the Dutch Reformed came to the new world just as much for economic reasons. Immigration generally peaked during agricultural crises in Holland, and like other patterns of European immigration, it mainly involved the rural poor—farmers who envisioned economic opportunity and the prospect of a better livelihood. As one immigrant observed, "The poorest here are better off than the richest in Holland. One works here for oneself and is no slave of anyone."[2]

Equipped with the dual incentive of religious freedom and economic opportunity, the Dutch Reformed settlers in the American Midwest came as the children of the *Afscheiding*.

Kuyper and the *Doleantie*

Before the largest wave of Dutch-American immigration later in the nineteenth century, another religious movement took hold in Holland. In the latter third of the nineteenth century, the Netherlands experienced a second revival of Calvinism under the leadership of Abraham Kuyper (1837–1920), the brilliant Dutch theologian and statesman. Trained at the University of Leiden, Kuyper was a theological modernist who converted to Reformed orthodoxy in the pastorate, and he sought to apply historic Calvinism to modern Dutch social life. He urged the *kleine luyden* to break out of the social and cultural isolation that characterized the *Afscheiding*. Kuyper urged them to confront the secularization of modern Europe with a coherent worldview, an "all-embracing life-system" that would fight the Enlightenment, principle against principle. To be worthy of this challenge, according to Kuyper, a Christian worldview must be as "equally comprehensive and far-reaching power" as modernism. The only worldview that could measure up to that task was Calvinism: "I found and confessed and still hold," Kuyper wrote, "that this manifestation of the Christian principle is given us in Calvinism. In Calvinism my heart has found rest. From Calvinism have I drawn the inspiration firmly and resolutely to take my stand in the thick of the great conflict of principles."[3] This second Reformed movement transformed Reformed orthodoxy from a religion into a worldview with an ambitious social agenda. Known as the *Doleantie*, or "complaint," it gave birth to what is now known as "neo-Calvinism."

Kuyper found Calvinism to work because of its "dominating principle." This was found not merely in the Reformation doctrine of justification by faith, "but in the widest sense cosmologically, *the sovereignty of the Triune God over the whole Cosmos*, in all its spheres and kingdoms, visible and invisible."[4] The keys to Kuyper's vision for Reformed cultural engagement were two seemingly contradictory principles. On the one hand, Kuyper insisted on the absolute separation, or "antithesis," between the Christian and the modern worldview that came to prominence in the French Revolution. The antithesis prompted Calvinists to draw sharp lines in theory between Christian approaches to social issues and those supported by non-Christian or "apostate" thought. But the antithesis described a difference in principle, on which non-Christians rarely acted with consistency. Restrained from the full expression of their epistemological self-consciousness, non-Christians were capable of genuine social good. This restraint, which Kuyper credited to the Holy Spirit's work of common grace, enabled Christians to cooperate with non-Christians in social causes.

The antithesis and common grace operated in Kuyper's social thought with less than peaceful coexistence, and in combination they seemed to yield conflicting wisdom on the proper course of Reformed social action. Yet for many of his followers, that paradox was regarded as a strength and not a weakness of Kuyper's thought. Indeed, most Kuyperians would agree with the claim of Edward Ericson that "exactly in this tension lies the genius of neo-Calvinism as an instrument of cultural analysis."[5]

Kuyper's tension also unleashed a longstanding and vigorous debate among his followers on how to reconcile these two principles. In Kuyper's own thought, these two were found in asymmetrical form, according to historian James Bratt, who observed that "Kuyper's appeal to the antithesis peaked in the first half of his career, the period of institutional formation, and declined in his later years, when [Dutch] Calvinists had to take their share of managing public life."[6]

Specifically, the tension between the antithesis and common grace tended to divide Kuyperians into conservative and progressive camps. The former were more influenced by the *Afscheiding* (Secession) of 1834 than the *Doleantie* (neo-Calvinistic revival) of 1886.

These two impulses found representation in conservative and progressive factions within Dutch immigration in the new world. The former were eager to maintain strict Calvinist ways, and the latter sought greater assimilation into American Protestantism. In the greater Chicago area, Dutch-American immigrants from Groningen especially were raised more on the piety of the antithesis than the sensibilities of common grace.[7]

When Abraham Kuyper made his one visit to North America in 1898, his itinerary included a stop in Chicago, where enthusiastic Kuyperians among the Dutch Americans warmly welcomed him. His main appointment was to the heart of American Calvinism, Princeton Theological Seminary, where he delivered the Stone Lectures. Those lectures, published as *Lectures on Calvinism*, became the manifesto of neo-Calvinism. For Kuyper, "Calvinism was not just another brand of Christianity but its highest, most systematic and coherent expression."[8] This language resembled that being used by one of Kuyper's listeners, B. B. Warfield, the great lion of the Princeton faculty, who had argued similarly that in Calvinism "theism comes to its rights."[9]

The distinguishing characteristics of Kuyper's Calvinism were its extension beyond the life and doctrine of the church, and the fact that it was more than a mere perpetuation of the past. As a world-and-life view, Calvinism was a roadmap for the future. The principles of Calvinism applied to social and political life as well: Calvinism offered a glorious "life principle." Proper attention to this principle and to its cultural features enabled American Calvinists to avoid the social decline that the Dutch Calvinists experienced in the eighteenth and early nineteenth centuries.[10]

Though a brilliant theologian, Kuyper would not produce the richest theological work of the neo-Calvinist movement that he launched. That distinction would fall to his younger colleague at the Free University of Amsterdam (which Kuyper had founded). Herman Bavinck (1854–1921) was perhaps the greatest of all Dutch Reformed theologians. Unlike Kuyper, Bavinck was the son of a Seceder minister, and he grew up in the spirit of *Afscheiding*. After a year of study at the Secessionist seminary in Kampen, Bavinck earned degrees at the University of Leiden, where he was exposed to modern scientific methods in theology and became acquainted firsthand with modern theology. When Bavinck taught at the Kampen Theological School from 1882 to 1902, he published his four-volume systematic theology, *Gereformeerde Dogmatiek*. Later (1902–21) he served as professor at the Free University, and over time he became an associate of Kuyper's. Bavinck's upbringing and theological temperament were vital in uniting the *Afscheiding* and the *Doleantie* together. More than Kuyper, Bavinck forged a coherent blend of the two Dutch Reformed movements, and he urged their collaboration for the cause of the Reformed faith in the Netherlands. With the publication of his *Gereformeerde Dogmatiek*, Bavinck emerged as the principal theologian of the neo-Calvinist movement.

Bavinck was a separatist but not a sectarian. In the words of a colleague at the Free University, he was both a "a Secession preacher" and a "representative of modern culture."[11] A half-century later, Cornelius Van Til described Bavinck in similarly admirable terms. "Bavinck was deeply concerned to make the Christ of Scripture speak to his age. In this sense he was a truly *modern* theologian." Van Til found a model for theological reflection in Bavinck's *Gereformeerde Dogmatiek*, as it demonstrated "true catholicity of spirit as well as unswerving loyalty to the truth." Reading Bavinck was an encounter with "true greatness of character," according to Van Til. The Dutch dogmatician was "humble before God, and courteous to his fellow-man" in refusing "to compromise his Savior whose voice he heard in the Scriptures."[12] These words foreshadowed the mature Van Til's apologetic goal of *suaviter in modo, fortiter in re* ("gentle in persuasion, powerful in substance"). Moreover, Van Til came especially to appreciate in both

Kuyper and Bavinck their discontent with merely restoring Calvinism to the Netherlands. Instead, they labored to broaden and deepen the principles of Calvinism, a goal that Van Til later set out for North American Calvinism as well.

Thus, Dutch Calvinism of the nineteenth century was born of two prominent movements: the *Afscheiding* in 1834, under the leadership of Hendrik de Cock, and Abraham Kuyper's *Doleantie* in 1886. In the Netherlands these two forces united and formed the Gereformeerde Kerken in Nederland in 1892. They were joined together in the new world through immigration that swelled the ranks of the Christian Reformed Church of North America (formed in 1857 from an exodus from the Dutch Reformed Church in America).

In his own reflections on this history, Van Til was careful not to draw too sharp a distinction between the two: "These differences . . . existed between two parties which both sought earnestly to be true to the Reformed Confessions."[13] Groningers (like the Van Til family) who settled in the greater Chicago area were partial to the *Afscheiding*, and as Van Til himself grew older he expressed even greater sympathy for the spirit of the *Afscheiding* than the *Doleantie*. Still, he warned against exaggerating their differences. Dutch-American historians generally agree and tend to portray these debates as family quarrels, noting that the boundaries among all variants of Dutch-American Calvinism—confessionalists, Kuyperians, and pietists—were generally quite fluid.[14]

The first volume of Bavinck's *Dogmatiek* was published in 1895, and in that same year, in the village of Grootegast in the province of Groningen, Mrs. Klazina Van Til gave birth to her sixth son on May 3. She and her husband Ite named him Cornelius.

Ite and Klazina Van Til raised eight boys on a traditional Dutch farm, consisting of a small thatched-roof house with a cow barn attached. (They also had one daughter, who died of a brain concussion from a childhood accident.)

Van Til remembered being a precocious boy. He recalled his mother's describing him as the biggest cry-baby of all her children. Others remember signs of uncommon intellectual giftedness in the young boy. A teacher of his in Grootegast remembered that "even as a little boy he was logical in his thinking [and] he questioned in an academic way."[15] These gifts did not hinder Van Til's life-long love for farming or quench his warm memories of farm life. His lectures were punctuated by agricultural metaphors such as furrows and corn shredders. Throughout his life he was an avid vegetable gardener and often expressed his preference for the vigorous routine of farm work over the sedentary pace of academic study.

An even more striking memory for Van Til was the strict Reformed piety that his father diligently cultivated in the Van Til home. Van Til captured this in his booklet, *Why I Believe in God*:

> Ours was not in any sense a pietistic family. There were not any great emotional outbursts on any occasion that I recall. There was much ado about making hay in the summer and about caring for the cows and sheep in the winter, but round about it all there was a deep conditioning atmosphere. Though there were no tropical showers of revivals, the relative humidity was always very high. At every meal the whole family was present. There was a closing as well as an opening prayer, and a chapter of the Bible was read each time. The Bible was read through from Genesis to Revelation. At breakfast or at dinner, as the case might be, we would hear of the New Testament, or of the "children of God after their families, of Zephon and Haggi and Shuni and Ozni, of Eri and Areli." I do not claim that I always fully understood the meaning of it all. Yet of the total effect there can be no doubt. The Bible became for me, in all its parts, in every syllable, the very Word of God. I learned that I must believe the Scripture story, and that "faith was a gift of God." . . . I was "conditioned" in the most thorough fashion. I could not *help believing* in God—in the God of Christianity—in the God of the whole Bible.[16]

Ite Van Til's household was a "Christian civilization" where Reformed faith and practice became "the atmosphere of our daily life." In the daily routines of farm life "there was a deeply conditioning atmosphere," the slow and steady work of God the "all-conditioner." As Cornelius grew up, there was "perfect harmony," he continued, "between my belief as a child and my belief as a man, because God is

Himself the environment by which my early life was directed and my later life made more intelligible to myself."[17]

Van Til was sent off to a Christian school at the age of five. His first recollection of the place was the memorization of the first question and answer to the Heidelberg Catechism, through which he learned that "his only comfort in life and in death" was that he "belonged, with body and soul, both in life and death, to [his] faithful Savior Jesus Christ." These were words that would trip easily off his tongue throughout his life. The catechism firmly imprinted Reformed orthodoxy on the young boy, who became known as "Kees" (pronounced "Case," and often spelled that way by his American friends), a child of the *Afscheiding*.

Emigration

Abraham Kuyper's influence in the Netherlands extended to his tenure as Prime Minister of the country, in which capacity he began serving in 1901. His ideas also took root in North America, especially after his visit at the end of the nineteenth century. Another year—1905—might also symbolize the trans-Atlantic transition of his thought. In that year, when Kuyper was ousted from national office, Ite Van Til brought his family to America.

Dutch immigration to the greater Chicago area began as early as the 1840s. Like similar movements of other ethnic groups, this one was born from mixed motives. Some settlers came in search of economic prosperity, which hopes were generally met. Eager to obtain their own farms and to escape the agricultural depression of the Netherlands, many Dutch discovered that prosperity rewarded their hard work. A letter from a Dutch immigrant in 1870 states:

> Those [Dutch] who belong to America are those who understand from the beginning that they are just like a tree planted in rich soil; first they have to live through a life struggle and also have the desire to do so. The ones who can and want to work and do not hesitate to take on anything, be it unusual or strange, or of little attraction, will succeed very well here.[18]

Religious zeal accompanied the economic hope. The centrality of the church in all areas of Dutch-American life indicated that religious concerns were never far from the surface. After the American Civil War, Dutch immigration expanded greatly, and most of the settlers came from the northern Dutch provinces that emphasized the confessional character of Calvinism. These settlers would help transform Chicago from a small town to the fifth largest city in the world by century's end.

As land prices increased, Dutch settlement continued to expand to the south of the city, then to the east, and eventually as far east as Lake County, Indiana, where land was considerably cheaper. In 1870, a congregation of the Christian Reformed Church was formed in Munster, Indiana.

Meanwhile, in the Netherlands, Ite Van Til despaired of sustaining his large family. As a dairy farmer he found it necessary to relocate his family often. During his early life, young Kees moved with his family to the town of Enumatil, then to Oldekerk for one year, and finally to a seventeen-acre farm in Zevenhuizen, in the province of Friesland.

Ite's oldest son, Reinder, had joined other Groningers in search of prosperity in the new world, where the vast fields of the American Midwest provided greater opportunities than the crowded conditions of Groningen. Ite and Klazina were dismayed to see their next oldest, Hendrik, inducted into the Dutch military, and they feared that their other sons—Sieze, Riemer, Klaas, Cornelius, Jacob, and Siepko—would eventually follow in turn. And so, in 1905, the Van Tils determined to set sail for the new world. In May the family boarded a boat of the Holland-American Steamship Company. While at sea, Cornelius observed his tenth birthday.

On May 19, 1905, the Van Til family arrived at the piers of the Holland-American line in Hoboken, New Jersey, on the west side of the Hudson River. This was an area so Dutch that "a person would think he was somewhere in the Netherlands."[19] The purpose of this stop was to further welcome and acclimate Hollanders, and to point them to Dutch settlements in the new world. In this way, the Dutch Reformed Churches took care that their immigrants would not be scattered as those of other European ethnic groups were.

The new world bedazzled the young Van Til. Years later, in typical immigrant rhetoric, he expressed his marvel at the opportunity America presented. America was *een luilekkerland* ("a land of plenty"). He enjoyed exotic new foods, such as bananas and oranges, which were plentiful and cheap. He was startled at the sight of an African American, his curiosity requiring his mother to scold him for pointing.[20]

The most difficult part of the journey, and the least impressive feature of the new world, then followed: a painfully slow twenty-seven-hour trip on the Erie railroad, which the family endured without a sleeping car, an unaffordable luxury for them. After the family survived that ordeal, Reinder met them in Hammond, Indiana, with his horse and buggy. The family then settled on a forty-acre prairie farm on Forty-fifth Street and Kleinman Road in Highland, Indiana.

The Americanization of this region during Van Til's time was powerfully depicted in the Pulitzer Prize–winning book *So Big* by Edna Ferber. This 1924 novel portrayed with great accuracy the Calumet area where fertile soil nurtured Dutch farms and Dutch families. Ferber described the struggle to earn a living from farming and the ways it exhausted the immigrants mentally and physically. Although the book was a sympathetic and even heroic portrait of Dutch-American immigrant life, it was marred in the judgment of many Dutch readers by the author's seeming ridicule of Dutch ways, including their broken English and a stubbornness in maintaining "backwards" farming habits.

Ferber did capture the thrift and industriousness of Dutch immigrants as they sought to recreate their old-world ways in the new world. The close-knit communities the immigrants established on the then American frontier were characterized by *gezelligheid*—the warmth and coziness of the old world. Their modest Dutch bungalows focused on family life in the dining rooms. So successful were they in clinging to their traditions that Dutch Americans were often accused of being "more Dutch than Dutch."[21]

As Chicago profited from post–Civil War prosperity, it became the land of opportunity for the hard-working Dutch. The sandy soil near the shores of Lake Michigan was conducive to the production of garden crops such as onions, carrots, cabbages, and turnips. Modest farms of forty acres could produce high yields, so long as large families could provide the cheap labor for planting and harvesting. The local German population created a regular demand for sauerkraut, and thus truck farming became a profitable enterprise. "Truck farms" described the process of hauling fresh produce on a daily basis to markets in Chicago and the other industrial areas in the Calumet River region along Lake Michigan. By the time the Van Til family arrived, railroads had greatly improved access to Chicago markets.

Ite Van Til settled his family in the fields of northern Indiana along the ridge that ran east to west in the upper part of Lake County. Munster was the "Town on the Ridge," on the south bank of the Little Calumet River, which flowed west toward Chicago. The main stagecoach route became known as Ridge Road, and rich soil attracted farmers on both sides of the ridge. After 1853, many Dutch farmers began establishing truck farms to supply a growing Chicago market, and residents built a church and a small school. In 1875, a three-room brick school was built.

To the east of Munster, the high sand ridge that formed the shoreline of the Calumet was described as "Highland" on early maps. Twenty-five miles southeast of the growing metropolis of Chicago, this open farmland expanded in population by constant immigration from Europe. Nearby, on the shore of Lake Michigan, was the city of Gary, Indiana, whose steel industry was establishing it as the second largest city in the state. Closer yet, the town of Hammond, Indiana, was evolving into an industrial center. The Van Til family found ample markets for their produce in these cities.

The Van Tils attended the Munster Christian Reformed Church two miles to the west of their Highland farm, traveling by horse and buggy. "On Sunday mornings," Van Til later remembered, "one of our two aged horses was hitched to the wagon and those of us who elected to go to the morning service jumped in, or rather, 'clambered up.' . . . When we got back home, the second horse was persuaded to draw the rest of the family to the second service."[22] A third service was added on Sundays when a full moon provided adequate light for travel.

Van Til often described his youthful self as mischievous. Among his most vivid memories was sling-shot hunting with a friend, a neighbor's chickens serving as targets. This would provoke the farmer to chase after the youths "as fast as his crotchety legs could carry him with a large manure fork in his hand and vengeance on his venerable face. We being of lighter weight and higher speed escaped with our lives in the old red-brick public school building."[23]

Van Til's youthful misadventures extended even during church, and he proved to be a handful for his first American pastor, William Borgman. "Dr. Borgman threatened to strike me with a stove-poke in the old church basement when I was in his catechism class," Van Til remembered.[24] Borgman was more than a strict disciplinarian; he also had the reputation of being a good preacher and an exceptional catechism teacher. Despite his adolescent pranks, Van Til developed a growing respect for his pastor's preaching.

The Munster church grew more crowded, and the distance to the church was difficult in a horse-and-buggy age. In 1908, Van Til's older brother, Reinder, boarded a train for Chicago to attend the meeting of Classis Illinois of the Christian Reformed Church. There he delivered a request that a new congregation be established in Highland. Despite some reservations from the Munster consistory, Classis granted the petition, and on April 28, 1908, the Highland Christian Reformed Church was organized with thirty-seven families. Ite Van Til was elected one of three elders, and he moderated the early meetings of the consistory before the first pastor arrived in January 1909. Minutes from those early meetings evoke the struggles with discipline in the frontier church. The consistory dealt with cases of drunkenness, lodge membership, and complaints from disgruntled members.

The church's modest first building included a wood stove and a horse stable. Its members gave sacrificially and rigorously observed the Sabbath and other Reformed habits from the old world. "There was a separation from the world," a semicentennial history of the church recorded, "forced on us to a great extent by our immigrant ways, but also by the militant mind of the church."[25]

For his first year in the new world, Van Til walked to public school in nearby Griffith, to the east of the family farm in Highland. He and younger brother Jake were enrolled in the first grade, and they became known as "Big Klompa" and "Little Klompa" for the wooden shoes they wore. Mastery of the English language came quickly and easily to the two boys, and within a year Van Til was at the head of the class spelling bee.[26]

But Van Til's public schooling would be brief, because another important old world feature that the family imported was a commitment to Christian education. The Munster Christian School was built in 1907, just west of the church. Mr. A. Cleveringa, the one-armed, bearded, serious-looking young teacher-principal, taught the class of forty by maintaining strict discipline. In 1910 Cornelius Van Til became the first graduate of the Munster Christian School. Although he showed academic promise as a young boy, further education was costly for a large farming family like the Van Tils. While some students continued their education in the Chicago Christian High School, most of them, including the Van Til boys, were destined for farming. So the fifteen-year-old spent his next four years working on his father's farm. Farm life was hard, but it did have its rewards. During this time Cornelius became acquainted with a neighbor girl whose family had a nearby onion farm, and he began an eight-year courtship with Rena Klooster.

Although most of Van Til's brothers were not recipients of a normal education, Ite and Klazina raised them in an intellectual and godly home. Older brother Reinder especially came later to regret his lack of a formal education. But the dairy farmer was "fiercely self-educated"[27] and was himself nearly as steeped in the writings of Calvin and Kuyper as was his younger brother. Reinder's intense intellectual curiosity impressed Cornelius at family reunions, and it prompted him to develop a life-long respect for the laity in the church.

For all of his studies, Van Til clung closely to the soil, and few pastimes gave him greater pleasure than harvesting tomatoes. Because the academic life was generally perceived as the vocation of the weak, his neighbors wondered why he was forgoing a successful career in which he was manifestly gifted. "Such a good farmer as Kees should not be wasting his time on books!" many townspeople advised the family.[28] For much of his adult life, Van Til spent portions of the summer months working on the family's farm, often putting his nephews to shame with his harvesting productivity in the hot August sun.

As Van Til grew up, he watched the changing character of life along the Ridge as the Calumet region experienced rapid industrialization. The population of the neighboring city of Hammond grew from 21,000 to 36,000 in the decade of 1910 to 1920, bringing economic opportunity and change to the region. Telephone service was introduced in 1915, and in that same year the Northern Indiana Gas and Electric Company installed power lines along Ridge Road. The automobile also became commonplace, replacing the horse and buggy by mid-decade.

Eventually, non-Dutch families settled in, and Dutch children moved away. In the two decades that preceded World War II, Munster's population increased from 600 to 1,751 residents, and Highland grew from 542 to 2,700 citizens. Small family farms gave way to industrial expansion, until the sprawling Chicago suburb swallowed up the entire Calumet region. By the 1920s Hammond, Indiana, was dubbed "the dumping ground of Chicago" as factory workers soon outnumbered farmers.[29] And Van Til observed firsthand the pluralization of American life even in his hometown. Unlike other Dutch-American enclaves, such as Holland, Michigan, or Pella, Iowa, the Calumet region of northwest Indiana quickly lost its distinctive ethnic identity. The changing character of his hometown may have served, ultimately, to prepare Van Til for service beyond the Christian Reformed Church and to define for him a Reformed identity beyond peculiarly Dutch practices.

Protective Isolation

Most of these changes, however, would occur after Van Til's Indiana days. His childhood life was still rural, revolving around the church as the center of community life, with his ethnic and religious identity reinforced by Christian schools.

The first half-century of the history of the Christian Reformed Church of North America was a time of protective isolation. Many immigrants lamented that some Dutch Reformed churches, especially in the east, incorporated such new world practices as Sunday schools and uninspired hymns. In order to protect themselves from the melting pot of American language, customs, and practices (a fate that befell the Reformed Church in America), members of the Christian

Reformed Church were in the habit of reminding themselves that "in isolation is our strength."[30] Isolation entailed Reformed practices that carefully reinforced Reformed convictions. Kuyper himself had warned about "de verflauwing der grenzen"—the fading away of Reformed boundaries.[31]

At the same time, the Christian Reformed Church expanded substantially, its growth generated largely by large-scale immigration between 1875 and 1905. During that period the denomination grew from 8,000 members to over 66,000, and denominational leaders conceded that certain forms of Americanization were inevitable. "We are quickly changing from Hollanders to Americans," observed B. K. Kuiper. "This process of Americanization by itself is not in the least a problem. It is a process that cannot and may not be held back. We shall become Americans and we must become Americans. It is an irresistible, moral duty."[32]

The ultimate question for Dutch Americans, as for any ethnic group, was not whether to Americanize, but how. How could the denomination become American and stay Reformed? The strategies that emerged differed in the extent to which American culture was judged to be conducive to Kuyper's grand Calvinistic vision. Most Christian Reformed observers saw American religion as too subjective, materialist, and pragmatic. It was indifferent to principle, especially to Reformed principles. Assimilation risked the incorporation of superficial forms of spirituality and doctrinal indifferentism. In a word, American Protestantism was Methodist.[33]

As the Dutch Americans negotiated the process of Americanization, Van Til's background in Groninger-heavy Northern Indiana would temper in him the optimistic triumphalism that was found in other American Kuyperians. Although the boundaries between the *Afscheiding* and the *Doleantie* were often blurred, Van Til's form of Dutch-American Calvinism tended toward more antithetical and confessional emphasis and was less interested in social or political transformation than in preserving sound doctrine.

In 1907, shortly after the Van Tils arrived in America, the CRC in North America celebrated its semi-centennial. Special celebrations marking the occasion were tempered by concern that the "spirit of our land" was making "deplorable inroads among us." Even the ever-optimistic Henry Beets observed that where the American tongue was gaining ascendancy, there was a loss of love for the Reformed faith and for "frequent and diligent attendance upon the means of grace."[34]

As conservative Protestants in the north began to wage war against liberal Protestantism, Dutch Americans shared their militant anti-modernism, but unlike fundamentalists, Dutch conservatism was accompanied by a strong confessional consciousness. The Americanization of the Dutch subculture, then, was a complicated process that entailed both a loosening and a tightening of behavioral expectations. The Reformed Church in America, the older Dutch Calvinist communion established in the seventeenth century, eagerly accepted many American habits, even permitting theater attendance and forms of social dancing. At the same time, the RCA embraced the cause of Prohibition along with other northern Protestants.

The Christian Reformed Church established some very strict regulations against worldly amusements, including the vices of theater attendance, dancing, and cards. But it did not advocate abstinence from smoking and drinking, as did its Dutch cousins in the RCA. As Swierenga writes, Christian Reformed "young men took up the weed as a rite of passage and it was said that 'you couldn't be elected to the consistory if you didn't smoke cigars.' The [consistory] room was blue with smoke."[35] Weddings and anniversary celebrations frequently involved alcohol, even on church property. (Van Til himself enjoyed an occasional cigar, especially at family gatherings. He later expressed bafflement at fundamentalist scruples against tobacco, and he quietly dismissed admonitions to abstain from tobacco.)

The protective isolation of Cornelius Van Til's Dutch-American religious upbringing paints a composite picture of a faith firmly rooted in a particular tradition, celebrating a heroic Dutch ancestry and instilling a militantly Reformed opposition to the world. It followed the premise that opportunity met with diligent work would find reward. The church of Van Til's youth instilled a robust faith that supplied not only resources from the past but also a roadmap for the future, especially in the neo-Calvinism of Abraham Kuyper.

This Christian Reformed isolation, however, began to break down in the twentieth century. The Dutch language disappeared from the pulpits, uninspired hymns joined psalms in public worship as the Christian Reformed increasingly began to enter the mainstream of American life. The question for many confessional antitheticals in the church, including Van Til, was whether the Christian Reformed Church would preserve its distinctive doctrine and practice.

As with other American ethnic groups, the ultimate sign of Americanization for the Dutch was their willingness to send their sons to fight America's wars. The small Dutch enclave in Highland proudly sent eight of its boys to serve in World War I, and later, six times that number would serve the Allied cause in World War II.

But the Highland Christian Reformed Church took even greater pride when in its first decade it raised two sons of the church for the gospel ministry. In 1914, Herman Moes and his second cousin, nineteen-year-old Cornelius Van Til, enrolled at Calvin Preparatory School in Grand Rapids, 150 miles to the north, as each of them sensed a call to the ministry and their families found means to support them.

2

"Fit Modesty and Unreserved Conviction"

*I*n 1931, Reinder Van Til's son, Henry, began his studies at Calvin College. His Uncle Cornelius (nicknamed Kees by family and friends) loaned him some money and offered him advice that included some reflections on Kees's own college years. "I have marveled oft," Uncle Kees wrote, "that a poor guy like myself should be able to get an education." The work was hard and the sacrifices painful, but the rewards were great. It was wise, Van Til continued, that

> for the sake of education for God you may want to impose upon yourself a certain period of unmarried life. Believe me, I imposed upon myself on that score. But even more it may be possible to marry before you are through studying. A consistent and thorough program of self-abnegation in the first years is by far the best method of obtaining more freedom of movement in later years.[1]

As able a student as he was, college life did not begin pleasantly for Cornelius Van Til. His first experiences away from home were extremely lonely, and a bout of homesickness was powerful enough nearly to prompt him to doubt his ministerial calling. The timely counsel of his second cousin, Herman Moes, also a son of the Highland Christian Reformed Church, persuaded him to persevere.

In his history of Calvin College, Harry Boonstra locates Van Til's time there as among the "transitional years" for the college.[2] During this period the school matured from its humble origins to an established four-year institution. By 1920, it had abandoned the preparatory school (which evolved into Grand Rapids Christian High School). In the middle of Van Til's student days the campus moved from Franklin Street and Madison Avenue to the edge of the city (at Franklin Street and Giddings Avenue). Athletic programs and other extracurricular activities were largely undeveloped, although this was of little concern to Van Til. As an older student (entering preparatory school as a nineteen-year-old), he showed little interest in the social life of the school. The college's yearbooks indicated that he participated in no interscholastic sports and in few of the college clubs.

While at Calvin College, Van Til secured room and board with Grand Rapids families near the campus. He faithfully attended Sherman Street Christian Reformed Church, where many of his classmates flocked. There he sat under the preaching ministry of R. B. Kuiper, a future colleague, whom Van Til later described as "a prince among preachers."[3] Van Til also attended the inaugural sermon by Herman Hoeksema at Eastern Avenue Christian Reformed Church in February 1920 and "greatly admired him as a preacher" as well.[4] Together, the pulpit eloquence of Kuiper and Hoeksema established Van Til's appetite for the preached word, and it raised high his expectations regarding the character of Reformed preaching.

By far Van Til's greatest collegiate accomplishment was editing the *Calvin College Chimes*, a student publication that began in 1907. In attaining this honor, Van Til numbered among a select company of Calvin students (later to include well-known authors such as Peter DeVries, Fredrick Feikema Manfred, and David De Jong). According to longtime Calvin College professor, John J. Timmerman, Van Til edited the *Chimes* with distinction. Timmerman cited particularly a January 1921 editorial in which the twenty-five-year-old college senior described the *Chimes* as "the expression of the soul of the student," an expression often laced with "the follies of youth, its boundless self-confidence, its destructively critical attitude towards elders and superiors."[5]

Van Til encouraged student respect toward instructors, and yet he qualified the authority his teachers possessed. The Reformed student had an obligation to speak the truth unflinchingly even in the face of disapproval by his superiors. The student was not to fear antagonizing the faculty or the board, who were both too "big-minded" to take offense. Van Til instructed his classmates to write with "fit modesty and unreserved conviction," and Timmerman added that while Van Til and his associates did not shirk their duty, later editors of the largely uncensored publication "have on occasion dropped even the pretense of modesty."[6]

This "unreserved conviction" prompted Van Til to criticize the Seminary Preparatory Curriculum in a bold 1921 editorial that lamented especially the emphasis on classical rather than biblical (koine) Greek instruction. Citing Abraham Kuyper's emphasis on the importance of koine Greek, Van Til lobbied for radical changes to render the program genuinely preparatory. "Till now," he regretted, "students entered the Seminary without any knowledge of modern philosophy, but carried with them a few faint remembrances of the Homeric dialect."[7] At the same time, Van Til was careful not to sound an anti-intellectual note. He acknowledged the value of a liberal arts education for those in seminary. In a February 1922 editorial, for example, he urged his classmates to appreciate the importance of the study of literature. "Many of us have no cultural but an agricultural background. Alas! The Muses did not hover over stumps and cornfields."[8]

The *Chimes* also provided an outlet for early expression of Van Til's commitment to Reformed militancy. "We are to be officers in Christ's army," he wrote in January 1922. "The din of battle resounds already in our ears; impatiently we trample, anxious to join the fray." Yet the classroom itself was not the place for fighting. "We are now in training," he cautioned.

> Now it is for us to become conversant with the methods of warfare; to practice the art of fighting well. . . . It is for us students . . . to

sink our stakes ever deeper into the rock-bottom truth of Christ, to open our hearts ever wider to the influx of the Spirit divine. Then our hearts will become filled with life and love, and we shall be men and women fully equipped for the service of our King.[9]

Van Til constantly exhorted his classmates to attend more diligently to their studies. "As students of this generation it is well for us to be conscious of the fact that as we approach the end of time, we are to be ever awake. . . . Life moves at an ever quicker pace." Consequently, "No loafers may find a place at Calvin." Van Til urged doubters to trust the wisdom of their instructors, "but by all means work."[10]

Other *Chimes* contributions foreshadowed many of Van Til's life-long interests. A 1921 study of the relation between faith and reason expressed his apologetic methodology in embryonic form, complete with a condemnation of Scholasticism, an outline of the noetic effects of sin, Calvin's "sense of deity," and Van Til's case for the restoration of human reason in the regenerated consciousness.[11] An Easter message in 1922 was a diatribe against modernist denials of the resurrection, which he seasoned with quotations from Abraham Kuyper and Herman Bavinck.

By the advent of his senior year in 1921, Van Til had acquired sufficient advanced academic standing to enroll simultaneously in his first year of seminary at the Theological Seminary of the Christian Reformed Church (later renamed Calvin Theological Seminary). For the fee of $50 per year, he studied under Professors Foppe Ten Hoor (systematic theology), Louis Berkhof (New Testament), Ralph Janssen (Old Testament), Samuel Volbeda (historical theology), and William Heyns (practical theology).

Van Til later recalled that Ten Hoor was a particularly exacting professor who demanded that students preach faithfully from the text of Scripture. When Van Til had the occasion to deliver two student sermons, first on Revelation 3:20 and then on Colossians 1, he recalled Ten Hoor's pointed criticism. "Everything the brother said was true," the professor noted, "but the text doesn't say that."[12]

Van Til characterized his college experience as the time of his discovery and devouring of the works of Abraham Kuyper. Yet there were at least two qualifiers to his nascent Kuyperianism. In William Henry Jellema, Van Til had a brilliant philosophy professor who put a premium on original thinking. "You fellows are little theologues," Van Til remembered Jellema as saying. "You believe everything Abraham Kuyper says. Now you've got to think for yourselves."[13]

Another restraining voice was Foppe Ten Hoor, a strong critic of Kuyper and the *Doleantie* movement in general. Perhaps Kuyper's chief American antagonist, Ten Hoor himself emigrated to America and began to teach at Calvin two years before Kuyper's famous American tour. Ten Hoor argued that the *Afscheiding* and the *Doleantie* presented two warring principles with irreconcilably different views on the nature and mission of the church. Ten Hoor was particularly concerned about Kuyper's loose sense of the church as an organism. This ecclesiology gave Kuyper license to compromise the mission of the church by seeking to transform culture beyond the walls of the organized church. He went on to dismiss the folly of Dutch efforts to export Kuyper's neo-Calvinism into American politics and culture. Ten Hoor also took Kuyper to task for his speculative philosophy and his eagerness to learn from worldly philosophers. This importation of secular thought into the church could only have the effect, Ten Hoor warned, of transforming the church into the world.

However, Ten Hoor's influence on Van Til and other Calvin students was limited. Ten Hoor's classmate (at the Kampen Theological School), Herman Bavinck, persuaded most Dutch Americans to see a fundamental unity between the *Afscheiding* and *Doleantie*. In contrast, Ten Hoor's views sounded extreme, and his anti-American isolationism was reinforced by his inability to provide instruction in the English language.[14]

Eventually, Ten Hoor even came out against Kuyper's formulations on common grace. In this criticism Ten Hoor had proved very influential on an earlier Calvin College student of his, Herman Hoeksema. Ten Hoor likely instilled some restraint in Van Til as well (for example, Van Til dissented from portions of Kuyper's doctrine of common grace). For the most part, however, Ten Hoor's anti-Kuyperian polemic did not rub off on Van Til at the time, though later in life Van Til regretted his failure to appreciate Ten Hoor's criticism. In a 1965 letter to Ten

Hoor's great-grandson, John R. DeWitt, Van Til expressed his long overdue indebtedness to Ten Hoor, whom he described as "a very keen theologian." In another letter nearly a decade later, Van Til was more explicit: "I did not realize I had been such a poor student for him. He was a splendid man. He fought Abraham Kuyper all his life and he was right on some basic things, at least so it appears to me now."[15]

One of the few student clubs that Van Til joined at Calvin was *Nil Nisi Verum* ("Nothing but the Truth"), where in his senior year he presented a paper on January 23, 1922, on the subject "Calvinism in the New World." As he surveyed the contemporary state of Reformed thought in America, Van Til conceded that Calvinism had fallen on hard times in the twentieth century and that it was a marginalized remnant of its former glory. This was to be expected, he argued, since "sinful human nature and Calvinism would never be congenial friends." It is significant to note that in this undergraduate paper, Van Til was already registering his dissent from the optimism that was growing within the Christian Reformed Church regarding American Calvinism. Still, he challenged other interpretations that dismissed Calvinism as "merely a passing view of life" that inevitably gave way to higher forms of religious expression such as modernism. Though small and embattled in a hostile American context, Calvinism "embodies the eternal truth of God that must be the guide for men everywhere and through all ages." To see it rise again, he challenged his Calvin classmates, "we should make the maxim of *ora et labora* once more part and parcel of ourselves." "Pray and work" were words that would become his credo well beyond his Calvin days.[16]

Van Til's Calvin College years generally antedated the more controversial times in the history of the school, both in terms of theological developments and the students' pursuit of so-called "worldly amusements." But Van Til did find himself in the midst of one controversy that eventually influenced his decision to leave Calvin. This was the dispute involving Old Testament Professor Ralph Janssen. Janssen was a graduate of Hope College in nearby Holland, Michigan, who later studied at the University of Chicago, eventually earning a PhD at the University of Halle in Germany. The suspicions that a German degree might normally provoke were overcome because of his additional exposure to Kuyper and Bavinck at the Free University in Amsterdam, where he was awarded a *Doctorandus* in theology. Janssen came to Calvin Theological Seminary in Grand Rapids in 1914, the same year Van Til began the preparatory school.

Over time, concerns grew that Janssen was teaching higher criticism in his Calvin classes. Four Calvin professors brought charges against Janssen based on their evaluation of student notes. Although the seminary's trustees rebuked the accusers for their failure to confer with Janssen first, the four persisted in presenting their charges before the Christian Reformed Synod of 1920. That Synod affirmed the board's satisfaction with Janssen's teaching, but set aside the board's requirement that the men approach Jansen first. This curious ruling stirred up much of the rancor that followed.

Herman Hoeksema then took up the cause against Janssen, along with two other Christian Reformed ministers, Henry Danhof and H. J. Kuiper. They too built their case against Janssen from student notes. Janssen reassured his critics that he was committed to the authority and inspiration of the Bible, using the tools he learned from Kuyper and Bavinck, and he insisted that his critics' flawed evidence did not accurately reflect his views. In 1921 the Calvin board granted Janssen a leave of absence while it convened a special committee to investigate his views. Janssen was rightly skeptical of the prospects for a fair hearing, given that two members of the committee not only were vocally opposed to him (Hoeksema and Danhof) but were also trafficking in views that denied common grace and were becoming increasingly controversial as well (for which they themselves would be deposed from the church three years later). Eventually the Janssen case came to the Christian Reformed Synod of 1922. The accused professor appeared before the Synod only to read a prepared statement, which expressed his frustration at not receiving a fair trial. Synod proceeded to depose him from office.

The Janssen case became a bitter controversy within the seminary and the church. In evaluating the case over the distance of many years, interpreters may be tempted to regard it as a battle between antitheticals and progressives in the Christian Reformed Church, or perhaps the CRC version of the fundamentalist-modernist controversy that was about to beset the northern Presbyterian church. However, that is an anachronistic perspective on the debate, because those parties did not emerge in a pronounced way in the denomination until after World War II. Instead, this controversy resembled other complicated struggles in the Dutch-American circles by entangling many participants in conflicting loyalties.

For his part, Van Til the student did not publicly express his judgment for or against Janssen, and he likely had a measure of sympathy for both parties. (Only after the passing of many years did he pronounce Janssen's views as liberal.[17]) Whatever support he may have extended toward Janssen was likely shaped by R. B. Kuiper, Van Til's pastor at Sherman Street CRC and his future colleague on the faculty of Westminster Seminary. Kuiper, who was Janssen's brother-in-law, was outraged at the Synod's deposition of Janssen. Although he too later conceded that Janssen's views were tainted by higher criticism, Kuiper denounced the procedures that prevented a full and fair hearing of the charges. The consistory of his Sherman Street Church registered its protest against the Synod's action, and Kuiper himself left the CRC for the Reformed Church in America, where he pastored a Kalamazoo, Michigan, congregation for three years before returning, somewhat repentantly, to the CRC.

Van Til's primary interest in the case was limited to the student response to the controversy. In the March 1922 issue of the *Chimes*, Van Til wrote his last editorial on "Students and Controversies," a blistering attack on the attitude of his classmates on the Janssen affair. Even in his student days, Van Til never backed away from a spirited debate. Controversies, he wrote, were important learning opportunities in theological education. His dismay was directed at the way in which Calvin students reacted to this and other such controversies. Calvin students, he charged, had failed to display the proper attitude toward controversy. Van Til's classmates were passing themselves off as experts on a deeply complicated subject, with "premature judgments" and "rashness" that were borne out of a "lack of reflection." "To pose as orthodox or on the other hand as progressive," was harmful and dangerous, he warned. "Surely, we wish to be orthodox, but we must first learn what real orthodoxy is. Surely, we wish to be progressive, but we must first have a basis to progress from. And to be mature in judgment, even were the givens all in our possession, is manifestly out of place for students."[18]

Student smugness, he warned, results in trafficking in extremes, with the "spirit of the mob." Such arrogance would lead to "intellectual and spiritual retardation" and should be awarded with "Certificates of Incompetency." Van Til even had a word for his instructors, urging them to mind the difference between discipling students and propagandizing them. Tentativeness and humility characterized the proper student attitude toward controversy. He urged an attentive listening to all the arguments in the debate, "lest we be swept off our feet and carried along with the current." As a model of this careful deliberation, he called to mind the recent visit from a Princeton Seminary scholar: "remember Dr. Wilson" (that is, Robert Dick Wilson).[19]

The Janssen case became the precipitating factor in directing both Van Til and his close friend and classmate John DeWaard to Princeton Seminary, a place where, even as students, they would not shirk the difficult questions. Their assessment of Calvin Seminary was confirmed by others. According to George Stob, "fear of the mark of heresy" prevented the Old Testament department at the seminary from "free and unembarrassed discussion of biblical problems" for the next thirty years. Janssen himself moved to Chicago after his deposition, and he left the Christian Reformed Church a bitter and disillusioned man.[20]

The Janssen controversy led to a second conflict a few years later that confirmed for Van Til the wisdom of leaving Grand Rapids. The Christian Reformed Synod of 1924, meeting in Kalamazoo, Michigan, condemned the teachings of Herman Hoeksema and Henry Danhof, two of Janssen's opponents, for their failure to affirm the doctrine of common grace, which Synod articulated by way of formulating and adopting its "Three Points." Once again Van Til found himself in the middle of the controversy. He had friends and family on both sides and he had tremendous respect for Hoeksema. Though he was in essential agreement with the Kalamazoo decision, he was never quite settled with its particular formulations. Among the family involved was his brother, Reinder Van Til, a self-educated layman who was very widely read in theology. Reinder left the CRC for a time and joined the Protestant Reformed denomination that Herman Hoeksema founded. Cornelius's visits home to Highland, Indiana, during this time were occasions of fierce family discussions over the doctrine of common grace.[21] Two decades later, in 1947, Van Til publicly entered this controversy with the publication of his book *Common Grace*. As chapter 6 will note, his critics would accuse Van Til of rejecting the CRC Synod's 1924 formulation.

To Princeton

In 1922, after seven years of study in Grand Rapids, Van Til packed his bags and enrolled at Princeton Seminary. Whatever disagreements he expressed, his years at Calvin were filled with warm memories. For decades thereafter, he commended the school to others, and eventually he sent his son there. He even picked up the Christian Reformed practice of calling it "Onze School" (our school), indicating a sense of ownership that Van Til employed as a loyal and grateful alumnus. Even so, he took a bachelor's degree from the college and a year's work at the Theological School of the Christian Reformed Church and traveled east with his childhood friend and fellow Calvin graduate, John J. DeWaard.

The first man that Van Til remembered meeting at Princeton was Professor Geerhardus Vos (1862–1949), who immediately impressed him as a "remarkably erudite man."[22] This was fitting, because Van Til's odyssey from Grand Rapids to Princeton followed in the footsteps of Vos himself. Vos had taught at the Theological School of the Christian Reformed Church from 1888 to 1893, when he accepted the call to a newly established chair of biblical theology at Princeton Seminary (having previously declined an invitation from Kuyper to teach at the Free University). In coming to Princeton, Vos would join the northern Presbyterian church, but he continued to exercise significant influence within the Christian Reformed Church.

Though Vos left both Grand Rapids and the Christian Reformed Church in 1893, Van Til's decision to head for New Jersey and away from the protected isolation of his Dutch subculture was no indication of a renunciation of the CRC on his part. Unlike, for example, many southern Presbyterian ministerial candidates who rarely returned home once they traveled north to study at Princeton, Van Til had every intention of returning to the CRC. He had plenty of precedents to assure him that he could go home again. Among them were his New Testament professor at Calvin, Louis Berkhof (who earned a Princeton degree in 1904), his pastor in Grand Rapids, R. B. Kuiper (Princeton, 1912), and his cousin, Herman Moes (Princeton, 1920).

Berkhof especially whetted Van Til's appetite for Vos, frequently remarking that Vos was the greatest influence in the shaping of his theology. In addition to the prospect of studying under Vos, Van Til was also influenced by a visit that Professor Robert Dick Wilson paid to Calvin in 1921. When Wilson lectured on "Some Old Testament Problems," the Princeton scholar left Van Til awestruck. "Dr. Wilson is an expert in the Semitic languages," Van Til wrote in the *Chimes*. "He made it clear that none but experts are to discuss philological questions. The students looked like pigmies, as indeed they are."[23]

Wilson accompanied J. Gresham Machen to Westminster Seminary in 1929, and he passed away after the school's first academic year. He is remembered by generations of Westminster students through his portrait on campus, upon which are inscribed his oft-quoted words, "I have not shirked the difficult questions." Wilson's case for a Princeton education was persuasive to Van Til particularly in the midst of the Janssen case, as he feared that Calvin students were shirking difficult questions.

When he arrived at Princeton in 1922, Van Til came to another school in transition. A year before, the great "Lion of Princeton," B. B. Warfield, had died at the age of sixty-nine. His younger colleague, J. Gresham Machen, described the end of Warfield's thirty-four-year tenure as nothing less than the death of the seminary. Writing to his mother about Warfield's funeral, Machen lamented that "it seemed that the old Princeton—a great institution—died when Dr. Warfield was carried out."[24]

Among the changes taking place was a push for more practical theology in the curriculum. Van Til encountered students chafing at the rigorously classical curriculum of Princeton. Much of the discontent was focused on the difficult classes taught by Geerhardus Vos, and Van Til resented the movement to reduce Vos's classes to electives. He was encouraged to meet a kindred spirit who also appreciated Vos when John Murray enrolled at Princeton in 1924.

Van Til also joined the checker club at Princeton, the meetings of which commenced whenever the word "Tightwads!" was heard echoing through Alexander Hall on Saturday nights. This was J. Gresham Machen's announcement that students were studying too hard and that it was time to put the books aside and join him in his room for oranges, nuts, cigars, and checkers.

Van Til drew close to Machen, despite the fact that because he was a transfer student with advanced standing that included Greek instruction, he never had Machen in the classroom. The increasing demands on Machen's schedule also restricted the contact he had with students. He had just published his first book, *The Origin of Paul's Religion*, and he was becoming a popular speaker in both academic and lay circles. In fact, the academic year that Van Til arrived, 1922–23, was described by Ned Stonehouse, Machen's biographer, as his "watershed year," when he would publish both his New Testament Greek grammar and his most well known title, *Christianity and Liberalism*. This was soon followed by what Stonehouse called Machen's "Valley of Humiliation," where he bore reproach in the church because of vocal opposition to his pulpit supply at Princeton's First Presbyterian Church and his subsequent embarrassment at being denied the chair of apologetics at Princeton. Nevertheless, Van Til managed to establish a friendship with Machen, and he grew in his esteem for Machen's championing of Reformed orthodoxy.

Van Til was remarkably productive in his Princeton days. Equipped with a year of advanced standing, he secured four degrees in five years, including his ThB from the seminary in 1924 and an MA from the university in that same year, followed by a ThM in systematic theology in 1925 and his PhD in 1927 (awarded after he defended his dissertation on "God and the Absolute").

Van Til quickly distinguished himself as a student. In his first year (as a middler student), he won a $75 prize for a paper he submitted to Dr. Caspar Wister Hodge on "Evil and Theodicy." The essay contrasted

Christian and non-Christian theories of evil and its origin. The only adequate theodicy, Van Til maintained, had to account for the centrality of evil in human existence as thoroughly and deeply as it could be conceived. "We are prepared to notice," Van Til wrote,

> that every theologian that has conceived of evil as touching only the circumference of man's being cannot gain an adequate theodicy. On the other hand, that theology in which evil is presented not only to have touched man's moral nature so that his will has been perverted but also the intellectual part of man's makeup, so that it renounces once for all all rights of being competent to judge, and thus assumes a thoroughly receptive attitude to the Scripture, is able to render a satisfactory theodicy.

A lengthy section on Augustine demonstrated his own acceptance of the "core of the Biblical teaching on sin." This was explicated more fully by Calvin, who

> had an intensely deep realization of the wretchedness of sinful man. The heinousness and hideousness of sin he did not underrate. His utter helplessness of himself he clearly apprehended. "Saved by grace" reverberated as a constant echo throughout the compartments of his soul, when once he found his Savior. Now his logical mind could not help trace this sense of restoration back to its inception, the predestination of a sovereign God.[25]

Reformed Protestantism after Calvin rejected the Reformer's teaching on human depravity in waves of Arminian, deistic, Quaker, and perfectionist heresies. A solution could only come from "a return to the much-despised Calvinism," and a rearticulation that borrowed from the "inimitable trio of Kuyper, Bavinck, and Warfield." In that train Van Til found confidence to affirm a robust Calvinism. "God must be his own theodicy," Van Til insisted, and Van Til could not countenance any effort to soften the mystery that attends the problem of evil.[26]

> In his inscrutable will [God has] planned the reality of sin for the revelation of his glory. To say that God only permitted evil and has

53

not planned it is only a fruitless attempt to justify Him by our own
logic, because further thought cannot rest in the idea of a permission
of evil by one who could prevent it. God does not need our little
fences for his protection, nor do they do us much subjective good,
rather harm.[27]

The middler prize was followed in the next year by Van Til's winning a $700 senior prize for his essay "The Will in its Theological
Relations," a lengthy handwritten study that filled three composition notebooks. After reviewing the history of philosophy regarding
the problem of human freedom, Van Til asserted that only covenant
theology successfully avoided "all tendency toward Pantheism and all
forms of necessitarianism on the one hand and all forms of plagiarizing
thought on the other hand."[28]

The outlines of Van Til's transcendental approach to apologetics
began to emerge in this work. He located the "philosophical basis for
covenant theology" in a "transcendental realism" that avoided the
pitfalls of both pragmatism and idealism. (These were the two prevailing options in American philosophy in Van Til's day, and Van Til
characteristically treated them as general tendencies and not specific
schools of thought. The former denied that facts in the world were
related, and the latter related them into a framework of interpretation that was pantheistic. Both approaches claimed that autonomous
humanity could interpret the created world in a neutral fashion.) Once
again Van Til observed the differences between the states of human
consciousness, and he refused to establish human reason as the absolute
and final standard of judgment.[29]

Van Til argued that the theological basis for covenant theology is
the doctrine of the self-contained ontological Trinity. Just as the relations among the divine persons of the Trinity are covenantal, so too is
God's relation to every aspect of temporal existence. To be a creature
is to be in covenant relation with one's Creator. The foundational
importance of creation, and its intimate connection with covenant,
recurred as a constant emphasis in Van Til's work.

Humanity, then, is in covenant relation with God, a relationship
of absolute dependence. As Van Til reiterated in almost everything he

subsequently wrote, autonomy and creatureliness are incompatible, no matter how intoxicated modern thinking is with the former. Our absolute dependence upon an absolute God allows us "a finite covenant personality" with "exactly enough room for the highest and only possible form of freedom conceivable for a creature." Human freedom, then, "is not thereby abridged but realized." This freedom required the rejection of the counterfeit emancipator of the modern mind, Immanuel Kant.[30]

Van Til expanded these ideas in his 1926 ThM thesis, which he wrote for C. W. Hodge (grandson of Charles Hodge and successor to B. B. Warfield). Here he emphasized the Kuyperian principle of the antithesis between covenant keeping and covenant breaking, and he drew conclusions about the epistemological expression of this antithesis. Van Til developed this into his notion of "Reformed epistemology." (This term receded in his later work and is not to be confused with its use in the work of Alvin Plantinga and others.) Van Til contrasted various ways of knowing that corresponded to the fourfold state of man as revealed in Scripture. As the Westminster Standards summarized that teaching, human consciousness proceeds from a state of innocence (creation in the garden) to a state of sin (with the fall of Adam and Eve) to a state of grace (for those regenerated by the Spirit) and eventually to a state of glory (with the consummation of history). Non-Reformed epistemologies (Catholic, Lutheran, or Arminian) cannot account for those varied states. Reformed epistemology entails an Adamic consciousness, a non-regenerate consciousness, and a regenerate consciousness. This thesis, which Van Til further developed in his syllabus on Christian epistemology, reinforces his interest in developing a distinctively Reformed apologetic. Reformed theology requires a Reformed apologetic.

Taken together, these three seminary papers are impressive works that show a strong unity and coherence of thought, with convictions that were uncommonly firm and established for a seminary student. The papers comprise the foundation for Van Til's lifelong themes: the ontological Trinity, the organic connection between creation and covenant, the reverent and creaturely use of reason, and the radical antithesis between believing and unbelieving epistemologies.

Also evident in these student papers is Van Til's careful appropriation of both Kuyper and Warfield and his search for a middle ground that affirms and rejects aspects of both thinkers. Although interpreters often portray him as a hybrid of Kuyper and Warfield, Van Til himself generally included Bavinck in his list of interlocutors. Indeed, Bavinck is arguably the greatest of all of these influences, the evidence for which grows as Bavinck's dogmatics is translated into English. As this survey of Van Til's seminary scholarship indicates, he was less concerned with distinguishing himself from these antecedents than with applying their best insights with a rigorous consistency.

Readers of Van Til are familiar with his genealogy of non-Reformed apologetics: Aquinas led to Bishop Butler's analogy, which begot Charles Hodge, who produced Buswell and Clark. But the common assessment that Van Til rejected old Princeton (Warfield) in favor of old Amsterdam (Kuyper and Bavinck) is an oversimplification (which, admittedly, Van Til himself committed in casual conversation). Instead, he would identify weaknesses in the work of all of these men, especially in the remnants of scholasticism that lurked in their thinking. (*Scholasticism* was another term that Van Til employed imprecisely. Generally it represented for him the Thomistic identification of aspects of nature and natural understanding that had not been affected by sin.) The Reformed epistemology that was latent in all three theologians ultimately permitted no zone of neutrality, no epistemological common ground. In bringing the Reformed tradition to more consistent epistemological expression, Van Til could state with truthfulness that with respect to the "inimitable trio of Kuyper, Bavinck, and Warfield," he stood on the shoulders of giants.

Meanwhile, life at Princeton was not all theology and philosophy. Throughout these years, Van Til continued his correspondence with Rena Klooster of Munster, Indiana. Their long courtship culminated in their wedding at the Munster Christian Reformed Church, on September 15, 1925. The church's pastor, Jan Karel Van Baalen, performed the ceremony, which was followed by a dinner in the town hall. Van Til then quickly returned to Princeton with his bride to work on his doctorate at Princeton University.

Princeton's PhD in philosophy, begun in 1887 under President James McCosh, was still a young program when Van Til enrolled. Most of its students were recent graduates of the college, and many were part time, as the program lacked the prestige of other schools such as Johns Hopkins. Tuition-free cross-registration policies were extended to Princeton Seminary students, which prompted many seminarians to populate the university's graduate programs. (John DeWaard, for example, joined Van Til and earned a masters degree in philosophy.) Over time, the graduate school dean, Alexander Fleming West, grew critical of the quality of seminarian work, and by 1932 the faculty adopted stricter rules that limited the number of courses a seminarian could take. The number of seminarians in the graduate program in philosophy then quickly declined, going from as many as thirty-two in 1932 to a mere three students in 1935.

Thus Van Til was privileged to study under liberal policies that were eliminated soon after his graduation. His Calvin education under William Henry Jellema prepared him well for his university experience, and he remembered Dean West's commenting on his transcript when he applied to study philosophy: "Not much of it, but it's good what's there. I'll give you a chance."[31] At the university, Van Til worked under the Scottish personalist A. A. Bowman, who rewarded Van Til's mastery of modern philosophy with a graduate fellowship. Bowman was a non-Christian who made a deep impact on Van Til's thinking. Though Van Til rejected the philosophical idealism of his mentor, he was impressed at its methodological consistency. When Van Til reviewed Bowman's books in the *Westminster Theological Journal*, he marveled at how "perfectly consistent" was his former professor's thought.[32] This is a characteristic that Van Til himself would display throughout his life. K. Scott Oliphint has observed the unrelenting consistency in Van Til's thought, and he notes that Van Til never altered the substance of his method at any point in his teaching. "Van Til," wrote Oliphint, "while developing, expanding, and elaborating his approach throughout his career as an apologist, never wavered from his fundamental conviction that God is the presupposition behind all thought and all life. Whatever man thinks and whatever he does, God is there sustaining and maintaining."[33]

In 1927 Princeton University granted Van Til the PhD in philosophy for a dissertation on "God and the Absolute." Upon graduation, Van Til received a call from the Spring Lake, Michigan, Christian Reformed Church.

The Spring Lake church was formed in 1882 so that its members would not have to row across the Grand River to attend services in Grand Haven. Van Til was called as the twelfth pastor of the seventy-family congregation. He later recalled his one brief pastorate with fond memories. Two features of his experience stood out for him. First, Van Til maintained his predecessors' practice of *huisbezoek* (family visitation.) To accomplish this task, Van Til fell into the habit of walking great distances, because he served without the use of an automobile. Many of Van Til's later students struggled to maintain his strenuous walking pace when he strolled with them on the campus of Westminster Seminary. Second, Van Til placed great stress on catechetical instruction in his pastorate. So strong was his preparation for catechism classes that when he reflected on it later, he computed that his catechetical teaching load at Spring Lake far exceeded his Westminster teaching load.[34]

Cornelius and Rena enjoyed a happy and contented year at Spring Lake. His walking days came to end through the generosity of the congregation when it surprised the Van Tils with the keys to a new Chevrolet. Van Til often contrasted his warm pastoral memories with the rancor of his subsequent theological controversies. In 1950 he wrote to his nephew Henry, "I dreamt last night that I had accepted a call to Spring Lake and that I was telling someone that I expected to stay there for the rest of my days."[35]

His pastoral relationship drew to a close in less than a year when Princeton Seminary called him as an instructor in apologetics in 1928. Van Til did not see the invitation as a choice between two vocations. Both the pastorate and a professorship were at heart the same calling. Every minister, he once wrote, had a "V.D.M. degree" (that is, a "Verbum Dei Minister," or "minister of the Word of God"): "When therefore I became a teacher of apologetics it was natural for me to think not only of my Th.M. and my Ph.D. but above all of my V.D.M. The former degrees were but means whereby I might be true to the latter degree."[36] Preaching and teaching, for Van Til, were not two distinct vocations, and often the preacher emerged in his classroom lectures.

Instead, the dilemma for Van Til was geographical. Rena loved the Midwest, and she missed her family terribly when she married and moved east. The temptation to stay close to Munster surely weighed heavily on Cornelius. But Van Til decided to accept the call to Princeton, and he joined the faculty in 1928 as an instructor in apologetics, a decision that would change the course of his life and bind his story with that of his mentor, J. Gresham Machen. On September 23, 1928, Van Til preached his farewell sermon to his Spring Lake flock. His carefully chosen topic, based on 2 Corinthians 11:2, represented another lifelong concern of his, the importance of Christian education. To the youth in the church he said, "Young people, I am jealous over you. Many things attract us away from Christ. . . . But give unto Christ your whole heart, for he requires it of you." To their parents he made this appeal: "Now that you have so nobly begun the work of Christian instruction, continue to pray and give it to your children. There is nothing I know of more useful to help in exposing the hearts of children to Christ."[37]

The conditions that prompted Princeton's call to Van Til contained the seeds of the seminary's decline. In 1926 the General Assembly of the Presbyterian Church in the U.S.A. had failed to confirm Princeton's appointee to this position, who was J. Gresham Machen himself. Seminary President J. Ross Stevenson urged the Assembly's non-confirmation because he had identified Machen as the source of unrest and discord at the seminary. Had Machen not suffered the humiliation of the General Assembly's veto of his appointment, Van Til would not have been offered the post two years later. (Furthermore, had Machen transitioned successfully into that field before he formed Westminster Seminary in 1929, he would not have solicited Van Til's services. Thus Machen's defeat in the church was crucial in creating the career path for Van Til, both at Princeton and later at Westminster.)

If Van Til understood the irony of his appointment, he never expressed it in print. His interest may have been consumed with finding his approach welcomed in the seminary. Van Til succeeded William Brenton Greene, and he planned to redesign the instruction away from the apologetic tradition of Princeton Seminary. Thus it was potentially awkward when Greene learned of Van Til's appointment. But Van Til remembered that Greene had only two questions when Van Til paid a visit to his office.

> "Mr. Van Til, do you love the Lord Jesus Christ?"
> "I certainly do, Dr. Greene," Van Til replied.
> "Mr. Van Til, are you willing to teach the Reformed Confessions *ex animo*—without doubt?"
> "I certainly will."
> "Well, I am so thankful to the Lord that I have a man who will faithfully carry on my work."[38]

After one year, Van Til's teaching was so impressive that Princeton offered him a full professorship. Meanwhile, under orders of the Presbyterian General Assembly, Princeton was undergoing a radical reorganization that included the addition to its board of two signers of the modernist 1923 Auburn Affirmation, which denied the importance of doctrines such as the inspiration of Scripture and the virgin birth of Christ. When Van Til solicited advice from Machen over whether to continue at Princeton, Machen persuaded him that the seminary was lost to modernism. Van Til would not insult Machen by staying at Princeton, so he resigned his post and declined the offer of the chair in apologetics.

Van Til quickly adopted Machen's rhetoric concerning the death of Princeton. He employed strong language to lampoon the claim made by President Stevenson that the addition of Auburn Affirmationists would render the school "thoroughly Reformed." It would have as much of a Reforming effect, Van Til suggested, as if a Presbyterian church were to add two Methodists to its Session.[39] (Years later, he would describe the changes with another damning metaphor: "It was as if two communist sympathizers had been elected to the Supreme Court of the United States."[40])

To Westminster

There was no alternative for Van Til but to return to the pastorate. After a year at Princeton, Cornelius and Rena Van Til returned to the Spring Lake Christian Reformed Church in June 1929. (The pulpit had remained unfilled since his departure the previous September.) The next month witnessed the birth of their one child, Earl Calvin Van Til. It also was the beginning of Machen's three-month courtship of Van Til for his new seminary in Philadelphia, Westminster Theological Seminary.

In announcing his plans for a new seminary, Machen had counted on the recruitment of several conservative Princeton faculty. Some of the older members of the faculty (such as Vos, W. P. Armstrong, and C. W. Hodge) were sympathetic to Machen's cause, but they were unable to find their way to joining Westminster. Machen secured the services of O. T. Allis and Robert Dick Wilson. But he needed one more, and he pressured Van Til to sign on as well.

From the Seaside Inn in Seal Harbor, Maine, Machen desperately telegrammed O. T. Allis on August 2 regarding Van Til: "We must do everything in the world to get him."[41] Machen also telegrammed Van Til from Seal Harbor and applied direct pressure. Van Til's refusal to join Westminster, Machen explained, "would be a crushing blow to our whole movement." Machen knew he needed to take Princeton professors with him to Philadelphia in order to claim continuation of the Princeton tradition. Yet Van Til was more than a Princeton statistic. "Far more important . . . is the unique value of the service you could render to us. . . . Seldom is any enterprise so dependent upon the decision of one man as our movement is dependent upon yours." Machen continued: "I beg you therefore not for our sakes but for the sake of the gospel cause to rejoice our hearts by accepting [the] invitation. We shall be almost terrified to lose heart if you do not come with us." He concluded by assuring Van Til that all the details that might stand in the way could be worked out.[42] Not only was Machen persuaded that Van Til was the only man for the job, but he despaired at the embarrassment of failing to recruit him.

Allis made a recruitment trip to western Michigan, but without success. Van Til telegrammed Machen that "my decision is irrevocable," but he politely added that he would "gladly entertain [Machen's] phone call."[43]

Machen refused to give up. He suggested to Allis that they offer Van Til the choice of teaching systematic theology or apologetics, and that he be consulted about the hiring of John Meeter, then a Princeton student, as an assistant. Machen was prepared to make even further concessions. "We should make his salary whatever is necessary to get him. He should understand that he does not need to stay any longer than he and Mrs. Van Til desire and that he will be doing rescue work for the Princeton tradition this year."[44]

Ned B. Stonehouse, a Calvin College and Princeton Seminary graduate who had accepted Machen's invitation to teach New Testament, knew the obstacles that stood in Van Til's way. He prepared Machen to accept defeat by explaining why Van Til could not see his way to come to Westminster:

> Van Til is heart and soul Christian Reformed, and thinks that he should give his life to the Christian Reformed Church. He does have a splendid reputation in the church at large and also at the school, and no doubt will be asked to fill any vacancy which may occur in the department of philosophy of the college or the department of theology or apologetics in the seminary. It appears that no such vacancies will occur in the near future. But Van Til says that he would not be fair to you and the others at Westminster if he were to take the work of apologetics only as a temporary thing, and should leave after a short period of time from two to ten years of service.

Certainly Stonehouse was right about CRC interest in Van Til. He went on to suggest the only possible chance that Machen had to twist Van Til's arm at this point: "It is clear to me that the only way in which he can be won is by your coming personally and trying to convince him that you must have him in view of the *present* need, and that you are willing to regard the appointment as a *temporary* one."[45]

And so Machen paid Van Til a personal visit, and this trip finally succeeded in securing Van Til's services. Under the headline "Seminary Loses Fourth Teacher," the *New York Times* reported Van Til's appointment to apologetics at Westminster and went on to quote a statement by Machen about the new board at Princeton: "Men and women who really hold to the Bible and to the Confession of Faith of the Presbyterian Church can have no confidence in the signers [of the Auburn Affirmation]. The Affirmation and the historic Christian faith are two contradictory things. A man can be true to one or to the other, but he cannot possibly be true to both."[46]

Van Til had warm memories of the privilege of working with Machen in the early years of Westminster Seminary:

> How good it was for those of us whom he had chosen to labor with on the faculty, . . . to be with him daily and often to go out to lunch with him after the Saturday morning faculty meeting. He did not preach at us telling us to do this or to do that. He left us free in the true sense of the word, freedom to develop our work for ourselves. But we could not help but imbibe something of his spirit of unreserved devotion to the one goal of lifting up the banner of Christ on top of the highest mountain.[47]

Perhaps as a recurring tribute to his mentor, the mountain-climbing and flag-waving metaphor became a favorite of Van Til's. Growing up in the plains of the Midwest, Van Til did not have the mountaineering experience of Machen, who was an avid sportsman. But in coming to Westminster he was, in a sense, to become a mountain-climber for the rest of his life.

3

From Dutch Reformed to American Presbyterian

*I*n September of 1929, after months of agonizing decision making, Van Til finally determined to leave western Michigan for Philadelphia and the cause of conservative American Presbyterianism. But it was not a clean break from his past. For several more years he maintained his ministerial credentials in the Christian Reformed Church, hoping to see the establishment of a congregation of the Christian Reformed Church in Philadelphia. He maintained lifelong friendships in the CRC, where most of his extended family remained. He considered several invitations to join the faculty at Calvin College and Seminary, and he would eventually teach at the seminary for a semester in 1952.

What drew Van Til to Westminster, as much as Machen's persistent pleading, was his confidence that Machen was constructing a solidly Reformed institution. Machen's opening address confirmed that Van Til had made the right decision. Van Til found encouragement and inspiration in these words:

We rejoice at the approximations to that body of truth which other systems of theology contain; we rejoice in our Christian fellowship with other evangelical churches; we hope that members of other churches, despite our Calvinism, may be willing to enter into Westminster Seminary as students and listen to what we have to say. But we cannot consent to impoverish our message by setting forth less than what we find the Scripture to contain; and we believe that we shall best serve our fellow-Christians, from whatever church they may come, if we set forth not some vague common measure among various creeds, but that great historic Faith that has come through Augustine and Calvin to our own Presbyterian Church. Glorious is the heritage of the Reformed Faith. God grant that it may go forth to new triumphs even in the present time of unbelief![1]

Machen was proud of the faculty he assembled at Westminster and lauded all of their accomplishments. Although Armstrong, Hodge, and Vos chose not to leave Princeton, Machen did persuade three members of the Princeton faculty to migrate with him to Philadelphia. He was also gratified for the Christian Reformed representation on the faculty (that included R. B. Kuiper, Ned Stonehouse, and Van Til), and he observed at the opening of classes that "the Grand [River] is flowing into the Schuylkill [River]."[2] It was an acknowledgment of an intimate relation that Westminster began to develop over the next few decades with another Reformed community. In the midst of Machen's increasing isolation from mainline American Presbyterianism, it was no small comfort to him that there was another expression of Reformed orthodoxy in America.

Machen reserved his highest praise for his junior colleague in apologetics. Writing in the Christian Reformed magazine the *Banner* in 1930, Machen noted that Van Til enjoyed "a brilliant career as a student at Princeton Seminary and Princeton University, where he . . . made such a signal success as a teacher at Princeton Seminary last year and is continuing that success in the fullest measure now."[3] To be sure, the letter to a Christian Reformed audience served a public relations purpose, and Machen was eager for the church to see that her son was engaged in productive service.

The CRC regretted the brain drain to Philadelphia even while it congratulated Machen for selecting three of its finest for his distinguished faculty. An editorial in the *Banner* expressed relief that Kuiper and Van Til each had committed for only one year, and it hoped that they would soon find themselves returning to western Michigan. At the same time the editorialist predicted only one way in which Westminster could succeed. "We cannot foresee a bright future for Westminster unless it will take the lead in a movement to separate the conservative from the liberal element . . . and organize into a new Presbyterian Church, which will stand foursquare for the faith of the fathers." Such a development would make it harder for Kuiper and Van Til to leave, the *Banner* conceded, but it took the high road in imagining that scenario: "We are not unwilling to sacrifice our very best men if thereby we can help to make Westminster a stronghold of Calvinism in a country where positively Calvinistic schools are so rare."[4]

Another noteworthy feature of the editorial was its assent to Machen's claim that Westminster was the continuation of Princeton "in spirit, if not in name." This was no small acknowledgment, considering the steady flow of CRC ministerial candidates to Princeton in the past. However, this was not the unanimous assessment of the CRC toward Westminster. The skepticism of some in the church who suggested that the school was started for "trifling reasons" prompted Van Til to write a lengthy article in the *Banner* to outline the rationale for the seminary.[5] Moreover, the general CRC enthusiasm toward Westminster and Van Til would contrast with the attitude from certain quarters of the church two decades later.

Apologetics: Warfield, Machen, and Van Til

Students of the apologetic methodology of Cornelius Van Til have long puzzled over the apparent contrast between his approach and the "classical approach" of the Princeton apologetic tradition. This has prompted speculation concerning the question of how Machen and Van Til got along during Westminster's early years. That Van Til's appointment represented a radical shift cannot explain why Machen was so delighted in that appointment. As early as 1928 Machen saw Van Til's potential when he observed that "Van Til is excellent material from which a professor might ultimately be made."[6] If some interpreters exaggerated the affinities between the two by suggesting that Van Til prompted Machen's movement away from evidential apologetics, others have less ground in proposing that their differences were irreconcilably great. Allan MacRae, an early member of the faculty of Westminster, maintained that Machen privately told him in the "the strongest language" that he "stood with Warfield and against Van Til." Machen, MacRae recalled, was too busy during Westminster's early years to address the "harmful effects" of Van Til's teaching. Had Machen devoted the time to studying the matter, he would certainly have asked Van Til to leave.[7]

The longstanding debate over apparent differences between Machen and Van Til tends to obscure the more basic similarity between the two. What Van Til learned from his teacher and what Machen admired in his student was an unrelenting insistence on the coherence of both Christian theology *and* apologetics. Christianity is a *system* of truth, and Westminster promised to present that system with a methodological consistency that Princeton, now tainted with Auburn Affirmationists, could not.[8]

As anti-indifferentists, Machen and Van Til were cut from the same cloth. If, as Machen contended, indifferentism to doctrine made no heroes of the faith, Van Til went a step further in arguing that indifference to apologetic method made ineffective defenders of the faith. If Van Til devoted greater reflection to the question of apologetic consistency, the impulse was already in Machen. Van Til suffered Arminian apologetics no more gladly than Machen welcomed evangelical moderates. Reformed theology could do better than that.

Perhaps the differences between the two appear stronger from an anachronistic point of view. In the context of the Presbyterian controversies of the 1920s, Machen's and Van Til's messages bore greater underlying continuities. Although Van Til's distinctive approach was far from completely developed at this point, when Francis L. Patton described Machen's apologetic methodology in 1926, it sounded much like a Van Tilian approach:

In order to defend Christianity, one must have a definite conviction in respect to what Christianity is; and no man, I think, is better acquainted than Dr. Machen is with the current forms of minimizing theology, which, in some respects, are the most insidious foes of Christian faith, inasmuch as the gist of their teaching seems to be that the fruits of Christianity will continue to flourish after the axe has been laid at the roots of the tree that bears them.[9]

Machen himself stated (in a letter declining an invitation to become president of Bryan College), "Thoroughly consistent Christianity, to my mind, is found only in the Reformed or Calvinistic faith; and consistent Christianity, I think, is the Christianity easiest to defend."[10] The importance of methodological consistency is something Machen himself inherited from Warfield, as Ned Stonehouse observed:

There is little wonder that [Warfield's] incisive and lucid analysis and expression, developed on the background of encyclopedic scholarship and penetrating thinking, appealed to Machen. There was a breadth of vision in his point of view which removed him far from all taint of sectarianism and yet was combined with a steadfast commitment to and love of the truth which gave no quarter to a vapid doctrinal indifference and latitudinarianism. As a student and evidently in his early years as an instructor Machen had not come under the full impact of Warfield's approach, and had supposed that a minimizing apologetic for a broad Biblical Christianity would best meet the needs of the day. But as his letters and other testimony establish he came more and more to see that Warfield's position was the only strong position, and that Calvinism, or the Reformed Faith, had the advantage, not only of being the Biblical view of Christianity, but also of constituting the faith, which was incomparably the easiest to defend.[11]

In light of the pervasive indifference, latitudinarianism, broad-churchism, and theological minimalism in the Presbyterian church at the time, Van Til's apologetic approach stood out as it flowered from the central feature of Machen's convictions. Van Til's stress on theological precision and consistency was no departure from the approach of his mentor. Van Til simply applied Warfield and Machen's insights more fully in his own apologetics. Apologetics entails defending the self-same faith that one confesses: the Reformed faith of the Westminster Standards. This is the only faith worth defending, and as Warfield and Machen understood, it is the easiest to defend.

Another important similarity was this: for both Machen and Van Til, consistency, in turn, required controversy. Van Til embraced the calling of a controversialist reluctantly. Years later he would trace the importance of theological and apologetic consistency to the work of Calvin himself, in an article that he aptly entitled, "Calvin the Controversialist."

Where Van Til may not have lived up to his mentor was in the clarity of expression. Van Til defended Machen's cause with a distinct and at times idiosyncratic vocabulary. Consider, for example, his analysis of the Auburn Affirmation. Writing to a popular audience (readers of the *Banner* in 1930), he described the Affirmation as "clearly anti-Christian and anti-theistic. It denies the absoluteness of God, of Christ and of Scripture, it is based on the principle of relativism which is paganism."[12] This language possessed none of the simplicity of Machen's *Christianity and Liberalism*. Van Til's use of highly philosophical terminology (for example, denoting liberalism as "post-Kantian thought") often lost some of his readers, and it failed to communicate with the direct effect of Machen's more biblical appeal.

For all these underlying similarities, Van Til was still fully aware of the different direction he was taking in apologetics at Westminster. After his first year at Westminster, he and Rena and Earl moved to Munster, Indiana, where Van Til spent the summer of 1930 preparing to teach the second-year apologetics course, Christian evidences, for the first time. He wrote to Machen to secure confidence that he would teach as Machen wanted the course taught. In his response, Machen could not have constructed a more encouraging letter. He began by relating that he held but the "vaguest kind" of thoughts on the matter, but went on to suggest that the course consist of "essentially a defence of the possibility and actuality of the supernatural as it is recorded in the Bible, and of the supernatural revelation that the Bible contains." He went on to express his confidence that Van Til would teach the course competently. "Your choice of topics is sure to be better than mine ever would be." Going even further, Machen hoped to submit to Van Til's instruction. "I wish I could take your course in Evidences. I need it, and I am sure it is greatly to the benefit of the Seminary that you are offering it."[13]

Finally, Machen urged Van Til to enjoy the summer by availing himself of the badly needed season of rest, and he included a personal note of gratitude to Van Til. "Your presence has meant more to our cause than I can possibly say. I do not know what would have become of us if you had not stood by us in this crisis. Thank God that you made the decision that you did!"[14]

Van Til thanked Machen for his assurances about evidences. "I was somewhat ill at ease but you have reassured me." These letters not only shed important light on the relationship between the two men, but also reveal a young and somewhat insecure instructor as he cautiously took on the old-Princeton apologetic tradition. If Machen did not entirely embrace Van Til's approach, he clearly gave Van Til his blessing on proceeding.[15]

Over the course of their labors together at Westminster, Machen grew in his awareness of Van Til's apologetic differences with Warfield. Although Machen was unfamiliar with Kuyper (Machen had never read Kuyper, according to Van Til), he was eager to learn from Van Til and expressed, in Van Til's words, his "absolute confidence in me and wanted my approach."[16] Apologetic methodology was not the only field in which Machen leaned heavily on Van Til. When asked to evaluate the new theology of crisis arising from Europe in the writings of Karl Barth and Emil Brunner, Machen claimed that his knowledge was too limited for an expert appraisal and he referred inquirers to Van Til.[17]

Early Work at Westminster

The Machen–Van Til correspondence in the summer of 1930 contained even more good news for the young professor. Machen's latest crisis involved the emergency created by the sudden decision of R. B. Kuiper (who taught systematic theology) to leave Westminster in order to accept the presidency of Calvin College. Machen scrambled to find a successor, and his efforts to dislodge C. W. Hodge from Princeton again failed. He had another candidate in mind, a recent graduate from Princeton who, like Van Til, had spent a year at Princeton as an instructor. Machen advised that Van Til could avoid a trip to Philadelphia for a faculty vote if he would merely assent to Machen's selection.

The candidate was John Murray, Van Til's former Princeton classmate, and Van Til was thrilled at the choice. He offered to cooperate in every way with Murray's coming, and he was even willing to surrender the junior systematics course if Murray preferred to teach it. The hiring of Murray in 1930 was thus the start of a remarkable thirty-seven-year collaboration between the Dutchman and the Scotsman. Their interests, personalities, and teaching styles contrasted sharply in many ways, and yet as these two became the twin towers of Westminster's faculty, they developed a close bond and an ever-deepening friendship.

The division of labor at Westminster, especially within the theology department, enabled each professor to rely on the other's strengths. In the words of Edmund Clowney, Van Til felt the "freedom to focus on philosophical issues because of his confidence in Murray and other Reformed exegetes."[18] Murray held Van Til's apologetics in high esteem, though he employed a more biblical theological vocabulary than Van Til's highly philosophical terminology. Van Til always quoted Murray with approval, and he expressed special appreciation for Murray's "seemingly impeccable holiness of conversation."[19] Together, the two young scholars expressed common indebtedness to the biblical theological approach of Geerhardus Vos, and each oriented his own approach to systematic theology around the history of redemption.

Van Til's emphases found corroboration and support in Murray. Murray embraced Van Til's understanding of analogical knowledge and his notion of the interrelation of general and special revelation. Murray affirmed the self-attestation of Scripture and even articulated a form of circular reasoning in his article in *The Infallible Word* (1946) in what John Frame described as "the most explicitly Van Tillian passage in Murray's writings."[20] In short, the two were united in apologetics, and Van Til counted on Murray to offer exegetical support for many of his formulations.

One of Van Til's roles at Westminster was to serve as its watchdog on Princeton Seminary. The inevitability of Princeton's decline after 1929 was an essential part of Westminster's rationale for existence, though evidence was not readily at hand. When Westminster opened its doors in 1929 with 50 students, Princeton still had 177 students enrolled. Moreover, Princeton's board had pledged at the time of its reorganization "to continue unchanged the historic policy of the Seminary and to do nothing whatever to alter the distinctive traditional position which the Seminary has maintained throughout its entire history."[21] Van Til was anxious to challenge that claim and cast doubt about the future direction of the school. In the pages of *Christianity Today* and the *Presbyterian Guardian*, Van Til conducted a three-stage attack on his former employer. He first took aim at John E. Kuizenga, who filled the chair of apologetics at Princeton that Van Til himself had declined. By "adapting the Bible to the needs of modern non-Christian psychologists and philosophers," Kuizenga was urging, in Van Til's judgment, "a new type of apologetic" at Princeton that was no longer in harmony with the systematic theology of Hodge and Warfield. Whether or not Van Til noted the irony of those words (given that others had made the same charge of apologetic innovation about him), he sharply contrasted Kuizenga with his predecessor, William Brenton Greene: "The practical difference is that the old apologetic was a *help* and the new apologetic is a *hindrance* to the spread of the gospel."[22]

Van Til's next target was Donald Mackenzie, who succeeded Geerhardus Vos in Princeton's chair of biblical theology. In reviewing Mackenzie's book *Christianity—The Paradox of God*, Van Til attacked Mackenzie's reckless use of paradox and chance, which failed to clarify any difference from evolutionism or irrationalism. Van Til concluded that "we cannot be sure from Professor Mackenzie's book whether he would worship a mysterious aspect of the universe . . . or the God of Christianity."[23] Mackenzie used the pages of *Christianity Today* to fight back. Van Til's lengthy review, he countered, was a perversion of his position and a dishonoring of the Princeton tradition. Van Til's unworthy motives, Mackenzie went on to charge, displayed less zeal for the Reformed faith than antagonism to his former employer. As the Auburn Affirmation continued to "haunt" Van Til "like a nightmare,"

Mackenzie said,[24] Van Til created a new heretic "unknown to the Westminster divines"; Mackenzie termed it a "modern Princetonianist."[25]

Van Til's anti-Princeton polemic continued in the *Presbyterian Guardian*.[26] In his view, if Kuizenga and Mackenzie symbolized the decline of Princeton, they paled in comparison to the 1937 hiring of E. G. Homrighausen to the chair of Christian education. This was because Homrighausen was Princeton Seminary's first overt Barthian. Van Til had first critiqued the theology of Karl Barth in a 1931 book review in *Christianity Today*. Expressing there sentiments that would echo throughout his career, Van Til charged that Barth's anti-theistic theology destroyed historic Christianity, and he urged that "every branch of the Reformed churches" would "resolutely disown Barthianism as an offshoot of Reformed theology."[27]

In following the dialectical theology of Barth, Homrighausen had explicitly denied the inspiration and authority of the Bible, because Barth taught that Scripture could at best merely "contain" the Word of God. In 1938 articles in the *Presbyterian Guardian*, Van Til wrote that "there seems to be no justification for optimism in regard to Princeton Seminary." He noted that only two Princeton faculty from its pre-1929 days remained, and he scolded the school especially for its hiring of Emil Brunner. In a 1940 assessment of the arrival of Princeton's new President, John A. Mackay, Van Til observed that though Brunner had returned to Europe, Princeton had not improved.[28]

Well into the next decade, in 1943, the *Guardian* continued this theme in a series of articles entitled "Whither Princeton?" The series was designed especially to challenge the assessment of Clarence Bouma, editor of the *Calvin Forum*, who pronounced Princeton's Barthian phase as "on the wane."[29] Van Til's contribution focused again on E. G. Homrighausen, by that point Princeton's most popular professor. While Homrighausen had grown somewhat critical of Barth, he was still, Van Til warned, deeply indebted to dialectical theology.[30] This article foreshadowed Van Til's future debates with the *Calvin Forum*, and especially his clash with Bouma, which some came to call the "Clarence and Casey show."

Van Til steadily developed a name for himself through his relentless attack on Princeton and especially through his early criticism of Barth.

An early indication of his growing reputation was the invitation that Columbia Theological Seminary extended to him to deliver the Smyth Lectures in February 1936. This was a prestigious lecture that in the past included Warfield's studies on counterfeit miracles and Machen's work on the virgin birth. Van Til spoke on "God and Human Knowledge," contrasting the Reformed faith with current forms of unbelief in philosophy, biology, psychology, and education. Columbia professor William Childs Robinson lauded Van Til's presentation for his "loyalty to the Reformed faith" and his "comprehensive acquaintance with the many fields of modern thought." Though Van Til was less renowned than previous speakers, Robinson welcomed the seminary's exposure to a scholar of "Dutch extraction," and he concluded that "students and faculty agree that they seldom had a lecturer who secured their interest as completely as Dr. Van Til."[31]

Before his lectures, Van Til extended his trip south to include a brief vacation in St. Petersburg, Florida. While in Florida he received a telegram from his Westminster colleague Paul Woolley on January 8, 1936, informing him of a disruption taking place at the seminary. Thirteen of the twenty-eight members of the seminary's board had resigned at a special meeting on the previous day, including Samuel Craig, editor of *Christianity Today*, and Clarence Macartney, the prominent pastor of First Presbyterian Church in Pittsburgh. What prompted the exodus was the increasingly aggressive stand that Machen took with respect to the crisis in the Presbyterian church, including his formation of the Independent Board for Presbyterian Foreign Missions in 1933 and the more recent organization of the Presbyterian Constitutional Covenant Union, which was widely interpreted as a stepping-stone to the establishment of a new church. In the minds of the minority of the board, these actions had harmed the cause of conservatism in the Presbyterian church, and these members had grown impatient with Machen's leadership. In the words of Samuel Craig, "Dr. Machen is a very gifted man but as a tactician we venture the opinion that he is about the world's worst."[32] At the same meeting Old Testament Professor O. T. Allis also resigned from the faculty.

Van Til expressed deep regret at the departure of Allis, who had become a good friend. (Having inherited some wealth, Allis became an independent scholar until his death in 1973, when Van Til conducted his funeral.) Van Til feared the promotion of Allan MacRae in the light of Allis's departure, but otherwise he was remarkably unperturbed about the shakeup at Westminster. In letters to his friend, John DeWaard, he wrote, "I am happy things have turned out as they have" because "Westminster will go on and go on strong."[33] To be sure, Van Til was writing to encourage DeWaard (the pastor at First Presbyterian Church in Cedar Grove, Wisconsin), because DeWaard had just been elected to the seminary board in the wake of these resignations. Still, Van Til genuinely expected that these changes would confirm the seminary in a more solidly Reformed direction and enable it to take greater leadership in the Presbyterian controversy that was coming to a climax.

A New Church

Shortly before Machen's trial and suspension from the ministry in the Presbyterian Church in the U.S.A. in 1936, he attempted to transfer his ministerial credentials from the New Brunswick Presbytery into the Philadelphia Presbytery. McAllister Griffiths and Edwin Rian tried to persuade Van Til to join the PCUSA at that time. Their hope was to add Machen, R. B. Kuiper, Van Til, and Charles Woodbridge all at once, thereby establishing a strong orthodox consensus in the presbytery. Van Til declined to leave the Christian Reformed Church at that time, but he watched with great interest the final stages of the Presbyterian controversy. He attended Machen's debate against Robert Speer (the evangelical moderate secretary of the Presbyterian Board of Foreign Missions) in the New Brunswick Presbytery and his subsequent trial, which Van Til described as a "farce."[34]

As he watched the controversy unfold from the secure vantage point of membership in the Christian Reformed Church, Van Til did not suffer the ignominy of being suspended and defrocked like Machen and his friend, John DeWaard, who was humiliated in his exile from his Wisconsin church. When the Presbyterian Church of America (later renamed the Orthodox Presbyterian Church) was founded in Philadelphia on June 11, 1936, Van Til was not one of the forty-three ministerial members of the new church. However, by signifying his intention of joining the Presbyterian Church of America, he was enrolled, with eight other ministers as an associate member with privileges of the floor. Weeks later he joined the Philadelphia Presbytery of the Presbyterian Church of America in its first meeting, on June 30, 1936. Van Til described the excitement of walking out of one church with David Freeman to form a new one, and the unique honor bestowed on him in that first service: "My hat has the distinction of having been used for the first offering."[35]

In contrast to the struggle that Van Til underwent in deciding to join the Westminster faculty, he transferred into the new church quickly and without lengthy deliberation. Perhaps Van Til had already begun to perceive signals of ominous similarities between the CRC and the PCUSA. For example, Machen's frustration with Speer had a counterpart in Van Til's dealings with Henry Beets, the stated clerk of the CRC. Beets's generally cheerful optimism downplayed the importance of Reformed militarism, provoking Van Til to observe that "Beets may in some sense be called the Dr. Speer of the Christian Reformed Church. He has followed a middle of the road policy."[36]

When the new church was formed on June 11, Van Til and R. B. Kuiper sent a telegram to the Synod of the Christian Reformed Church that had convened two days earlier, which read: "Presbyterian Church of America organized yesterday as true spiritual succession of Presbyterian Church U.S.A. General Assembly meeting now. Will conclude its sessions tomorrow. Machen is moderator. Our Synod could strengthen hands of brethren by sending greetings."[37]

The Synod responded with Christian greetings and invited the new church to send a fraternal delegate to the Synod, which would continue to meet until the next week. The invitation was quickly accepted. H. McAllister Griffiths, the stated clerk of the General Assembly, informed the Synod in a subsequent telegram that the Presbyterian Church of America had commissioned Cornelius Van Til as its fraternal delegate.

Van Til arrived in Grand Rapids on Tuesday morning, June 23. With his ministerial credentials in transition, he addressed the Synod as his former church: "Till last week I was a minister in good standing in the Christian Reformed Church of America and now I am such no more. I have not left the Christian Reformed Church because I disagree with its teachings. On the contrary I have left because I do agree with them. It is in order in some small measure to propagate the teachings that I am now a minister in the Presbyterian Church of America."[38]

His farewell words expressed both personal and corporate gratitude for the noble testimony of the church he was leaving. He went on to describe the formation of the new church in terms familiar to his listeners: "The same idea that controlled the men of the *Doleantie* when they said they were not beginning a new church but simply renouncing 'het synodale juk' of the corrupt organization of the *Hervormde Kerk*, has also controlled the men who now seek to carry on the true spiritual succession of the *Presbyterian Church in the U.S.A.* under a new name."[39] In these words Van Til invited the Synod to picture the new Presbyterian church as a reprise of Dutch separatism. The Presbyterian Church of America represented the *Afscheiding*, and Machen was the Kuyper of American Presbyterianism.

Van Til pressed home this analogy forcefully.

> I am asking that you sacrifice the popularity with, and perhaps even the recognition of, large churches and influential men in America. I need not elaborate this point. It will be understood by any child of the *Afscheiding* or of the *Doleantie*. But any child of these movements, if he can justify his own existence, can also justify the existence of the Presbyterian Church of America.[40]

The CRC reception was important for the young church. Others welcomed it with hostility or indifference, he noted, invoking Machen's language, but Van Til was confident of better things from his forefathers. "We need your encouragement and your help."[41]

Van Til's history lesson was not lost on the Synod. Responding on its behalf, William Kok noted,

> You have reminded us of our own history, and in our own history certainly lies a basis for our sympathetic attitude toward the organization which you represent in our midst this morning. . . . Our sympathy will continue as long as we both remain loyal to the faith

once delivered to the saints. And it will be our continued prayer that God may bless the Presbyterian Church of America; that God may make it a power for good, and that in it we may find an ally in our struggle to maintain ourselves upon the basis of the truth as we conceive of it.[42]

These words were reassuring to Van Til in two respects. First, they constituted the warmest ecclesiastical greeting that the new church would receive. Second, they confirmed his hope that he had not burned a bridge in joining Machen.

It is worth observing that at no time during the final stages of the Presbyterian controversy did Van Til consider returning to a CRC pastorate, as he had when he left Princeton Seminary in 1929. In pledging his loyalty with northern Presbyterian conservatives, Van Til was following Machen's lead, because Machen had declined opportunities to join the southern Presbyterian church in the height of the Presbyterian controversy. No doubt Machen prevailed upon Van Til to lend his assistance to the new church, and Van Til gladly obliged. Any thoughts he may have entertained at this time about returning to the Midwest he kept entirely to himself. Those opportunities would arise in the future.

As many interpreters have noted, Van Til sought to combine the best of the Dutch and Scottish Reformed traditions. This would have an effect on the Orthodox Presbyterian Church. Never fully or simply the spiritual successor to the northern Old School Presbyterian tradition, the OPC would cultivate, under the influence of Van Til, a spirituality that benefited from Dutch Reformed sources as well. The OPC would send its sons and daughters to Christian Reformed schools, including Calvin, Dordt, and Trinity Christian colleges.

Personally, Cornelius Van Til maintained throughout his life a twofold impression of the church of his youth. On the one hand, it was as a model of robust Calvinism for the Orthodox Presbyterian Church. On the other hand, the CRC served as a warning against the dangers of progressive Calvinism, especially of yielding to the seductions of Barthianism.

Militant Calvinism

The ease of Van Til's migration to Presbyterianism was also due to developments in his thought in his first seven years at Westminster Seminary, an experience that confirmed a Presbyterian consciousness in him. He began to feel particularly at home with the Westminster Standards and, like Geerhardus Vos before him, came to appreciate the Standards' more overt description of the covenantal relation between God and man, especially in their teaching on the covenant of works.[43] Van Til's embrace of the Westminster Standards was unqualified. While he continued to express a love for and fidelity to the continental Reformed confessions, the Westminster Standards became the system and the very vocabulary that Van Til used to express his theology with increasing ease and familiarity. This is evident as early as his ThM work on Reformed epistemology, in which he adopted the Westminster Confession's language of humanity's fourfold state as the basis of his epistemological approach. Later evidence of his affinity for the Standards can be found in his contribution to the 1946 Westminster faculty symposium, *The Infallible Word*. Van Til's article, "Nature and Scripture," outlines and defends a distinctively Reformed approach to natural revelation based on the first chapter of the Westminster Confession of Faith.[44] Whenever Van Til defined historic Christian orthodoxy, he employed the language of the Westminster Standards. (One noteworthy occasion was his participation, with Nels Ferré, Alden Kelly, and Paul Tillich, in a 1955 symposium, "Where Do We Go from Here in Theology?" in *Religion in Life*. In Van Til's contribution, the dilemmas of modern theology find solutions from the Westminster Shorter Catechism.[45])

In other respects, however, the transition to the new church was not always easy for Van Til. In becoming an American Presbyterian, Van Til more often had difficulty with the modifier than with the noun. One goal that Van Til set out to accomplish was to bring a Christian Reformed teaching on Christian education to bear on American Presbyterians. He was dismayed at the apparent Presbyterian disregard for Christian schools, though his low estimate was something of an over-reading. American Presbyterians were by no means indifferent to

Christian education, but their efforts had traditionally concentrated on Sunday school programs and higher education initiatives that included an impressive array of Presbyterian colleges and seminaries. What they tended to overlook was the importance of Christian day schools.

In a 1936 article, "How Shall We Feed Our Children?" Van Til urged a twofold approach to Christian education. The task of exposing unbelief must be accompanied by "the constructive work of building up our own people in an understanding of and love for a full-orbed Christianity."[46] Van Til argued that children will remain in the church and another generation will arise only though an aggressive program aimed at the education of all levels. To ignore this, he warned, was as naïve as jumping off the Empire State building with "prayers for a safe landing." Van Til went on to suggest that the formation of the new church was a futile enterprise if attention were not paid to Christian education. After all, why preserve orthodoxy, he asked, merely for one more generation? "Humanly speaking, then, one cannot honestly be enthusiastic about the future of the Presbyterian Church of America unless its people will realize that a new and far more intense policy will have to be adopted in the field of Christian education." This entailed not only the elimination of modernism but also shedding from the church all "non-Reformed elements."[47]

Van Til set out to speak about the importance of Christian education wherever he was invited to do so. Later that year, he spoke in Philadelphia before a group that subsequently formed a society for a Christian school. In these talks he focused on common themes: John Dewey was the "murderer of Christianity" and evolution was the greatest contemporary threat to Christian education.[48]

Another disturbing feature of conservative American Presbyterianism for Van Til was its sympathy toward premillennialism. It amazed him, as much as it did colleagues such as Kuiper and Murray, that Westminster faculty attacks against Arminianism and dispensationalism provoked storms of reaction. "The thing that worries me most," he wrote to John DeWaard, "is the premillennial question. [Charles] Woodbridge and others . . . [believe] all schools of eschatology have equal right. Now if I am not mistaken this is not the historical attitude of the Reformed churches. In the Dutch tradition at least those holding the [premillennial view] were merely *geduld* [tolerated]." Van Til chafed at the equal footing that premillennialists demanded.[49]

For their part, the fundamentalists began to accuse the Westminster faculty of being out of touch with American Presbyterianism, and there was a sense in which they were right, at least with respect to Van Til. Presbyterian premillennialism was fairly well established by the time Van Til joined the OPC. It was represented on the faculty at Princeton Seminary as early as 1905 with the appointment of Charles Erdman, the son of a prominent dispensationalist, who taught premillennialism in his popular English Bible course. For Machen, the presence of a dispensational-leaning course in English Bible in the Princeton curriculum represented a decline in the school, both in its Reformed orthodoxy and in its biblical scholarship.

Yet Machen allowed the premillennial issue to recede to the background in order to fight the larger battle against modernism. As a result, dispensationalists populated the board of Westminster Seminary and eventually the Independent Board for Presbyterian Foreign Missions. Only when O. T. Allis exposed the dangers of dispensationalism in an *Evangelical Quarterly* article in January 1936, did the controversy come out in public.

Van Til himself could never understand the appeal of premillennialism, dispensational or otherwise. This was a lifelong frustration for him, which he often vented in suspicion toward J. Oliver Buswell. Buswell (1895–1977) was born the same year as Van Til, and like Van Til he grew up in the American Midwest. After studies at the Universities of Minnesota and Chicago, McCormick Theological Seminary, and New York University, Buswell was ordained in 1918, and he ministered to congregations in Minnesota, Wisconsin, and Brooklyn. He was president of Wheaton College from 1926 to 1940, and briefly (from 1936 to 1938) a member of the OPC.

Buswell was a successful president of Wheaton who brought academic credibility and accreditation to the school. However, college supporters thought he publicly embarrassed the school when the Presbyterian church disciplined him for his involvement in the Independent Board. A showdown that he forced within the Wheaton College board in order to secure its vote of confidence unexpectedly resulted in his dismissal from the school. (Eventually Buswell became a founding member of the faculty of Covenant College and Seminary.)

Van Til's relationship with Buswell began when the second General Assembly of the Presbyterian Church of America convened in Philadelphia on November 12, 1936. The Assembly began with a sermon from Machen as the retiring moderator. His sermon on "Constraining Love" (based on 2 Cor. 5:14–15) contained his vision for the new church when he exclaimed, "What a privilege to carry the message of the cross, unshackled by compromising associations, to all the world."[50]

In an effort to symbolize the unity of the church, Van Til, at Machen's suggestion, nominated Buswell to the office of moderator. The nomination demonstrated Van Til's and Machen's willingness to establish eschatological freedom in the church. The limit of Van Til's esteem for Buswell, however, was not lost on a reporter covering the assembly for the *New York Times*. When a subsequent motion was made to declare Buswell's election unanimous, Van Til interceded. According to the account in the *Times*, the motion was lost "when the Rev. Dr. Cornelius Van Til of the Westminster Theological Seminary asked that no precedent for unanimous selections be established."[51]

The most pressing matter confronting the commissioners to that Assembly was the report from the Committee on the Constitution on the adoption of the Westminster Confession of Faith and Catechisms as the doctrinal standards of the five-month-old church. The debate centered on whether or not the church should include the 1903 confessional revisions in its version of the standards. While it was generally agreed that those revisions were Arminian and anti-Reformed, some commissioners argued that maintaining the old constitution of the church (including the 1903 revisions) would bolster the church's claim of being the "spiritual successor" to the Presbyterian Church in the U.S.A., and thus help congregations in their legal battle to maintain their property. Machen himself feared the outcome of this debate, and he privately expressed concern that what lay ahead for the church was a "calamity beyond words."[52]

But Machen knew that he could count on his younger colleague. At a crucial point in the debate, Van Til spoke in opposition to the appeals he heard for expediency, reflecting, perhaps, Machen's vision of liberation from compromising associations. "Shall we be Arminians before the courts this year, with the full expectation of being Calvinists next year?" Millions of dollars of church property, he averred, "could not justify the dishonesty" of adopting Arminian standards for the church. Van Til's arguments prevailed, and the *Presbyterian Guardian* described the outcome of the debate in this way: "When the vote was taken by roll-call on this all-important matter the result was the adoption of the Westminster Confession of Faith and Catechisms, without the obnoxious 1903 revisions, by the decisive majority of 57 to 20."[53]

Death of Machen

Machen and his listeners did not know that when he delivered his General Assembly sermon it would be the last time most of them would hear him preach. After preaching at a small church in Bismarck, North Dakota, Machen caught pneumonia and died on January 1, 1937. Van Til's letters to John DeWaard described how devastated Van Til was at the news of Machen's sudden death. "No one man has meant so much to me," he wrote on the next day. A few days after the funeral, he wrote, "I have never felt so forsaken."[54]

Later, in his "Letter from America" in *De Reformatie*, he described Machen as indispensable to the seminary, to the *Presbyterian Guardian*, and to the Presbyterian Church of America. "Enough about that—God has taken him. God will continue his work. To be disheartened would be sinful."[55]

Van Til was particularly depressed on the train ride back to Philadelphia from the burial service in Baltimore. "Would everything that Machen had done go, as it were, with him into death?" he wondered. He was comforted by Mrs. Frank Stevenson, the wife of the president of the board. The greatness of Machen, she reminded Van Til, lay in his wisdom not to center Westminster around himself. God would raise up new men to his work, she told him. "They may not be of the caliber of Machen, but as long as they were of the spirit of Machen" the work would go on.[56]

A few days later, Van Til paid a visit to his family in Highland, Indiana. He repeated to his father, Ite Van Til, how disheartened he was at Machen's death and his fear that the work could not continue without his leadership. "My father," Van Til recalled, "old and well stricken in years, simply quoted the passage of Hebrews, 'He that cometh to God must believe that he is and that he is a rewarder of them that diligently seek him.' That was all he said! I was rebuked and chastened. Did I still finally trust in Machen's greatness as a scholar and as a man or did I trust in the Christ to whom Machen constantly pointed us?"[57]

Even while Van Til and his colleagues were grieving, they were aware of the enormous task before them. Their calling was to continue Machen's cause, which demanded a rationale for both institutions, the seminary and the church. This fell largely on Van Til's shoulders, who at the time of Machen's death was the senior member of faculty at the age of forty-one.

And so Van Til performed many tasks that likely would have fallen upon Machen to do. He fulfilled Machen's term on the Committee on Christian Education of the church, and he assumed several of Machen's speaking obligations. This included the sermon he preached on May 28, 1937, at the service in New Haven, Connecticut, when John Murray was ordained by the Presbytery of New York and New England.

Meanwhile, Van Til's critics used the death of Machen as an opportunity to attack Van Til's work more openly. In early 1937, Van Til engaged in lengthy correspondence with J. Oliver Buswell, after Buswell raised the question of Van Til's compatibility with Machen. Conceding that Machen had claimed to learn a lot from Van Til in the last years of his life, Buswell posed this question to Van Til: "In excluding the underlying assumptions of Orr, Hodge, and Wilson, do you also exclude the underlying assumptions of *The Origin of Paul's Religion* and *The Virgin Birth of Christ*?"[58] (These were two books written by Machen.)

Van Til's response to that question is worth quoting at length:

> As to the point whether I can recommend Dr. Machen's works I may say that I can do so and have done so heartily. . . . The point . . . is not that factual apologetics is useless but that it alone and by itself is insufficient, if we are considering the question of a logically consistent and comprehensive apologetics. If I deny vigorously that you can run

100 miles I have not therein denied that you can run at all. Because I have said that factual apologetics is, say, half of the work, I have not said that that half is not important. If someone could prove that the human species has actually derived from animal species, Christian-theism would be disproved. It is therefore important to show that the facts do not warrant any such idea. But even when that has been done the whole work has not been done. A discussion of the philosophy of fact will have to accompany a discussion of the facts themselves. If Dr. Machen has shown that the resurrection of Christ is an actual historical occurrence he has done an inestimable piece of service. But if then the pragmatic philosopher comes along and says that this is an interesting item in this strange world but that it has no universal significance, the factual discussion is in itself for that man quite fruitless unless it is supplemented by a discussion of the philosophy of fact.[59]

Buswell continued to attack Van Til, and the two, who were never close, grew further apart after Buswell left the Presbyterian Church of America with Carl McIntire, Allan MacRae, and other fundamentalists in 1937. Perhaps none of Van Til's opponents more thoroughly misunderstood him than Buswell, who continued to make the public and undocumented claim that Van Til rejected Charles Hodge's system of theology. Reckless comments like this prompted Van Til's colleague, Paul Woolley, to call Buswell "an incompetent reader of Van Til."[60]

The course of years did not find Van Til warming to Buswell. He agreed with and often quoted Louis Berkhof's assessment that Buswell's doctrine of sin was "pure Arminianism." In a letter to Henry J. Kuiper, Van Til wrote that Buswell's "writings show that his Calvinism is a very broad sort of thing, at points scarcely if at all, distinguishable from Arminianism."[61] Toward the end of his life, Van Til continued to distrust Buswell, and he worried that talk of a merger in the 1970s between the Orthodox Presbyterian Church and the Reformed Presbyterian Church, Evangelical Synod, would result in the triumph of Buswell's premillennialism in the church.

Allan MacRae, a former Westminster colleague, also went public against Van Til after Machen's death. When he left the Presbyterian Church of America, MacRae claimed that a small group alien to

American Presbyterianism had taken both the seminary and church hostage. To a certain extent, he was referring to Murray, whom Mac-Rae had failed to persuade to abstain from the use of intoxicating beverages.[62] But much more were his words pointed to Van Til, whose densely philosophical apologetics were "never going to reach anybody." In accusing the Westminster faculty of crushing the "broad evangelical tradition," MacRae heaped scorn on Van Til, whose teaching was "very unfortunate and harmful." Van Til's effect on the students was to lead them away from solid apologetics toward theorizing that would never reach the unsaved world. MacRae even went so far as to suggest dishonesty on the seminary's part when it solicited funds from premillennialists only to convert students to amillennialism before their graduation.[63]

In the debates that followed, Buswell and others failed to pass a declaration that indicated that the church did not oppose premillennialism. The majority of the General Assembly was content that the constitution of the church provided adequate safeguards for "eschatological liberty." Buswell and MacRae left the church in 1937, and MacRae joined the faculty of Faith Theological Seminary.

Van Til was happy to see MacRae leave Westminster, and he contrasted the exodus of Allis and MacRae in a letter to Henry Van Til: "Allis left us gracefully, [but] Allan [MacRae] left us disgracefully."[64] In the departure of Buswell, MacRae, and others from the church, Van Til saw antecedents in Dutch Reformed church history. On the one hand, the *Afscheiding* provided a Reformed rationale for Machen's movement, as it was simultaneously an act of "secession and return." It was a return to doctrinal and confessional fidelity. But as previously noted, the *Afscheiding* of 1834 itself also splintered into different parties. Both wings shared a resistance to antisupernaturalism, but they sought different solutions. Dutch Seceders in the south were pietistic, premillennial (even dispensationalist), and nonconfessional and tended toward ecclesiastical independence. So doctrinally broadminded did this movement become that its ministers were accused of harboring Arminian tendencies. In the north, in contrast, the concern was for confessionalism and a desire to return to Dortian orthodoxy. These two parties in Dutch Reformed history had analogies with the Presbyterian division of 1937, and thus the departure of Buswell, MacRae, and McIntire rendered the church more militantly Reformed.

Debrecen

Even as Van Til struggled with affairs in the new church, he continued to win recognition that began to take on an international scale. In October of 1938 he was invited to the University of Debrecen in Hungary to receive a *professor honoris causa* (honorary professorate), as that Reformed institution was celebrating its four hundredth anniversary. Edwin Rian, the media-conscious field secretary for Westminster Seminary, was quick to make use of this award for publicity purposes. Writing in the *Presbyterian Guardian*, Rian noted that the invitation provided evidence that the seminary had "a Calvinistic theologian of international prestige." He added that no other American school had been invited (implying that Princeton Seminary would not be represented).[65]

Rian's boasting aside, it was curious that Van Til was chosen, given that he was still a young and relatively unpublished professor. It seems that his popularity and success in the classroom would scarcely have attracted attention in eastern Europe by this time. It is possible that Debrecen had made previous arrangements to invite Machen, and Van Til substituted after the untimely death of the seminary's founder.

Still, Van Til eagerly accepted the opportunity, and Westminster obliged him with a month's leave of absence. His travel to Europe included speaking engagements in Scotland, Ireland, Norway, France, and the Netherlands. Rian anticipated a windfall for the seminary, including the enrollment of many more international students. Moreover, Van Til's distinction would demonstrate "anew that theologians the world over consider Westminster . . . a center of Christian learning." And most importantly, it would prove the school's critics wrong:

> Many opponents of the institution have continually prophesied its demise, and especially now that Dr. Machen is no longer on the faculty. At such a time this honor by a foreign university of high standing makes it very clear that such prophecies are only the

product of wishful thinking. The seminary will continue its teaching of the Bible as the Word of God and will continue its opposition to unbelief, strengthened in the knowledge that the gospel will ultimately triumph.[66]

Two ironies accompanied Van Til's European trip in 1938. First, Van Til never made his final destination. He did not deliver his address at Debrecen, because he determined at the last minute that the winds of war rendered travel to eastern Europe too dangerous. Second, Van Til likely grew to resent the attention that Rian sought to bestow upon him. As the next chapter indicates, Rian's ambitions for the seminary and church, so blatant in this article, would ultimately clash with Van Til's vision for both institutions.

In the years following Machen's death, Van Til sought in many ways to avoid becoming the focus of attention, both in the seminary and in the church. When the Westminster faculty chose a new chairman to fill the shoes that Machen had worn since the founding of the school, Van Til was a natural choice. But as Edward Heerema recorded, "Van Til was not interested in the position, feeling with characteristic humility that the administrative duties involved in the position of chairman did not suit whatever gifts the Lord had given him." Instead, the faculty chose R. B. Kuiper (who had returned to the Westminster faculty), a decision with which Van Til was very pleased.[67]

Van Til's unassuming manner was also evident at the General Assembly, where he never served as moderator. At the fourth General Assembly, in 1938, he was nominated, and R. B. Kuiper bested him by ten votes. At the sixth General Assembly, meeting at Westminster Seminary on May 10, 1939, Van Til was elected moderator, winning a majority on the first ballot. However, he was away from the floor at the time of his nomination, and when he learned of his fate, he requested that he be relieved of the office because of "definite reasons." Those reasons, unrecorded in the Assembly minutes, perhaps related to his interest in focusing his energy on the public lecture he delivered that evening on "Modern Psychology of Religion in Relation to Christianity." The Assembly granted this unusual request, and after four more ballots, it elected Everett DeVelde as moderator.[68]

No subsequent General Assembly nominated Van Til to serve as moderator, and he was the only founding member of the Westminster faculty never to have moderated an Orthodox Presbyterian General Assembly. Still, in the words of Charles Dennison, "Van Til was nothing if he was not a faithful churchman—always present but somewhat retiring in the courts of the church."[69] Indeed, Van Til's involvement at the General Assembly was remarkable. He attended fourteen of the first fifteen Assemblies (missing one because of a sabbatical), and he served at twenty-four Assemblies throughout his years in the OPC (he declined those that involved extensive travel, especially to the West Coast). His last General Assembly was the thirty-eighth Assembly (1971) in Wilmington, Delaware, when he was seventy-six years old.

4

Reformed or Evangelical?

*I*n the January 10, 1940, issue of the *Presbyterian Guardian*, Van Til wrote a favorable review of Henry Meeter's book *Calvinism, An Interpretation of its Basic Ideas*. He commended it especially for its popular presentation of the Reformed faith. "Calvinism is not presented as a half-way position between other views; on the contrary, emphasis is placed upon the fact that Calvinism at every point interprets experience from a principle of its own."[1] These words express a recurring theme in Van Til's work: the Reformed faith must establish its integrity as a self-sustaining system. It required no supplement from other expressions of American Protestantism. This claim would place him in the thick of controversies as the new church (which changed its name to the Orthodox Presbyterian Church in 1939) wrestled with the Reformed and evangelical elements in its identity.

By this time, Van Til, now forty-five years old, was firmly established at Westminster Seminary and a recognized leader in the Orthodox Presbyterian Church. As Van Til led both institutions to recover slowly from the blow of the death of Machen, he settled into lifelong habits in his personal and professional life. In 1938, the *Westminster*

Theological Journal debuted, providing Van Til an important publishing outlet for reviews and articles, some of which he developed into books. According to Moisés Silva, Van Til was the most controversial author in the journal's early years, especially in his exposition of the doctrine of common grace.[2] Also by this point, Van Til had written almost all of his classroom syllabi, at least in first edition. Though he would spend the rest of his long career at Westminster revising and expanding them, he had outlined the main themes of his teaching, and he would subject none of them to significant retraction.

Equally entrenched were healthy routines in his home. In 1941 the Van Til family moved from a rented house in Glenside, Pennsylvania, when Van Til purchased the first and only home he would ever own—on Rich Avenue in Erdenheim, close to the seminary campus. He pronounced it "quite suitable" for his family, and it was far better than he had expected to find.[3] The three-story brick home at the end of a short, quiet street became his residence for the next forty-six years until his death in 1987. During that time he and Rena would open their home to many guests. For a time, when their son Earl was on military assignment in France and Germany in 1952, they welcomed boarders such as their daughter-in-law, Thelma, and her infant daughter. Later in that decade, Van Til's nephew, Fred Klooster, and his wife, Leona, also stayed in the home while Klooster pursued his ThM degree at Westminster Seminary. (Leona DeWaard Klooster was the daughter of Van Til's close friend, John DeWaard). Throughout the years, the Van Tils also provided hospitality to countless students and guests of the seminary.

Van Til was characteristically self-deprecating in his description of his personal life. In letters to friends he boasted of his laziness, and he often described his work as the easiest job in the world. Indeed, his schedule permitted him to be home often, where he usually ate breakfast, lunch, and dinner. Yet Van Til's regimen, far from rendering him idle, enabled him to maintain vigorously disciplined work habits, and he was deeply committed to a daily writing schedule. Moreover, each of his three daily meals was accompanied (both before and after) by family prayers, a pattern that Ite Van Til had indelibly imprinted upon his son. After every meal, it was also Van Til's regular habit to wash the dishes.

Van Til's reading habits were impressive. "His head was always in a book," remembered Lena Klooster from Van Til's frequent visits to the DeWaard home.[4] He read the *New York Times* daily, and he subscribed to the Sunday edition to read its book reviews (on Monday). He received several English and Dutch weekly magazines, and, he confessed, several Christian Reformed publications, such as the *Banner*, *Missionary Monthly*, and the monthly *Calvin Forum* would also "tempt me from my work."[5]

Writing was laborious and painful for him. He derisively referred to himself as "Dr. Syllabicus."[6] He often despaired at producing anything more than his classroom notes. Van Til chose the term "syllabus" for want of a better term. "Paper" sounded too ephemeral, and "manuscript" wrongly implied that the work was heading for a published state. In an introduction to a new edition of Van Til's syllabus on apologetics, William Edgar of Westminster Seminary observed that "readers expecting elegant prose may be disappointed. This book remains a course syllabus and is not intended to showcase particular literary merits. It may sound more like a rehearsal than a concert performance."[7]

Some of his critics came to mock these publications. One referred dismissively to Van Til's "scattered writings."[8] Van Til, however, grew comfortable with this method of publication. Students came to Westminster with a wide variety of exposure to the field of philosophy, and his classroom syllabus leveled the playing field by providing background material. Moreover, it freed Van Til to conduct a wide-ranging classroom discussion, which he much preferred over a lecture method of presentation.

So difficult was it for him to write for publication that he often considered contenting himself with the production of his syllabi and leaving it for his successors to write for general readership. As attractive as that temptation seemed, the challenge of articulating a Reformed apologetics kept the fire in his bones. "The riches of the Reformed faith have only fairly been tapped when it comes to Apologetics in our own time," he wrote to a friend.[9]

In the midst of this struggle, he would take solace in gardening, a pastime at which he was enormously successful. Often, the productivity of his garden atoned for the barrenness of his typewriter. In the heat of the controversies that unfolded over the next two decades, Van Til found great contentment in the comfort and stability of his home life. "As long as the family is intact I can stand quite a bit of 'gaff' from would-be Reformed theologians," he wrote to his nephew Henry.[10]

Van Til also maintained close ties with his extended family. His summers generally involved a migration to Munster, Indiana, for Rena's sake, though it was difficult for him to accomplish much writing there. He stayed close to his father, especially after the death of his mother in 1930. His habit was to write to Ite Van Til every Saturday. After the failure of the bank owned by Hendrik Van Til (Cornelius's brother) in the Depression, Ite, then in retirement, lost most of his life's savings. Cornelius bought his father's Ridge Avenue home in Highland and ensured a dignified life for his father in his last years.[11] Van Til also made financial contributions to the theological education of his nephews Fred Klooster and Henry Van Til. He even organized the family's post-war relief to cousins in Groningen, providing for them food, clothing, and tobacco.[12]

Another sign of Van Til's generosity was the distribution of his publications. Because his works were in the form of syllabi, he lacked a publisher to provide for their marketing and distribution. Every year Van Til received dozens of personal inquiries from readers worldwide who were frustrated in their search for his semi-published works. He gladly obliged each request, including a suggestion of the cost of production, and he only asked that the reader pay whatever he or she was able.

Van Til the Teacher

John Murray preferred not to teach the introductory systematic theology course (prolegomena) to juniors at Westminster Seminary, and he welcomed Van Til's willingness to teach it. Van Til's syllabus-based teaching method was markedly different from the lecture style of his colleague, and Murray often joked that "Van ruined the students" before they came to Murray's classes as second-year students.[13]

As different as the two were in temperament and teaching style, they served well together, and together they "formed the poles around which the world of Westminster was to turn," for more than three decades, according to William White.[14] The respect that each held for the other deepened through the years of their collaboration.

Although Van Til mocked himself as an easy grader, his early students consistently regarded his courses as difficult. Two Westminster alumni who went on to long ministerial careers in the Orthodox Presbyterian Church recorded characteristic experiences in Van Til's classroom. Henry Coray remembered that he and his classmates sat under Van Til with open mouths as Van Til dazzled them with his encyclopedic history of philosophy. Elmer Dortzbach described Van Til as having brought him "kicking and screaming" into the "delightful rigors" of the Reformed faith. Van Til left Dortzbach "devastated before the Scriptures as [they were] so beautifully and consistently proclaimed." Scores of other ministerial candidates would begin at Westminster, like Coray and Dortzbach, as struggling and even antagonistic students, later to evolve into Van Til's ardent defenders.[15]

One student who recorded a different experience was John Gerstner. Gerstner came to Westminster in sympathy with Van Til in his first semester, but he eventually graduated with deep disagreements. Apologetic differences would continue between the two during Gerstner's long career at Pittsburgh Theological Seminary, but he never wavered in his assessment that Van Til was among his best instructors. Van Til was a "fabulously interesting professor" and "a delightful person to listen to." Gerstner especially appreciated Van Til's pedagogy. "He didn't give lectures, and he didn't recite things. You were supposed to have read the material and we'd thrash it out all the time."[16]

Behind the lectern, Van Til charmed and enlightened students with chalkboard graffiti, and his teaching earned him the esteem of his colleagues as well. His longtime associate in the apologetics department at Westminster, Robert Knudsen, observed that the best of Van Til often emerged in the classroom and that "only a partial glimpse of the man is evident from his literary output."[17] Church historian Paul Woolley was most impressed with Van Til's gentleness in the classroom. Though he would speak boldly, with firm convictions and unambiguous viewpoints, he "lack[ed] the flaring temper that troubles so many of us." Woolley added his admiration for Van Til's boundless energy and devotion, all of which produced an "intellectual genius" that "stands out from his academic peers by the penetrating quality of his analytic judgment."[18]

Defining the Orthodox Presbyterian Church

Even as Van Til was settling into these highly disciplined patterns of home and work life, a growing spirit of discontent was emerging in certain quarters of the Orthodox Presbyterian Church over a perceived isolation of the denomination. One party, led by Edwin Rian, executive secretary of Westminster Seminary, feared that the OPC was heading in a sectarian direction and needed to reposition itself to exert greater influence in American culture. If the church were really aiming to be the spiritual successor to the PCUSA, Rian urged that it become more culturally relevant. A captivating public speaker, Rian persuaded the eighth General Assembly in 1942 to establish a special "Committee of Nine" with an ambitious agenda "to study the relationship between the Orthodox Presbyterian Church to society in general, and to other ecclesiastical bodies in particular" in order to suggest "ways and means whereby the message and methods of our church may be better implemented to meet the needs of this generation."[19]

Rian was especially disappointed that the OPC was so small. In its first six years it had grown to barely over six thousand members in seventy churches. While others shared his frustration, Rian's appeal begged the question of how the church should promote its growth without weakening or compromising its Reformed commitments. Though many were swayed by Rian's public eloquence, Van Til numbered among the skeptics.

The General Assembly barely chose Van Til to the Committee of Nine, on the fifth ballot, as the penultimately elected member. The committee held nine long meetings over the course of the following year, and when it reported to the following General Assembly, Van Til and ruling elder Murray Forst Thompson dissented from the conclusions of the committee majority. Van Til and Thompson filed a minority report, which Van Til read before the 1942 Assembly, which met in Rochester, New York. While acknowledging the need to make the church's witness more effective, Van Til unleashed strong criticisms of the proposed "super committee" to oversee denominational affairs. The "centralization of power" proposed by the majority, he wrote, "was bureaucratic and unpresbyterian," and it would usurp the Reformed polity of the church's standards. Moreover, the social gospel that was embedded in the committee's proposals would actually impede the effective witness of the church, which, he argued, comes only from "vigorous proclamation of our distinctive faith."[20]

After a lengthy debate on the floor of the Assembly, Van Til and Thompson achieved two key victories. Their recommendation to dissolve the committee prevailed, and the Assembly also voted down the majority's recommendation to encourage greater OPC cooperation with evangelical churches. Van Til and Thompson opposed this too because cooperation with non-Reformed churches would "inevitably lead to the impairment of our unique witness."[21]

As the *Presbyterian Guardian* described the debate, the denomination, now confirmed in its Reformed identity, "knew in what direction it wanted to go."[22] That was certainly overstating matters, and controversies soon to unfold would demonstrate that the church's direction was still highly contested. But what was clear from the Rochester Assembly was the direction in which Van Til was unambiguously pointing the church.

Though Van Til thwarted Rian's agenda for the OPC, the battles between them were not over. They then turned their attention to the challenge of Christian higher education. Van Til joined twenty-six other ministers and educators in an investigation into the possibility of launching a Reformed university. Numbered in that company were his Westminster colleagues Murray, Stonehouse, and Kuiper, as well as representatives from Calvin College and the Christian Reformed Church (including his former professor Samuel Volbeda).

The secretary of the Christian University Association was Edwin Rian, and Van Til joined others in questioning whether Rian was qualified to lead in the formation of a university that was self-consciously Reformed. Although the project soon died (amid charges of financial improprieties on Rian's part), it occasioned further refinements of Van Til's approach to Christian education in his disagreements with others in the association. Against some members who advanced a classical model of education, Van Til countered that a truly Christian education would not challenge the modern mind with the wisdom of ancient or medieval times. Rather, a Reformed approach must present the simple choice of covenant keeping or covenant breaking, or between those who worship and serve the Creator and those who worship and serve the creature.

On the heels of Van Til's antagonism with Rian came a controversy surrounding the ordination of Gordon H. Clark. Because of Van Til's leadership at Westminster Seminary and his ecclesiological prominence in defeating the Committee of Nine, most analyses tend to overstate his involvement in the debate, even to the point of describing it as the "Clark–Van Til controversy." (Worse yet was the infelicitous description of the "heresy trial of Gordon Clark" by James Daane.[23])

This popular nomenclature is misleading, and it is worth observing that Van Til very nearly avoided any role in this debate. When systematic theologian Louis Berkhof, Van Til's former professor at Calvin Seminary, retired in 1944 (after a long career that began in 1906), Van Til was the overwhelming choice of the Christian Reformed Synod to succeed him, far surpassing the votes of six other candidates. (This was not Van Til's first time to be tempted to leave Westminster. In early 1936, the president of Gordon College in Boston invited him to join that faculty, but at the time he expressed "no intentions of leaving."[24]) Letters poured in to Rich Avenue from friends, family, and former students with advice for his decision making. His arm was severely twisted in two directions, and strong opinions suggested very different ways for him to exercise the greatest influence for the Reformed faith.

Together, these appeals formed a remarkable testimony of how fluently Van Til continued to live in two different worlds. His many Dutch friends and associates argued that Van Til's faithful labors on behalf of American Presbyterianism should draw to a conclusion after fourteen years. He had performed heroic service in the OPC, but it was now time for the son of the church to return home, where there were already faint signals of growing sympathy to the work of Karl Barth. "Don't disappoint us," wrote Peter Eldersveld to Van Til. "We need you more than Westminster does." Berkhof himself wrote to Van Til making it clear that Van Til was his personal choice.[25]

Van Til's OPC friends countered with the urgent reminder that his work was unfinished because the church's Reformed identity was still to be established. "There is not a wholesome respect in our church for Reformed leadership," John Hills, a minister and former student wrote. He acknowledged that Van Til would be accorded greater respect if he moved to Grand Rapids. "If you were to leave us, I could not find it in my heart to censure you." But Hills pointed out that the church had suffered already the loss of an influential Dutch Reformed minister when Theodore Jansma left the OPC to return to the CRC in 1943, and he did not know whether the OPC could sustain a bigger blow in Van Til's departure. Hills concluded with an appeal for Van Til to transcend his ethnicity; as small as it was, the OPC still represented the greater hope for the cause of American Calvinism.[26]

In the course of his decision making, nothing made a greater impact on Van Til than the counsel of John Murray. As he urged Van Til to stay in Philadelphia, Murray was bold enough to advise that Van Til not abandon his calling in apologetics because he was simply not qualified to specialize in systematic theology, as the Grand Rapids appointment called him to do.

Murray's words were appealing because Van Til's pen was beginning to bear fruit in articulating his distinctively Reformed defense of the Reformed faith. In 1944, at the suggestion of former student H. Evan Runner, Van Til wrote his widely distributed pamphlet entitled *Why I Believe in God* for the Committee on Christian Education for the OPC. In this dialogue with an imaginary skeptic, Van Til admitted that God was for him the "all-conditioner," who thoroughly shaped his belief in God. He then demanded that the unbeliever make a similar acknowledgment. "If you want to say that belief was poured down my throat, I shall retort that unbelief was poured down *your* throat."[27]

Religious neutrality, in other words, was impossible. If one is not for God one is against God, and to be without bias is simply to have a particular kind of bias. Apologists do injustice to unbelievers when they withhold this truth from them, as Van Til parodied:

> We really think you have colored glasses on your nose when you are talking about chickens and cows, as well as when you talk about the life hereafter. We should have told you this more plainly than we did. But we were really a little ashamed by what would appear to you as a very odd or extreme position. We were so anxious not to offend you that we offended our own God. But we dare no longer present our God to you as smaller or less exacting than He really is.[28]

Thus, the blindness of unbelief was not only the product of anti-Christian conditioning; it was also fueled by the Christian who practiced a non-Reformed approach to apologetics.

Why I Believe in God became Van Til's simplest explanation of his apologetic methodology. Its highly autobiographical account charmed its readers, many of whom found his writings otherwise dense and forbidding.

Debating the Theology of Gordon Clark

Van Til heeded Murray's counsel, and he declined Calvin's offer. Less than a decade later, he would take another invitation even more seriously. Meanwhile, his decision to stay at Westminster set up his confrontation with Gordon Clark.

As a ruling elder in the church since its inception in 1936, Gordon Clark (1902–85) was well known in the denomination, and it was he who nominated J. Gresham Machen as the moderator of that first Assembly. (Clark's nomination of Machen does not mean that he was an especially close intimate of Machen's. Machen was surely everyone's choice as the inaugural moderator of the church, and Clark simply beat other nominators to the floor. Similarly, Van Til's nomination of Buswell as the moderator of the second assembly was no indication of a close bond between those two.)

As a popular professor of philosophy at Wheaton College (1936–43), Clark directed many of his students to Westminster, and he used Van Til's apologetics syllabus in his senior course in Christian philosophy. "The capstone of his whole teaching at Wheaton was to bring us to Van Til," observed Edmund Clowney, a Wheaton graduate. Though Clark expressed disagreements with Van Til, he believed that no one was Van Til's "peer in trying to set forth a thoroughly Christian philosophy."[29] During the early years of their relationship, both men muted their criticisms of each other, and before the controversy erupted, Clark visited the Van Til home occasionally as the two labored to work their differences out, though without success. Although the debate enacted a heavy toll on their friendship, Van Til maintained the highest regard for Clark and his work.[30]

Greater differences began to emerge when Van Til solicited Clark's feedback on his metaphysics syllabus. In his response, Clark wrote that there was nothing objectionable in the human pursuit of comprehensive knowledge of God. Clark argued that it was sinful to aspire to God's being but not to his knowledge. Van Til countered that this ambition destroyed the Creator-creature distinction, because God's being and knowledge were coextensive.

Even as their disagreements widened, Clark continued to maintain contacts with Van Til and Westminster Seminary, and in 1941, he was the seminary's commencement speaker. Van Til was not there to hear him, however, and this was the only one of the first fifty-two Westminster commencements that Van Til failed to attend. (Van Til was not avoiding Clark. Instead, he was concluding a year-long leave of absence. He and Rena went to California, as he traveled and spoke on the West Coast.)

Difficult days for Calvinist faculty at Wheaton College followed the firing of J. Oliver Buswell in 1940, and Clark chafed under the administration of Buswell's successor, V. Raymond Edman. On February 15, 1943, Clark resigned from Wheaton under pressure. The *Presbyterian Guardian* printed Clark's letter of resignation along with Edwin Rian's account of the folly of Wheaton's action in losing an eminent professor whose views were consistent with historic Calvinism. In Wheaton's forcing his resignation, Rian declared that the college "set itself against practically every Reformed and Presbyterian church body in the world."[31]

Later that same spring Clark published "On the Primacy of the Intellect" in the *Westminster Theological Journal*. Van Til again pressed Clark on the Creator-creature distinction, fearing that Clark's argument failed to distinguish between a Christian and a pagan understanding of the intellect. Van Til cited Calvin and Warfield to argue that the intellect was no less fallen than other human faculties. Further conversations confirmed for Van Til his suspicion that Clark's thought was deeply grounded in Greek philosophy; Van Til summed up Clark's position in the Socratic motto that "knowledge is virtue."

To be sure, Van Til was willing to affirm the primacy of the intellect in a certain sense: coming to faith is no mere act of emotional enthusiasm. But Van Til believed that faith is deeper than mere assent, because the Word of God makes an impact on the believer's heart. Van Til feared that Clark's exclusive emphasis on assent to doctrine denied the demands that Scripture places on the whole man. The Bible shapes what one knows, but also what one loves and how one behaves.

After leaving Wheaton, Clark pursued ordination in the OPC in order to consider a pastoral call, despite his lack of formal training in theology. Several of his supporters in the Philadelphia Presbytery sought to process his ordination in an expeditious manner in order to spare Clark the burden of making several trips from Wheaton to Philadelphia. At the meeting of the Presbytery in July 1944, Ned B. Stonehouse of Westminster Seminary conducted a four-hour theological examination of Clark, after which the Presbytery approved him for licensure by a vote of thirty-four to ten (an affirmation that barely met the required three-fourths majority). It then proceeded to license Clark and ordain him on August 9, 1944. Several presbyters then filed a complaint against his ordination in the Presbytery, launching the lengthy battle in the Orthodox Presbyterian Church that reached the General Assembly in 1945.

The Clark controversy played out in the church on three levels. In its most narrow terms the debate was procedural: Had the Presbytery of Philadelphia licensed and ordained Clark properly? Presbyteries occasionally committed procedural mistakes and were corrected routinely in the young church. What raised the stakes in this case were theological issues that prompted the close vote on Clark's licensure: Did his doctrine of the incomprehensibility of God do justice to the Creator-creature distinction, or was it premised on a Greek (and therefore pantheistic) construction of the knowledge of God and man?

Beyond polity and theology, the debate was concerned on yet a third level, which connected it to Van Til's previous battles with Edwin Rian. Discontent continued to spread in the church over its seemingly narrowly Reformed direction, and the focus of much of the concern fell on the role of the faculty of Westminster Seminary in shaping the mission of the Orthodox Presbyterian Church. Should the church cooperate with other forms of conservative Protestantism in America? Or ought it to preserve its distinctively Reformed identity? How could the church best combat the modernism of its day: by joining the emerging evangelical movement or by defending and propagating the Westminster Standards? At first glance, these issues do not seem directly related to the epistemological divide between Clark and Van Til. However, they were prominent concerns of members of the church who became Clark's supporters.

Eventually the 1946 General Assembly determined that the Presbytery of Philadelphia had erred in violating the Form of Government by failing to provide sufficient time between Clark's licensure and ordination. The Assembly "implored" the Presbytery to acknowledge its errors, which the Presbytery did, confessing that in its haste to ordain Clark it had failed to account "for the sharp differences of opinion concerning Dr. Clark's theology, and thereby contributed to the disturbance of the peace of the church." (The Presbytery registered its contrition by the slim margin of 16–14.)[32]

Strictly speaking, the General Assembly never addressed the substance of the complaint against Clark. Instead, it assigned the theological issues of the debate to study committees that reported over the course of three years, and these reports were distributed to congregations for their study. Several issues were involved (including the relationship between divine sovereignty and human responsibility and the free offer of the gospel), and chief among them was the doctrine of the incomprehensibility of God. The two principal documents before the church were the Complaint (against the Presbytery of Philadelphia and its action in licensing Clark) and the Answer to the Complaint. The dispute centered on this question: Did the doctrine of the incomprehensibility of God require a qualitative difference between the content of God's knowledge and man's knowledge?

Clark's failure to acknowledge that qualitative difference, according to the Complaint, collapsed the Creator-creature distinction that lay at the heart of a biblical doctrine of creation. By his very nature, God is incomprehensible to man in every sense. In so arguing, the complainants sought to affirm both the incomprehensibility of God and the genuineness of human knowledge of God. That knowledge, though not identical at any point with divine knowledge, is analogous to divine knowledge and an expression of genuine truth from a creaturely point of view. Clark sought to underscore the certainty of human knowledge, but for his opponents this came at too high a cost because it ultimately compromised God's transcendence:

> We dare not maintain that his knowledge and our knowledge coincide at any single point. Our knowledge of any proposition must always remain the knowledge of the creature. As true knowledge, that knowledge must be analogical to the knowledge which God possesses, but it can never be identified with the knowledge which the infinite and absolute Creator possesses of the same proposition.[33]

In response, Clark claimed that he protected the Creator-creature distinction. Only God possesses omniscience, and human knowledge "would always be temporal, and could never include either the immediate intuitive knowledge of God or the knowledge of all the relationships and implications of any and all propositions." He challenged the scriptural basis for the qualitative difference between divine and human knowledge, and he insisted that any theory of knowledge that granted to man a mere analogy of God's knowledge plunged the church "into unmitigated skepticism."[34]

Van Til did not author the complaint (although he signed it along with several others, and his ideas were certainly embodied in it). Not once did he take the floor of Presbytery to speak, and he did not write anything during the controversy. Nor did he serve on any of the General Assembly study committees. Several reasons account for Van Til's silence in this process. As a member of the Philadelphia Presbytery, he was disqualified from serving on the study committees to address the complaint. Moreover, he was actively involved in work on a major book on the theology of Karl Barth. Finally, though he would publicly express himself after the controversy (in a 1949 syllabus), Van Til was more than content with the labors of John Murray, who was a member of the Presbytery of New York and New England. Murray served on the study committees appointed by the General Assembly, and his prominent role in the debate has led some participants to suggest that it was better described as the Clark-Murray debate.[35] Murray argued that a qualitative difference prevailed between divine knowledge and human knowledge on every proposition.

Still, because Murray and other complainants employed Van Tilian distinctions and vocabulary, Clark's supporters successfully established Van Til as Clark's principle antagonist.[36] This tactic proved effective for Clark's defense, because Van Til already had a reputation of being a difficult professor for students to understand. The voices of Murray and others may have presented the case, Clark's defenders argued, but the Complaint against Clark embodied the obscure apologetics of Van Til.

Robert Strong, minister of the Willow Grove, Pennsylvania, Orthodox Presbyterian Church, which Van Til and his family attended, was among Clark's most vocal supporters. So intent was he to turn the debate into a referendum on Van Til's views that he charged Van Til with reluctance in claiming responsibility for the complaint, even hinting at cowardice on Van Til's part. "Although he did not write [the complaint]," Strong later wrote, "he did agree with it to the extent that he signed it, and so what it offers he really offers. Fault that can be found with it is fault that can be found with the point of view offered by Dr. Cornelius Van Til."[37]

Strong described the Clark ordination as "a very great victory" for the church because it recognized that "there could be some difference at minor points without a man's loyalty to the system of doctrine [of the Westminster Standards] being impeached."[38] This was a revealing statement, because Clark himself never conceded that his views required an exception from the church's standards. Strong's observation suggests that his ultimate interest in the debate centered on the tension previously described between the more Reformed and the more evangelical camps in the Orthodox Presbyterian Church. Strong argued that Clark's supporters were willing to draw a broad "circle of charity" to include many within the fellowship of the church, contrary to the narrow circle drawn by the faculty of Westminster Seminary, who were acknowledged as the intellectual leaders of the church.

Frustrated that the procedure drained the resources of the church for over two years, Strong dismissed the debate as an unfortunate controversy that wasted time through "an intensive study of an arcane area of Christian philosophy" and was thus a "tragic chapter in the history of the trouble-beset Orthodox Presbyterian Church." He continued to emphasize Van Til's role, even anachronistically citing Van Til's 1949 "Introduction to Systematic Theology" syllabus to accuse Van Til of engaging in a "strife over words," and he went on to characterize Van Til's language as vague, uncertain, and even skeptical.[39]

Strong's focus on Van Til disguised his own active role in the broader battle. Intent on redirecting the OPC and Westminster Seminary toward broader evangelicalism, Strong formed a coalition of like-minded evangelicals and established a "Program of Action" that claimed to recover the lost ideals he said had characterized the OPC at its founding a decade earlier, including the active cooperation with other denominations and parachurch organizations that were combating modernism. In order to achieve these goals, the "Program of Action" established four "specific objectives":

1. The ordination of Gordon Clark
2. Affiliation with the American Council of Christian Churches
3. An official deliverance against the use of alcoholic beverages
4. Denominational control over Westminster Seminary and the *Presbyterian Guardian*.[40]

Many subsequent studies of this controversy have followed Strong's lead in failing to reckon with the broader ecclesiastical debate. In his book *Van Til: An Analysis of his Thought*, John Frame mentions neither the evangelical coalition that Strong formed nor its infamous "Program of Action," and he disregards John Murray's leadership in the battle for the soul of the Orthodox Presbyterian Church. The effect is to reduce the debate to misunderstandings between two obscure and strong-willed apologists, and thus Frame concludes that the episode represented a low point in both Clark's and Van Til's careers.[41]

It is too strong to cast the debate in the terms employed by Edward Heerema, R. B. Kuiper's son-in-law, when he described the OPC at this time as divided into "left wing" and "right wing camps." Yet Heerema's analysis, in his privately published and distributed pamphlet entitled "Whither the Orthodox Presbyterian Church," serves to highlight the larger evangelical agenda at work in Clark's defense.

In Heerema's recounting, the Clark faction consisted of those who were engaged "in an all-out offensive to gain control of the OPC and related agencies like Westminster Seminary." Strong organized a boycott of Westminster Seminary and circulated claims about its faculty. Among these were charges that professors were "blindly following the prejudiced leadership of Dr. Van Til in opposing Dr. Clark," and that the faculty consisted of "a bunch of ingrates toward Dr. Clark," who were either "jealous" or "afraid" of him. Heerema charged this group with "spread[ing] poison through the church" and "speaking more viciously and more bitterly [about Westminster] than they would about a modernist seminary."[42]

Heerema sought to distance Clark himself from the egregious tactics of his supporters, though not always carefully enough. Heerema's "Whither" contained the absurd claim that Clark was an Arminian. Clark, after all, was dismissed from Wheaton for his outspoken Calvinism, and the controversy had some in the OPC suspecting him of hyper-Calvinism. It is better to suggest (as Michael Hakkenburg argued) that evangelicals in the church, many of whom did not share Clark's strongly Reformed convictions, used his case as a convenient instrument to vent their frustration at the direction they feared the OPC was headed.

The debate over the ordination of Gordon Clark, therefore, was part of a larger battle over the denomination's Reformed character. Clark was an instrument in the agenda of a faction in the church that was discontented with its Reformed identity. Ultimately, what was at stake for the likes of Robert Strong was whether the church's ecclesiology would be Reformed or evangelical. Although Strong and his allies secured the ordination of Clark against the complainants, they lost the greater battle when other aspects of their "Program of Action" collapsed.

In the years that followed, Clark's sympathizers left the church and headed in a number of different directions. Several ministers, including Strong, joined the southern Presbyterian church. Edwin Rian, a supporter of Clark who generally maintained his silence throughout the controversy, made an ostentatious recantation and rejoined the northern Presbyterian church (after claiming to have discovered the errors of OPC sectarianism while rereading Calvin's *Institutes*). Still others joined the Bible Presbyterian Church, founded in the previous decade by Carl McIntire.

Clark joined Strong and others in criticizing the narrowness of the Orthodox Presbyterian Church. In the January 10, 1945, issue of the *Presbyterian Guardian*, Gordon H. Clark labeled the OPC a "sectarian oddity." He accused the eight-year-old church of diverting its chief emphasis away from opposition to modernism. As a result, the church had "earned an unenviable reputation" and "assumed the position of an isolationist porcupine."[43] In 1948, Clark himself transferred his ministerial credentials into the United Presbyterian Church of North America. After the UPCNA merger with the mainline northern Presbyterian church in 1958, he affiliated with the Reformed Presbyterian Church (General Synod), which, through a merger with disaffected members of McIntire's Bible Presbyterian Church, formed the Reformed Presbyterian Church, Evangelical Synod (RPCES). Clark taught philosophy for nearly thirty years at Butler University in Indianapolis and for ten years at Covenant College in Lookout Mountain, Georgia, from which he was retired at the time of his death in 1985.

It was on behalf of the Reformed identity of the OPC that Van Til, Murray, and others on the Westminster faculty argued so passionately in this debate. By the controversy's end they had persuaded the church that its Reformed militancy needed to express itself in careful distinction from Reformed evangelicalism. It is in this sense that Van Til "won" the debate, and in the larger context of Reformed ecclesiology, Van Til's role in the Clark controversy, far from being an embarrassment, should be interpreted as one of his finest moments.

Van Til demurred from writing extensively about the controversy because he was more than content with the output of Murray and the General Assembly study committees. He could hardly improve on this assessment:

> The infinite transcendence of God and His consequent incomprehensibility should always constrain us in the profound sense of mystery, awe, and reverence. It is at the highest reaches of our apprehension, understanding, and contemplation that we are most deeply, gratefully, and adoringly aware of the transcendent and incomprehensible glory of God. It is then that we are most truly conscious that God dwells in light unapproachable and full of glory, and we are constrained to exclaim, "Great is the Lord, and greatly to be praised; and his greatness is unsearchable."[44]

Van Til was also pleased that his nephew, Fred H. Klooster, wrote a thorough assessment of the controversy in 1951 for his dissertation for the Free University of Amsterdam. Van Til welcomed this analysis, and especially the pastoral conclusion that Klooster drew:

> The doctrine of the incomprehensibility of God should not be a dry, dead doctrine. . . . Incomprehensibility in Scripture is set in relation to very practical problems. . . . It is used to comfort the people in exile. It is declared in relation to the problem of suffering. Job is dumb before the mighty Creator when he sees that he cannot even comprehend the greatness of God's works.[45]

In 1957 Clark revisited the debate in the pages of *Bibliotheca Sacra*. There he unapologetically repeated the charges that Van Til denied that believers could know the truth, and he attributed this to a "neo-orthodox influence" on Van Til.[46] This was so for Clark because truth must have a univocal, identical point of coincidence in the knowledge of God and man.

For many of Clark's supporters, Van Til's criticism of Clark was difficult to reconcile with his concurrent opposition to Karl Barth. "Exceedingly strange it is," wrote Robert Reymond, that as ardent a foe of Barthian irrationalism as is Van Til comes nevertheless to the same conclusion concerning the nature of truth for man as does Barth. The only difference in this connection between Van Til and Barth is that Van Til insists that truth is objectively present in biblical propositions while for Barth truth is essentially existential. But for both religious truth can appear, at least at times, paradoxical.

Reymond thus summarized Van Til's "radical view of analogy" as "pure equivocism," and he posed the question, "Is it any wonder that Clark contends that Van Til's position inevitably leads to skepticism and total human ignorance?"[47]

Clark himself allowed the possibility of a non-Barthian root to Van Til's thought, but one that was hardly more palatable. Analogical thinking also had it roots in Roman Catholicism, he noted. In tying Van Til to Aquinas's doctrine of analogy, Clark ignored the painstaking efforts of Van Til to distinguish the two.

Even more glaring was Clark's ignorance of the history of the doctrine in Reformed thought on the subject. If Clark and Reymond resisted the notions of mystery, Van Til found himself at home with that expression, because of his deeper commitment to revelation and covenant. Van Til was comfortable even to the point of embracing the language of his mentor, Herman Bavinck, that "mystery is the life of all dogmatics."[48] Because the finite cannot contain the infinite, Bavinck underscored that the revelation of the infinite God to the finite creature cannot be exhaustive of the being of God, and so God remains incomprehensible. Van Til did not embrace Bavinck's teaching completely, and he criticized Bavinck for failing to describe a distinctively Christian approach to incomprehensibility. "The Christian and the non-Christian notions of mystery are as the poles apart," he wrote, and "Bavinck sometimes speaks as though the concept of the incomprehensibility of God entertained by Christian theology and that entertained by pagan philosophy were virtually the same."[49]

Mystery is a consequence of the Creator-creature distinction, which for Bavinck (and Van Til) is ever accompanied by the Creator-creature relation, by virtue of humanity's covenant standing with God. Thus the incomprehensibility of God is to be supplemented with the communicability of God, and the result is analogical knowledge. Bavinck wrote, "But though God is thus beyond our full comprehension, and description, we do confess to having the knowledge of God. This knowledge is analogical and the gift of revelation. . . . This truth is beyond our comprehension; it is a mystery but not self-contradictory."[50]

The communicability of God rescued Van Til's thought from skepticism; he argued that we are not left to choose between univocal knowledge and equivocal knowledge. Van Til may not have expressed himself in the clearest way, and some confused readers tripped over the seeming incomprehensibility of Van Til. But little of what he wrote was genuinely novel, and the debate revealed the large extent to which conservative American Presbyterians were unconversant with their Reformed heritage. Klooster observed that the OPC controversy was "instructive because it took place in an American church in which the elements of the Reformed tradition of America, Scotland, and the Netherlands are present." And he went on to add that though irrationalism had become more prominent by this point, "it is just as necessary to realize that rationalism impairs our knowledge of God."[51]

Recently, Scott Clark (no relation to Gordon) of Westminster Seminary California echoed Klooster's point by locating Van Til's views within the context of Reformed scholasticism. Post-Reformation Reformed orthodoxy posited two kinds of knowledge, God's knowledge and the knowledge that God revealed to humanity. This "archetypal/ectypal" distinction "became the basis for Protestant theological method," and scholastic theologians introduced the necessity of speaking analogically about the knowledge of God, and of understanding theology as it is revealed to us as an analogue of what is proper to God. Scott Clark has argued that Van Til's doctrine of the incomprehensibility of God was an effort to maintain this distinction, although Van Til employed a different vocabulary.[52]

Speaking analogically of God was not merely permissible but necessary for Reformed theology. As Van Til himself went on to argue, "we are entitled and compelled to use anthropomorphism not apologetically but fearlessly. We need not fear to say that God's attitude has changed with respect to mankind. We know well enough that God in himself is changeless. But we know that we are able to affirm that our words have meaning for no other reason than that we use them analogically."[53]

Scott Clark's analysis also explains why Herman Hoeksema took Gordon Clark's side in the debate, an allegiance that surprised and disappointed Van Til. Scott Clark notes that the CRC debate at the 1924 Synod (which condemned Hoeksema's denial of common grace) divided those who accepted the Reformed archetypal and ectypal distinction (Hoeksema's critics) from those who denied it (Hoeksema and his supporters).

While Van Til included analysis of Gordon Clark's rationalism in subsequent revisions of some of his syllabi, he generally regarded the episode as a closed chapter. Reluctant to open up old wounds, Van Til would later decline the opportunity to contribute to a Festschrift for Clark in 1966.[54] At the same time, both men sought ways of demonstrating that they did not bear personal animus against the other. For example, when Van Til later developed his analysis and critique of what he termed the "new evangelicalism," he was careful to exclude Clark from that company.[55] In the 1970s, Clark accepted an invitation to speak at Westminster Seminary, and Van Til was among the first on campus to greet him.[56]

If Van Til emerged fatigued from these battles, he was surely tempted by another way of escape that was offered to him. In 1947 William Hendriksen, professor of New Testament at Calvin Seminary, urged him to consider another opportunity to return to Grand Rapids, this time for a position in historical theology, to replace D. H. Kromminga, who had died that spring. In weighing Hendriksen's suggestion, Van Til could imagine switching fields and becoming enthusiastic about church history. "And to think of working in the church of my youth has its constant appeal for myself and for my wife," he wrote to Hendriksen. Still he felt attached to the field of apologetics, and "the need here [at Westminster] is as great as ever. We do have a beachhead for the Reformed Faith here and even the very janitors ought to stay. The adversaries are many."[57]

Van Til expressed his gratitude for the cooperative spirit between the two schools, and he expressed his hope that Calvin not appoint someone "who has in any degree imbibed the new Princeton spirit."

The pressure of these invitations, especially the 1943 overture from Synod, was strong, but not nearly as tempting as the offer that was still to come.

Presuppositionalism

One of the curious features of Van Til's engagement with Clark is that it involved two thinkers who both espoused the apologetic method of "presuppositionalism." In the analysis of Ronald Nash, Clark was a "rational presuppositionalist," and Van Til a "revelational presuppositionalist." The Clark controversy demonstrated the ambiguity of the term *presuppositionalism* to describe Van Til's distinctive approach to apologetics. (Several decades later, the ambiguity would return by the employment of the term by Francis Schaeffer.) While Nash (a protégé of Clark's) dismissed Van Til as a skeptic, Van Til concluded that Clark was more rationalist than presuppositionalist, and pronounced a plague on both rationalism and irrationalism as positions that rendered autonomous human reason supreme.

The term *presuppositionalism* was probably coined a decade before the Clark controversy by Allan MacRae, Van Til's antagonist on the early Westminster faculty, and it was intended as a term of derision. J. Oliver Buswell later popularized it in a series of articles in *The Bible Today* that ran in 1948 and 1949.[58] The term was not Van Til's choice, although he frequently referred to the necessity of reasoning by presupposition. The word *presuppose* appeared in passing in two early works of his, *Why I Believe in God* and *The Intellectual Challenge of the Gospel*. By 1955 he came to state the matter explicitly in his *Defense of the Faith*: "The best, the only, the absolutely certain proof of the truth of Christianity is that unless its truth is presupposed there is no proof of anything. Christianity is proved as being the very foundation of the idea of proof itself."[59] Still, it is striking to discover in Van Til how rarely he labeled his own work as "presuppositionalism." As MacRae and Buswell trafficked in the term critically and disparagingly, Van Til seemed to respond by acknowledging that, despite its vagueness and ambiguity, it was of some usefulness. However, he seldom chose to call his system by that name. He tended to refer to it simply as "Reformed apologetics," thereby stressing its consistency with Reformed theology and epistemology. On occasion he dared to label it privately to confidants in eponymous fashion as "Van Tilian apologetics."[60] (Later, in the context of his engagement with Herman Dooyeweerd, the expression "transcendental apologetics" gained currency.)

By the end of the Buswell–Van Til exchange in the *Bible Today*, an anonymous letter writer employed poetry to express frustration at the fruitlessness of the debate:

> Scotch is Scotch,
> And Dutch is Dutch,
> But Calvin was French, you see,
> And died at the age of fifty-five,
> Not older than "B" or "Van T."
> He wrote in the language of 1509—
> He wrote not English nor Dutch,
> He wrote in the words *he* understood
> And has been translated much.
> And the mind of the Scotch interprets Scotch,
> And the mind of the Dutch sees Dutch;
> But God's great grace is working on
> And souls respond to his touch.
> And when in the glorious crowning day
> The Scotch and the Dutch shall meet,
> They both will say "It is all of grace;
> We have reached the Mercy seat."
> But Buswell will drive his "Bus"
> And Van Til his "Van" will drive,
> But whether thru tunnel or over bridge,
> By *grace* they will both arrive.[61]

Two Circles

For all the controversy that Van Til's approach has generated, the point that he sought to make was deceptively simple: Reformed theology demanded a Reformed apologetic. Apologetics must be based on a Reformed doctrine of God and the Reformed doctrines of grace. It is inconsistently Reformed, therefore, to employ a less than fully

Reformed defense of Calvinism. Van Til wrote in review of Wilbur Smith's apologetic book *Therefore, Stand*:

> A generally evangelical apologetic to a large extent defeats its own purposes. True enough much good may be accomplished, both by an Arminian theology and by a generally evangelical method of apologetic. In this fact all who love the Lord will rejoice. But how much more good may be accomplished by the grace of God through a more consistently Biblical theology and a more consistently Biblical apologetic. A generally evangelical apologetic does not drive the natural man down into a corner with no hope of escape. It does not track him down till he is at bay. It does not destroy his last shelter. His fire is not altogether extinguished. . . . A plea for a vigorous apologetic ought therefore to be a plea for a genuinely Reformed apologetic. We may not be clear, indeed as to the full implications of a truly Reformed apologetic. But this fact does not justify us in refusing to point out to those who, with us, love the Christian faith that a generally evangelical apologetic, like a Roman Catholic apologetic, is inadequate for any time and especially inadequate for our time.[62]

American Presbyterian disquiet over Van Til's employment of presuppositional reasoning owed, as previously noted, to its unfamiliarity with the Reformed tradition, and especially unfamiliarity with Bavinck. Van Til imported many of his ideas from Bavinck, whose four-volume *Gereformeerde Dogmatiek* was largely inaccessible to the English-speaking world. Bavinck employed presuppositional language in his first volume:

> Apologetics cannot precede faith and does not attempt a priori to argue the truth of revelation. It assumes the truth and belief in the truth. It does not, as the introductory part or as the foundational science, precede theology and dogmatics. It is itself a theological science through and through, which presupposes the faith and dogmatics and now maintains and defends the dogma against the opposition to which it is exposed.[63]

On this basis Bavinck went on to critique rationalistic apologetic approaches that were premised on a denial of Christianity:

115

If Christian revelation, which presupposes the darkness and error of unspiritual humanity, submitted in advance to the judgments of reason, it would by that token contradict itself. It would thereby place itself before a tribunal whose jurisdiction it had first denied. And having once recognized the authority of reason on the level of first principles, it could no longer oppose that authority in the articles of faith.[64]

Van Til did not so much create a new apologetic as he refined Bavinck's approach, applying it to modernism, old and new. The most memorable feature of Van Til's teaching involved a diagram of the two circles that he drew in his classroom lectures. Van Til positioned the larger one above the smaller one, and the two did not overlap. The former represented God, and the latter the world that he created, which was always dependent upon God and his revelation. The two circles represented not only the creaturely and analogical standing of humanity and God's transcendence, but as Van Til connected them with two vertical lines, they indicated man's covenantal standing before God. By connecting creation and covenant in this way, Van Til established the similarity of the being and knowledge of man, as God's image bearer, with God's while denying their identity at any point. Gordon Clark, intolerant of any notion of mystery, committed the error of allowing the circles to touch.

The struggles of this decade enacted a personal toll on Van Til, and he experienced several setbacks to his health. His letters referred to a protracted illness in 1948. A heart condition in 1949, attributed to nervous tension, forced the cancellation of a planned trip to London, when his doctor ordered him to secure more rest in his schedule and "to take things easy at once."[65]

Church life was a struggle for Van Til as well. Van Til and his family continued to attend Calvary Church in Willow Grove, although it was ten miles away when the family moved to Rich Avenue. With gas rationing during the Second World War, driving to Willow Grove twice a Sunday proved difficult, so the Van Tils attended an Orthodox Presbyterian Church in nearby Germantown at night, which had the advantage of partially relieving the difficulties at Willow Grove. It was not easy for Van Til to sit under the ministry of Robert Strong, as he confided to his nephew: "Much of the pleasure of church attendance has left us since I have become keenly aware that my pastor is a ringleader of a group that is trying to steer the OPC into something less than a Reformed direction."[66]

Van Til continued to attend Willow Grove mainly because of his interest in the Christian school that was meeting there at the time. The battle between the Reformed and the evangelicals was raging on several fronts, and one of them was the Willow Grove Christian day school (which eventually became Phil-Mont Christian Academy). "Strong is virtually taking over the school," he wrote to his nephew Henry in 1945. "He's robbing my cradle."[67]

As Van Til persevered throughout these struggles, the Orthodox Presbyterian Church emerged more confirmed in her Reformed identity. If it was not the spiritual successor to the PCUSA, it was taking on a loftier goal. Van Til became the conduit for a more penetrating analysis of American Calvinistic theology, especially bringing to the forefront the insights of Dutch Reformed theology, which sought to advance the church beyond the old-Princeton tradition.

After the exodus of Rian, Strong, and others, Westminster Seminary established itself as a center of international Calvinism, if not American Presbyterianism. Van Til wrote to a Christian Reformed associate in 1949 that the "direction and control" of the OPC was "militantly Calvinistic."[68] Militancy resulted in some lean years at Westminster Seminary, and at times Van Til lectured to classes as small as four students during the decade. Yet he felt a sense of vindication as he addressed the Westminster commencement exercise in 1947 on the topic of "Facing the Future with Confidence." A month later he expressed before the Christian Reformed Synod the hope of strengthening the bond between the two Reformed churches.

Van Til's buoyancy by the controversy's end could be measured by an open letter he wrote to *Time* and *Life* magazines. In 1947, both magazines ran articles hinting at a "Calvinist Comeback" in American religion. Van Til's defiantly titled response, "We Are Not Ashamed of Calvinism!" (published by neither *Time* nor *Life* but later appearing in the *Presbyterian Guardian*), claimed that reporters were looking for Calvinism in the wrong places. Echoing the language of his earlier review of Meeter, Van Til identified true Calvinists as those "who hold to the system of Christian theism and do so seriously at every point."[69]

Only a full-orbed Calvinism could produce a Reformed renaissance in America, and it was futile to search for Calvinism among those who were its enemies. Van Til warned especially about one particular form of counterfeit Calvinism: "If there is anything that 'Calvinist Karl Barth' finds distasteful and untrue it is Calvinism."[70]

The New Machen
against the New
Modernism

*T*he year 1937 marked the centennial of the birth of
Abraham Kuyper. Dutch Americans observed the mile-
stone by evaluating Kuyper's success in America. Henry
Beets (1869–1947), longtime director of missions in the Christian
Reformed Church and editor of the *Banner*, was bullish in his assessment of the American appropriation of the great Dutch statesman
and theologian.

Cornelius Van Til was less so. In an article that he wrote in Dutch
for *De Reformatie*, Van Til offered a dissenting opinion. He was discouraged about the prospects for American Calvinism, because in his
judgment Reformed Americans showed little sign of appropriating the
real message of Kuyper's celebrated 1898 visit. "Calvinism is making
progress in America, according to Beets," Van Til wrote. "But let's look
at the facts." Yes, Van Til, conceded, Christian schools were growing in

America, and the spirit of Kuyper was alive in the Christian Reformed Church. But the fundamentalist-modernist controversy hindered the spread of Kuyper's thought. Liberals disdained historic Calvinism, and the fundamentalists showed little interest themselves. The Reformed Church in America and the southern Presbyterian church were both showing signs of modernist corruption, and conservatives in neither denomination were speaking up.[1]

The chief evidence for Van Til came from that former bulwark of Calvinism, Princeton Seminary, where Kuyper had delivered his Stone Lectures. For Van Til, a telltale sign of decline was the institution's fascination with another continental theologian. By 1937, he wrote in *De Reformatie*, "Karl Barth had conquered Princeton."[2]

After the 1918 publication of his commentary on Romans (the famous "bomb on the playground of the theologians"),[3] Barth became an enigma for the English-speaking theological world. Along with that of Emil Brunner, his early work exposed the inadequacies of liberal theology. Although a rift developed between the two in 1934 with the publication of Brunner's treatment on natural theology (to which Barth thundered *Nein!* in response), the two were together credited with the rise of crisis theology or dialectical theology.

Preliminary evaluations of Barth had been cautious and tentative. Even Machen spoke with great hesitation and uncertainty when he was asked to evaluate the work of Barth. After Barth's massive *Kirchliche Dogmatik* (*Church Dogmatics*) began to be released in 1932, Machen had little time to devote to it. He generally pleaded ignorance and referred inquirers to Van Til. Beyond time constraints, Machen believed that Van Til had the better philosophical background from which to evaluate Barth, and he found the "strange dialectic of Barth" terribly difficult to understand.[4]

If conservatives struggled to read Barth, they were not alone. The liberal *Christian Century* dismissed Barth's early work as "German fundamentalism," misreading both Barth's theology and his nationality. Still, the magazine was careful to assert that Barth's conservatism was a marked improvement over American varieties.[5]

In the pages of the *Banner*, Van Til continued to warn against American infatuation with Barth. The truly Kuyperian approach to Barth was rejection. Van Til noted Valentine Hepp's observation that the Reformed churches of the Netherlands "have shown that they are still alive to the spirit of Kuyper by rejecting Barthianism in a vigorous fashion." In contrast, Van Til lamented, Americans were "playing with Barthianism," and this in the spirit of being "truly progressive." It was no sign of progress that some were praising Barth in the same breath with Kuyper, Bavinck, and Warfield.[6]

Van Til could also cite Barth himself about the irreconcilability of the Dutch and the Swiss theologians. In volume 2.1 of his *Church Dogmatics*, Barth described the naiveté of conservative movements "inspired by Abraham Kuyper" particularly over the relationship between reason and revelation.[7] True Kuyperians, Van Til urged, must identify Barth as an enemy and not a friend, and the Reformed faith could not advance in America if differences were minimized. And so Van Til launched a sustained polemic against Barth that would extend over three decades.

Having the advantage of knowing Barth in the original German, Van Til's analysis became one of the earliest of English language assessments. (His 1946 book on Barth preceded by a whole decade the release of all but one volume of the English translation of Barth's *Kirchliche Dogmatik*.) What alarmed Van Til about other American responses was their willingness to identify isolated elements of Barth's theology that seemed amenable to orthodoxy, as though it were possible to accept a selection of Barth's system and to discard others. Barth himself insisted that his dialectical principle was of a whole cloth and thus indivisible, and Van Til was eager to oblige him.[8]

As indicated in chapter 3, Van Til's regular reports on developments at Princeton Seminary emphasized that neo-orthodoxy did not make the school safe for Calvinism. By establishing this overt link between Barth and Princeton, Van Til sought to defend against skeptics Machen's claim about Princeton's inevitable demise after 1929. This was a difficult case to make. In the judgment of other conservatives who stayed in the mainline Presbyterian church, neo-orthodoxy rendered obsolete the Presbyterian controversies of the previous decades. Moreover, the liberal trajectory that Machen had predicted of Princeton Seminary seemed not to have played out, especially after the arrival of John Mackay in 1936. Under Mackay's presidency, neo-orthodox professors were hired (including a brief tenure by Emil Brunner), and Princeton became for a time the locus of an American post-liberal movement, promising to transcend the tired categories of fundamentalism and liberalism. Princeton's Elmer Homrighausen testified that Barth had eroded his confidence in the shallow cultural optimism of modernism and encouraged his return to the older sources of Reformed ortho-doxy.[9] Crisis theologians espoused many conservative themes, such as the centrality of Scripture as God's revelation, the transcendence of God, the biblical account of sin and the fall, and the need for faith as an encounter with God through Jesus Christ, all the while embracing the higher critical conclusions about Scripture.

Van Til denied that Barth represented a corrective to Protestant liberalism, and he charged that every Barthian addition to Prince-ton's faculty only added proof of its concession to modernism. He mocked particularly the appointment of George S. Hendry to the Charles Hodge Chair of Systematic Theology in 1949, wondering how Hendry could assume a chair when he denied the very idea of systematic theology. The "Christ of the present day Princeton Sem-inary," Van Til warned incoming Westminster students that year, "is not the Christ of Charles Hodge, of Benjamin Breckenridge Warfield, and of Geerhardus Vos. . . . The Christ of modernized Princeton is not God."[10]

To Van Til's dismay, Mackay was particularly successful in gaining support from quarters in the Christian Reformed Church. That was due in part to Mackay's clever use of the phrase "neo-Calvinism" to describe the new Barthian phase at Princeton.[11] This term was also becoming a popular description for Kuyper's reappropriation of Reformed orthodoxy. Van Til himself did not commonly employ the phrase, fearing the conflation of "neo-Calvinism" and neo-orthodoxy among undiscerning readers. According to Van Til, Barth's theology could hardly own up to Mackay's description. It was neither a correc-tive nor a modification of Calvinism but a radical break with Calvin and the Reformation itself.

Van Til first published on Barth in 1931 and wrote several articles in the *Presbyterian Guardian* throughout that decade. His analysis was impressive enough for Machen to defer all inquirers about Barth to Van Til's more expert judgment. In a 1937 article for the *Presbyterian Guardian*, Van Til focused on Barth's doctrine of Scripture. At the heart of Barth's teaching was the activism of God, which reduced revelation to pure existential encounter. Revelation was found in Jesus Christ, who was the Word of God as the reconciling work of God. This Word came to us in our encounter with God through faith, not through anything complete or past. God's freedom demanded the activism of his revelation and forbade our binding him to any static or completed revelation. The written word, therefore, was itself a dead letter, Barth argued, and a petrification of the living word. Barth's activism was undercutting the most basic doctrine of the Reformation, Van Til countered, and Barth was robbing the Word of God from the people of God just as Rome had done.[12]

While subsequent American evangelical criticism of Barth focused heavily on Barth's defective view of Scripture, Van Til would not content himself with that point. Another article in the *Presbyterian Guardian* charged Barth with denying the biblical account of creation and the fall. Van Til wrote that despite "Barth's best intentions to call men back to the sovereign God of the Reformers he has in reality no 'sovereign God' to offer us."[13] A third article attacked Barth's Christology, noting Barth's dismissal of the work of Christ in history. For Barth, Christ's mediation was located in a realm distant from ordinary history, in what Barth insisted was a newer and higher historical reality. The resurrection happened in a time of pure presence; it was not an event in the past (*Historie*) but a present manifestation of Christ's supreme sovereignty (*Geschichte*). Thus Barth engaged in no theological quarrels about the past. Debates over an empty tomb involve the static order of speculation, not the active realm of revelation. Van Til charged that this was "playing fast and loose with the facts of redemption," and that Barth would have readily signed the Auburn Affirmation.[14]

During a 1941 study leave from Westminster Seminary, Van Til began work on a full-scale analysis of the dialectical theology of Barth and Emil Brunner. Published by Presbyterian and Reformed in 1946 under the title *The New Modernism*, it was a bold and direct assault on the teaching of the two men. "Our purpose . . . is frankly polemic," Van Til began, and then he carried out his assault in nearly four hundred pages. Despite Barth's confronting liberal theologians with the "wholly other" God, crisis theologians were not presupposing a self-contained ontological Trinity, and thus their god was "virtually identical" with the immanentism that Barth sought to correct. Notwithstanding Barth's claims to the contrary, Van Til charged that Barth stood with Schleiermacher in his denial of a God that was independent of creation.[15]

As the title suggested, Van Til's strategy was to link in the reader's mind the "new modernism" with the old, that is, the liberalism that J. Gresham Machen had exposed in his 1923 book *Christianity and Liberalism*. In case readers missed the connection, Van Til was explicit in his final chapter: "If the late J. Gresham Machen spoke of the necessity of making a choice between liberalism and Christianity, we should be doing scant justice to his memory if we did less today with respect to the new Modernism and Christianity."[16]

The book met with generally favorable reviews. Louis Berkhof, writing in *The Banner*, lauded it as a "masterpiece," though he warned that it did not "make for easy reading." The book was especially timely for Reformed scholars who were deceived into thinking that in Barth and Brunner were "the rising of a new star of hope" that would "lead to a rejuvenation of Calvinism." Despite their appearances, Berkhof believed that Van Til exposed them to be in fundamental agreement with modern "subjective consciousness theology" and thus great enemies to traditional Reformed orthodoxy.[17] Even James Daane, who was later to emerge as a fierce critic of Van Til, praised the book in the *Calvin Forum* as "the most searching criticism of the dialectical theology of Barth and Brunner that has yet appeared in the English language," and his assessment was that Van Til was "essentially correct."[18]

As one would expect, the *Presbyterian Guardian* was most enthusiastic about the book. H. Evan Runner lauded the author as "a true son of the Calvinistic Reformation" for his careful exposé of its counterfeit children. The former student of Van Til turned the review into a primer of Van Til's apologetic. Historic Calvinism, Runner noted, provided genuine meaning for man by asserting that he is not correlative with

124

God. With his gaze directed at Van Til's controversy with Clark, Runner noted that only the incomprehensibility of God renders belief in God rational, and only by presupposing God is human predication possible. Runner added that a particular strength was Van Til's attention to the deeper structures of Barth's philosophical thought. "System is of great importance," he wrote, and Barth's theology was a system "radically different from the system of truth found in the Scriptures."[19]

As much as Van Til sought to identify his work with Machen's, he struggled to reproduce his mentor's direct and simple approach. Van Til's prose was often dense and tedious. Still, mid-century American evangelical reaction to the book was swift and appreciative of the heavy lifting that Van Til performed. Francis Schaeffer spoke for many when he thanked Van Til, decades later, for speaking out against Barth in such a timely fashion: "You have pointed out for all the world to read that Barth's theology [was] wrong at its core, and not just in the details."[20] Van Til's work soon produced imitators, when, for example, Carl Henry's 1949 book *The Protestant Dilemma* followed Van Til in tracing the roots of Barth and Brunner's thought through Kierkegaard to Kant. According to Bernard Ramm, *The New Modernism* "became the official evangelical interpretation of neoorthodoxy." In George Marsden's study of this period in American church history, he observed that "few fundamentalists read the book, but many repeated the title."[21]

The rise in conservative Protestant estimation of Van Til furthered his ambivalence to the evangelical movement. On the one hand, he called on American evangelicals to join in the fight against "this new enemy." Meanwhile, he also tended to level the same method of criticism toward American evangelicalism, which he often considered synonymous with Arminianism. The only true antidote to Barth's activism was Calvinism. "Only the Reformed Faith holds to a God who is wholly self-contained," he wrote, and thus it alone has the resources to combat Barth's poison.[22] A collaborate case against Barth by Arminians and Calvinists was not possible, because the two did not merely differ over the arrangement of the top story of a theological house. Rather, they differed in foundational doctrines, and "Calvinists must build the whole of their theological house by themselves."[23]

Between Rationalism and Irrationalism

It is worth observing that Van Til's encounter with Gordon Clark (surveyed in the previous chapter) took place coterminously with his criticism of Barth. If Van Til's response to Clark, Rian, and other evangelicals elevated his leadership role in the Orthodox Presbyterian Church, his pioneering work on Barth established his academic standing within the international Reformed community, and it contributed to the growing prestige of Westminster Seminary. Although student enrollments were small at Westminster, especially during the years of World War II, Van Til's reputation succeeded in recruiting bright students. John Gerstner, E. J. Carnell, and Paul King Jewett were among several young men who enrolled at Westminster, primarily to study under Van Til. William Stanford Reid's biographer, A. Donald MacLeod, acknowledged that Van Til's "positive and aggressive stance was a welcome antidote" to the prevailing fundamentalism of other American conservative seminaries. Thus, for Reid and many students like him, "Van Til opened new doors to students" with his "searing and searching insights."[24]

Despite Van Til's careful criticism of Barth, Gordon Clark's supporters suspected Barthian elements in his theology. Robert Reymond of Covenant Theological Seminary in St. Louis challenged Van Til's doctrine of analogical knowledge, wondering how such an "ardent foe of Barthian irrationalism" could "come to the same conclusions concerning the nature of truth."[25] Clark himself made occasional references to Barthian tendencies in Van Til, even going so far as to suggest that Van Til's *Why I Believe in God* was a Barthian tract because it referred to creation, providence, prophecy, and miracles as "pointers" to God. This smacked too much of the Barthian scheme of Scripture as a mere pointer to God, who alone is infallible.[26]

Aware of the surface plausibility of such connections, Van Til strove to guard his vocabulary carefully to avoid "paradox," "myth," and other dialectical buzzwords. A good example can be found in this 1937 criticism of Barth:

> We may note, however, that the very heart of a Barthian theology, that is, its conception of the paradoxical character of human thought,

is radically opposed to Reformed theology. Reformed theology has taught that man is made in the image of God. Man, because finite, cannot comprehensively know God. Yet the knowledge that man has of God is true. The absence of the power of complete comprehension does not make human thought self-contradictory. It only means that man must point to God for complete comprehension. The very reason then why men conclude that human thought is self-contradictory is that they have set before it the impossible goal of complete comprehension. To conceive of human thought as self-contradictory is fundamentally antitheistic. Barth holds to the paradoxical character of human thought while Reformed theology holds to the analogical character of human thought.[27]

Still, the suspicions about Van Til's latent or unintentional Barthianism have lingered for a long time among evangelicals who have not taken the time to read Van Til carefully. Norman Geisler accused Van Til's "methodological fideism" of standing closer to Barth than to evangelical apologists, despite Van Til's regular appeals to evidence and reason. Ronald Nash likened Van Til's notion of divine logic to Barth's. In a 1984 book, R. C. Sproul, Arthur Lindsley, and John Gerstner wondered whether there was any difference between Van Til and dialectical theologians: "Van Til rejects the term, 'absurd' but defends the concept."[28]

Together, Van Til's encounters with Clark and Barth refined his apologetic approach as he structured his defense of Christian theism against the twin errors of rationalism and irrationalism. To be sure, Van Til did not treat these antagonists symmetrically. While the consequences of their views were both subversive of Reformed orthodoxy, Clark's errors were the faulty formulations of a Reformed theologian, and Barth was the proverbial wolf in sheep's clothing. Still, as far apart as they were, Barth and Clark shared the common error of a defective starting point, a non-Christian doctrine of creation. No theologian of Van Til's time had a more robust doctrine of creation or explored as fully as Van Til its covenantal character and its philosophical consequences. He often asserted that creation is the foundation stone of Reformed theology. "The most fundamental distinction of orthodox theology," he wrote in *The New Modernism*, "may be said to be that of Creator and creature."[29] To deny this is pantheism, of either a Greek type or a modern form. Defective views of creation yield non-Christian consequences, whether rationalistic or irrational. Thus unbelieving thought is of a dialectical nature.

For Van Til, creation did not merely establish the self-existence of God. The Creator-creature distinction, rightly understood, did not devolve into the Barthian skepticism of a "wholly other God" of pure transcendence. Just as integral to Van Til's doctrine of creation was the Creator-creature relationship. As Van Til learned especially from his Princeton Seminary professor Geerhardus Vos, creation was synonymous with covenant. To be fashioned in the image of God was to be in covenant with God. All of God's words and works entail his covenant relationship with humanity, and thus human beings were divided into two camps: covenant keepers who worshiped and served the Creator as his image bearers, and covenant breakers who worshiped and served the creature, in whose image they fashioned God. This way of articulating a philosophy of history, "baldly stated" by Van Til's own admission, was foundational for a Reformed apologetic.

Van Til confessed to his nephew, Henry Van Til, that his attention to Barth bordered on an obsession. He blamed Barth for wearing out his typewriter ribbons, and he conceded that his long hours of work only contributed to his health problems. His doctor told him in 1949 that he was suffering from battle fatigue not unlike a soldier, which brought to mind the struggles Nicholas Van Til, another nephew, was experiencing. "Nick used to see Japanese in his dreams. I see Buswell and Barth: which is worse?"[30]

Van Til was eager to take on Barth because Barth's superficial resemblance to orthodox theology rendered his work so deceptive. Readers of Barth, Van Til conceded, will find that "Barth believes in verbal inspiration, in a finished canon, in the necessity, sufficiency, authority and perspicuity of Scripture." But Van Til sought to demonstrate that Barth "pours new and radically different meaning into all of these ideas by means of his critical epistemology."[31] Several years later, Van Til reflected on his work on Barth in this way: "The most effective way to set the Reformed Christian position over against that of modern theology is to set it over against the one who appears to be nearest the Reformed Faith."[32]

Van Til's focus on Barth, however, was a means to a deeper point and a more penetrating critique. As Barth was committed to the philosophical assumptions of Immanuel Kant, he developed a distinction between history and revelation that prevented him from reckoning significantly with redemptive history. In a phrase (that Van Til was fond of quoting) found in the early work of Dutch theologian G. C. Berkouwer, Barth failed to allow for "the transition from wrath to grace in history." The basic structure of Barth's thought was Kantian, and Barth's embrace of Kant's "basic skepticism" yielded a theology that "would leave us without God and without hope in the world." By pledging their allegiance to Kant, Barth and Brunner and all of modern philosophy had the "fatal courage" of proclaiming the complete autonomy of the human mind. In Van Til's mind, this is what linked the new modernism with the old: their common origin in Kant's critique of pure reason.[33]

In rejecting Kant's autonomous interpreter, Van Til insisted that revelation was required for the human mind to interpret reality. Some of Van Til's readers identified this as a sign of idealism in Van Til, and indeed there are similarities to the idealist argument for the Absolute. But once again Geerhardus Vos was a more likely source for Van Til. Vos taught that humanity, as the image bearer of God in covenant with God, was always subject to God's revelation. Taking his cue from Vos, Van Til argued that there was no human knowledge that was not revelational.

Furthermore, the character of redemptive history that Vos taught Van Til likely shaped Van Til's understanding of the history of philosophy. Westminster students recalled that in nearly every class, Van Til found himself sketching the biblical story of salvation from Adam to Christ and also surveying the history of Western philosophy, beginning with Plato and Aristotle and ending with Kant. In eschatologically colored language, Van Til often suggested that in Kant the apostasy of non-Christian thought found its nearly consummate expression.

This is strikingly evident in an article entitled "Kant or Christ?" which Van Til wrote for the *Banner* in 1942. Here he virtually applied the theological language of federal headship to describe the monumental influence of Kant on modern philosophy. What all of modern thought held in common was its union with Kant. Whatever differences exist among modern theologians were but family quarrels among those operating, more or less consistently, in the Kantian tradition. Even ancient Greek philosophy, as it was premised on autonomous grounds, served as a type or foreshadow of Kant's thought. For this reason, Van Til went on to underscore the inadequacy for Christian apologists to retreat from Kant in order to find an epistemological safe haven in Aquinas or Aristotle. The scholastic effort to roll back the clock, manifested in either the Catholic theologians (such as Étienne Gilson or Jacques Maritain) or so-called classical apologetics, was to assume the same autonomous reasoning of non-Christian thought.

It may not be too great a stretch to imagine, therefore, that Vos provided Van Til with the tools to comprehend not only redemptive history but also the story of Western philosophy. In neither soteriology nor epistemology is neutrality possible. In this way Van Til expanded on Machen's distinction between historic Christianity and modern thought. Orthodoxy and modernism differed on the ultimate interpreter of reality; the "ultimate definitory power" that Christians assigned to God all of Kant's followers ascribed to "the mind of man." These "two creators" stood "face to face in mortal combat" because there could not be "two ultimate interpreters." Epistemologically, one is united to a federal head, and the choice was simply Kant or Christ.[34]

Throughout his work, Van Til attacked Kant's assumption of human autonomy, a subjectivism in willful rebellion against God. All of modern thought was in direct descent from Kant. In arguing this way, Van Til was admittedly painting with a very broad brush, and his sweeping genealogical claims left for little nuance. As Van Til applied this analysis to the disciples of Kant (such as Barth), he was often accused of misreading them, putting words into their mouths, and drawing improper and unnecessary conclusions.

Van Til dedicated *The New Modernism* to the memory of his father. In the year before the publication of the book, a month before his fiftieth birthday, he buried his father, who died on April 12, 1945, at the age of eighty-six. Van Til frequently remarked that Ite Van Til died on the same day as Franklin Delano Roosevelt, and he was gladdened to know that his father's eternal security was assured, unlike Roosevelt's.

Four years later, Van Til conducted the funeral for another father in the faith when Geerhardus Vos died on August 13, 1949. After Vos retired from Princeton Seminary in 1932, he lived for a time in southern California and then moved to Grand Rapids to live with his daughter, Marian Radius. Van Til frequently referred to Vos as his "finest teacher" and "the greatest and most versatile theologian that I have had the privilege of knowing."[35] He was a frequent visitor to the Radius home, and the honor of conducting the graveside service was, according to Richard Gaffin, "one of his most cherished memories."[36]

Van Til traveled to the Vos homestead in Roaring Branch, Pennsylvania, with his close friend John DeWaard, to join a small graveside gathering that did not include a representative from Princeton Seminary. Van Til preached from 2 Corinthians 5:1: "For we know that if our earthly house of this tabernacle were dissolved, we have a building of God, an house not made with hands, eternal in the heavens" (KJV). Van Til selected this verse because he remembered how Vos had exegeted it in class, and he could not have chosen a more fitting text. The verse stressed the Vosian theme of heaven as the aspiration of all disciples in the kingdom of God. Eschatological life, Vos had taught Van Til, is more than merely another stage in the culmination of the benefits of redemption; it is life of a different order. Van Til's appropriation of Vos prompted an important restraint on his use of Kuyper. The creation-fall-redemption paradigm of neo-Calvinism could not fully account for the qualitative difference of the resurrected life, life in the consummate state. Van Til embraced Vos's teaching that this present age is earthly and mortal. In contrast, the life to come, which believers enjoy even now in union with Christ, is "eternal in the heavens."

And so by the end of the decade, the torch had been fully passed to Van Til, not only from Machen but also from Vos. Van Til's goal was to preserve Vos's memory as much as that of Machen.

The Intellectual Challenge of the Gospel

The New Modernism was not only Van Til's first book but also among the first major publications of the Westminster faculty. Van Til had become by far the most well known of the distinguished faculty, and most of his colleagues at this point remained unpublished. Westminster Seminary was fully aware of Van Til's rising reputation and sought to promote his work wherever possible. The seminary sent him on the road often for recruiting purposes, and it also promoted a visit to England, in 1950, where Van Til delivered the Tyndale Lectures, which occasioned further exposure to his work.

Entitled "The Intellectual Challenge of the Gospel," Van Til's lectures were designed as a "brief synoptic picture of modern thought" and an outline of the message that the Reformed faith offered to the modern mind. It became one of his most succinct efforts to express his apologetic distinctiveness. He began by commending B. B. Warfield's "fine little book" *The Plan of Salvation*, which located Calvinism as the most consistent expression of Protestantism. Characteristically, Van Til linked this consistency to a proper assessment of creation. "It is the genius of Protestantism," he wrote, "to make the God of the Scriptures the final reference point of all predication. In Protestantism man is really taken to be the creature of God" and the Protestant "builds his system squarely upon the Creator-creature distinction."[37]

Van Til went on to "develop briefly the implications of Warfield's argument for apologetic purposes."[38] Though careful not to indict Warfield personally, he attacked classical apologetics for its failure to own up to the Protestant theology of creation, thus leaving unchallenged the root assumption of modern thinking. All of modern theology, he claimed, following the trend of Kantian philosophy, rejected a biblical account of creation, along with other metaphysical claims. Kant's followers (including Barth) were pursuing the wisdom of the world, which Catholic and Arminian apologetics each fail sufficiently to challenge, and only a consistent Reformed apologetic offered any hope of predication to modern man. Van Til ended his lectures on a note of humility and boldness:

> Let us again remind ourselves that what has been said does not mean that Christians are in themselves wiser than are other men. What they have they have by grace. They must be "all things to all men." But it is not kindness to tell patients that need strong medicine that nothing serious is wrong with them. Christians are bound to tell men

the truth about themselves; that is the only way of bringing them to recognize the mercy, the compassion, of Christ. For if men are told the truth about themselves, and if they are warned against the false remedies that establish men in their wickedness, then, by the power of the Spirit of God, they will flee to the Christ through whom alone they must be saved.[39]

When Tyndale Press published these lectures, the little booklet became Van Til's most widely distributed work. Van Til received appreciative feedback from many quarters, including Philip Hughes in South Africa. His former student E. J. Carnell congratulated Van Til for producing his clearest writing. The booklet found a receptive audience especially among evangelical college students on both sides of the Atlantic.

At about the same time, Van Til wrote another pamphlet, entitled *Paul at Athens*, that reiterated the same theme about creation. Again, what bears noting was the way in which Van Til assessed the significance of creation. He did not argue the scientific details of human origins or antiquity. Rather, creation led directly to the doctrine of the covenant. Human beings as creatures were called to submit minds and hearts to the revelation of God in Scripture. Thus, he wrote, "Paul only knows two classes of people, those who worship and serve the Creator and those who worship and serve the creature." Only the Reformed faith, Van Til claimed, does justice to Paul, because it reckons seriously with the idea that man is a creature of God who lives entirely by God's revelation. Life in total submission to God's revelation is life in the covenant, and so Van Til, following Paul, appealed to creation to convert covenant breakers into covenant keepers.[40]

Reviews of *The Intellectual Challenge* were not universally favorable. In a scathing notice in the British *Evangelical Quarterly*, Geoffrey W. Bromiley dismissed the lectures as "profoundly disappointing," based on "a mode of apologetic which is futile and even illegitimate." Bromiley's review came four years after blistering criticism of *The New Modernism* in the same journal by T. F. Torrance. Bromiley and Torrance wrote with vested interest as the co-editors of the English translation of Barth's *Dogmatics*, and they would regularly heap scorn on Van Til's assessment of contemporary theology.[41]

In Bromiley's later reflections on Van Til, he lumped him with "many of the critics who had not read much of Barth, or not read him carefully and scientifically enough to understand what they were reading." These enemies were either incompetent or intentionally deceitful in their misrepresentations.[42] Bromiley's remarks were grossly unfair, given the painstaking investment that Van Til made in a close reading of Barth in the original German. Roger Nicole, longtime professor of theology at Gordon-Conwell Seminary, claimed that Van Til's polemics against Barth carefully met the obligation of thorough acquaintance with Barth's work. "It has been my privilege to be at Dr. Van Til's office," Nicole observed, "and to see with my own eyes the bulky tomes of Barth's *Kirchliche Dogmatik*. As I leafed through these, I bear witness that I did not see one page that was not constellated with underlining, double-underlining, marginal annotations, exclamation points, and question marks galore." Every volume of Van Til's copies of Barth revealed the critic's "very careful scrutiny."[43]

If it was unfair to accuse Van Til of failing to read Barth, the criticism of Van Til's rhetorical overreach may have validity. Critics have observed that Van Til's rigorous assault on Barth led him and his students to overstatements that bordered on caricature. Often, wrote one, "the danger with Van Til's system was its difficulty in engaging in serious dialogue with those who challenged its presuppositions," and his methodology could be "reduced to a template, short-circuiting serious intellectual encounter and engagement with opponents."[44] Van Til typically pressed the logical consequences that his opponents would not concede, and then rendered judgments on the basis of that consequential reasoning. As another critic put it, "This dangerous procedure can lead one to attribute anything to an opponent."[45] Similarly Carl Henry, though appreciative of Van Til in his *Fifty Years of Protestant Theology*, suggested in a footnote that Van Til was too architectonic in his critique, and he wondered whether one should allow for some "blessed inconsistency" in Barth.[46]

If there was a method to Van Til's madness, the strengths of his approach also contained weaknesses. Though Van Til insisted on the need to explore the philosophical background of Barth's thought and to press Barth's assumptions to their logical conclusion, he conceded that this was a "hazardous undertaking."[47] For some readers, this yielded a tone-deafness to the postliberal elements in Barth and a failure to appreciate the ways in which Barth's theology rejected certain liberal premises.

And yet, Van Til's student and eventual colleague, Richard B. Gaffin Jr., offered countervailing testimony to this common charge. Gaffin's graduate studies in Germany sealed his appreciation for Van Til's assessment of modern theology. His exposure to German higher criticism vindicated the soundness of Van Til's approach, and it consolidated his commitment to it.[48]

Van Til was the object of especially harsh criticism in European circles. Th. L. Haitjema labeled Van Til's analysis of Barth a "horrible misunderstanding." Hans Urs von Balthasar, a leading Catholic interpreter of Barth, dismissed as "ridiculous" Van Til's attempt "to explain the whole theology of Barth and Brunner on the basis of their earlier positions and in terms of the philosophical principles that are supposedly at the root of their system."[49] American liberal reaction to Van Til, predictably, was no more charitable. The *Christian Century* panned Van Til's *New Modernism* as the narrowly polemical ranting of a fundamentalist and mocked Van Til for claiming Calvin as the last word in theology.

This early criticism only prompted Van Til to turn up the heat. In a 1954 article in the *Westminster Theological Journal*, he posed the question, "Has Karl Barth Become Orthodox?" Van Til evaluated claims that changes in Barth's thinking warranted a reappraisal. Van Til acknowledged that Barth was the victim of superficial "theological journalism" in early English-language appraisals, but his conclusion expresses his opposition to Barth in the strongest possible language:

> It is, we believe, to do Barth injustice and to the church irreparable harm, when orthodox theologians, for whatever reasons, fail to make plain that the dialectical theology is basically subversive of the gospel of saving grace through the blood of Christ. . . .
>
> Shall not preachers of the gospel call men away from this other gospel which is not the gospel? Is the church now any less responsible for setting the truth against error than it was at Nicaea, at Chalcedon,

not to speak of Dort or the assembly of the Westminster divines? No
heresy that appeared at any of these was so deeply and ultimately
destructive of the gospel as is the theology of Barth. Never in the
history of the church has the triune God been so completely and
inextricably intertwined with his own creature as he has been in
modern dialectical thought.[50]

Barth himself had chosen to ignore Van Til's criticism up to this point,
but this latest broadside did not go unnoticed. In a letter to Geoffrey
Bromiley, Barth complained that "in 1953 [sic] the fundamentalist
Cornelius Van Til wrote a whole book to the effect that 'I was possibly
the worst heretic of all time.'"[51] In volume 4.2 of his *Church Dogmatics*,
Barth likely had Van Til in mind when he wrote that while he could
discuss his views with some fundamentalists, there were "butchers and
cannibals [who] are beyond the pale (i.e. the one who summarily described
my theology as the worst heresy of any age.)"[52] By now, Barth, who certainly
proved he could tolerate criticism, could no longer abide Van Til.

Still, Van Til found vindication in other liberal and mainline circles.
In his *A Religious History of the American People*, Sydney E. Ahlstrom
struggled to distinguish Barth from other modernists. While neo-orthodoxy challenged some of the assumptions of liberalism, "neo-orthodox
theologians have been justifiably accused of putting down only a very
thin sheet of dogmatic asphalt over the problems created by modern
thought."[53] Even the editor of the *Christian Century*, in a three-part
series on the topic, argued that there was a strong kinship between
neo-orthodoxy and liberalism, and "far more common ground" than
readers recognized. Even the "exponents of neo-orthodoxy" failed to
recognize "the strong currents of liberalism in their own thinking."
Barthianism, he concluded, was simply the further unfolding of the
Protestant liberal agenda, even in those doctrines, such as Scripture
and sin, where Barth claimed to take liberalism to task.[54]

Coming to Terms with Evangelicalism

Because of his work on Barth (and despite his growing reputation for militance), Van Til became the darling of neo-evangelicals,

and he struggled to be gracious with his neo-evangelical friends and associates.

In 1951, in the height of the Orthodox Presbyterian Church's deliberation on membership in the International Council of Christian Churches, Van Til wrote an article in the *Presbyterian Guardian* on Reformed faith and action. Although his Westminster colleague Ned Stonehouse promoted the ICCC, Van Til would have no part of it, and he sternly warned that ICCC membership would silence the OPC's Reformed voice. Van Til also urged against entanglements with other evangelical or fundamentalist organizations, including the National Association of Evangelicals. These ecclesiastical ties were "lowest common denominator witnesses," and the Reformed could not afford them. Differences between the Reformed and evangelicals lay in their very understanding of the Christian faith, and both fundamentalists and evangelicals were involved in compromise with unbelief at every point.

Van Til pleaded for the church to protect its Reformed identity:

> Do Reformed Christians want their own witness to be identified before the world with those who cannot speak otherwise than words of compromise? Of course they do not. Then let them not either as churches or as individuals be joined to councils or associations where such compromise necessarily occurs, either through organizational or doctrinal relationships.
>
> Do Reformed Christians want their own witness, the only consistent witness to the Christian faith, to be heard in the world? Then let them band together with all Reformed men everywhere for a common testimony to that which can really challenge the wisdom of the world.[55]

The choices were simple for Van Til: "squelching" the voice of Reformed theology or raising its banner high. Van Til argued that the former was ecclesiastical suicide. This warfare required him to take on his friend, Ned Stonehouse, who was actively encouraging OPC participation in these alliances. Van Til himself declined a General Assembly request that he represent the church as an observer at an ICCC meeting. When Stonehouse expressed his willingness to attend instead, Van Til marveled at his colleague's ability to stomach the gathering.

Despite the distance he was carving between the two camps, neo-evangelicals frequently invited Van Til to speak. At the request of his former student, Harold Ockenga, he participated in the Plymouth (Massachusetts) Conference for the Advancement of Evangelical Scholarship in August 1945, a gathering of many evangelical intellectuals, including Carl Henry, Allan MacRae, and Clarence Bouma. Ockenga, pastor of Park Street Church in Boston, was hopeful of ushering in a renaissance of evangelical theological and social thought after World War II, and he recognized Van Til's importance for this cause. Van Til, slightly older than the other scholars in attendance, was a reluctant participant, and he expressed his skepticism about the presumption of Ockenga's venture in a letter to Henry Van Til.[56]

Still, when he was asked to speak to evangelical audiences, Van Til sought to find words of encouragement. He was often asked to evaluate the work of C. S. Lewis, and he responded respectfully and with gratitude for Lewis's American reception. He considered Lewis a "genius," and he was embarrassed to be considered in his company. "I rejoice in the fact that he is so widely read. I refer people to him whenever I can."[57] In private his analysis was more candid. In November 1953, Van Til read Lewis's *Surprised by Joy*, and he lamented that a generally "worthwhile" book was "vitiated by [Lewis's] wretched Arminianism."[58]

Lewis's popularity only served to heighten Van Til's passion for Reformed apologetics. He wrote to Theodore Jansma:

> I rejoice in Arminian preaching, but it is my business to preach and teach the Reformed faith. And when I do that I cannot avoid the responsibility of pointing out where Arminianism does not fully present scriptural truth. Now I try to follow the same line when it comes to apologetic argument. We need a Reformed Lewis. But we have none. I see none on the horizon. . . . I feel that a fully Reformed argument is always more effective than an Arminian or Romanist argument.

Douglas Johnson, an English friend of Van Til's, tried to interest C. S. Lewis in reading Van Til, but Lewis returned unread copies of Van Til's syllabi to Johnson, regretting that he lacked the time to read them.[59]

Van Til's struggles with evangelicalism were evident especially in the extensive letters he exchanged with E. J. Carnell and Carl F. H. Henry.

In both cases he sought cordially and yet firmly to express his theological differences, a delicate goal that he did not always achieve.

Edward John Carnell (1919–67) was a student of Gordon Clark at Wheaton College. Later he earned ThB and ThM degrees at Westminster, the latter in apologetics under Van Til; he also earned the seminary's Greene prize. From there he went on to earn a ThD at Harvard and a PhD at Boston University, and eventually he taught at Fuller Seminary, where he also served for a time as president. Van Til heaped praise on Carnell during his student days and regarded him as a brilliant student of philosophy and a fine apologist. The two were active correspondents when Carnell left for graduate work, but in Van Til's judgment Carnell soon began to drift from his Reformed bearings. Within four years of leaving Westminster, in 1948, Carnell published his *Introduction to Christian Apologetics*. He tried to prepare Van Til for the book in advance. "I trust that I have kept within the fundamental bounds of apologetics that you taught me in school," he wrote. "I have sincerely tried to follow out the implications of the Reformed Faith in the whole. . . . It is self-evident that I owe a great indebtedness to you for your work with me at Westminster. I hope you will not anathematize my volume."[60]

As Carnell anticipated, Van Til was profoundly disappointed by the book. In a letter to a Christian Reformed friend, he described it as "Clark through and through," and he regretted the necessity of reviewing it negatively. Van Til's depiction of his declining relationship with Carnell served as a harbinger of his role in evangelicalism at large: "Perhaps I was brought into the world to be a nuisance to others."[61]

Carnell's biographer, Rudolph Nelson, suggested that Carnell's rift with Van Til developed even during his Westminster student days, when Carnell declared, at least to some classmates, his allegiance to Clark over Van Til.[62] Nelson's claim finds credibility in Carnell's apologetics book, where there are many references to Clark and there is only passing mention of Van Til. If Nelson's claim was true, Carnell managed to keep his feelings a secret from Van Til, who corresponded with him frequently during Carnell's graduate days in Boston.

For a time, both men genuinely sought to reconcile their differences. Van Til expressed to Carnell's publisher, William Eerdmans, his desire "to win Carnell back to the Reformed truth in apologetics."[63] It was a deep disappointment for Van Til to see Carnell move further away from his Westminster orthodoxy, though he generally expressed the hope that Carnell could be won back. For his part, Carnell was also an eager correspondent. While working on his dissertation on Kierkegaard in 1948, Carnell wrote to Van Til and challenged his former teacher's rigorous presuppositionalism. "I think that you are too generous with the unregenerate man to suppose that he thinks consistently enough to be non-Christian in his whole system. On my view the unregenerate man is blinded—so blinded, in fact, that he is blinded to his own use of categories which are true only on Christian presuppositions—as the law of contradiction, e.g."[64]

Carnell's letter isolated the key difference between himself and Van Til: whether or not the law of contradiction was a valid principle of rationality for all men, independent of their covenant standing. Despite these differences he pressed Van Til to maintain a literary relationship. "This issue is so serious that I am happy we can begin personal talks on it," he wrote, adding a note of respect for his former teacher, "No one is more ready to be corrected in his thinking than myself. You are the senior member."[65]

Carnell continued to express his devotion to Van Til even while their differences grew. He wrote in August of 1948 that his failure to fully understand Van Til "makes me feel that there is a depth to your position which I have missed."[66] Five months later, he expressed the wish that "we could settle the semantical dust which has clouded up our two approaches."[67] Upon the publication of Van Til's *Intellectual Challenge of the Gospel*, Carnell, serving by this time on the faculty of Fuller Seminary, reiterated his frustration over their growing estrangement. "It is a source of no small continual irritation to me that our attitudes should be drifting apart as they are. You doubtless weary of classifying my approach with that of Butler, and I weary with equal boredom in hearing you do it."[68] Carnell went on to challenge his mentor to resume their correspondence on the issues that separated them. But at this point, Van Til, preoccupied with other matters, declined Carnell's offer. Carnell expressed his regret at this decision.

I understand your decision and accept it, but I had hoped that it might be one of affirmation. I believe that your emphasis has yet something to teach me. . . . I feel certain, however, that I could make a contribution to your thinking. Reformed apologetics is constantly making the claim that it alone can challenge the modern mind, but it seems perfectly apparent to me that Reformed theology is not challenging the modern mind. The modern mind isn't paying any attention to Reformed apologetics.[69]

Van Til's relationship with Carl F. H. Henry (1913–2003) presented a similar challenge. One of the founding members of the Fuller Seminary faculty, Henry expressed enormous respect for Van Til, especially for his early and comprehensive critique of neo-orthodoxy. As evangelicals by mid-century struggled to comprehend the dense prose of those whom Henry called the "neo-supernaturalists," he acknowledged Van Til's *The New Modernism* as providing "firm support" for fundamentalist concern.[70] In another book, Henry asserted that Van Til "served notice upon evangelicals that their *Nein* must be even more intense than any *Ja* to neo-orthodoxy." (He went on, however, to add that Van Til may have "overshot the mark" in portions of his criticism, owing to his method of "exposing the underlying philosophical principle" in Barth and Brunner.)[71]

In 1948 Henry paid the further tribute of dedicating his book *Remaking of the Modern Mind* to Van Til, placing Van Til in awkward company along with Gordon H. Clark and William H. Jellema (collectively, "three men of Athens"). Henry regarded his differences with Van Til as matters of style and not substance. "I have sometimes felt that there is a difference of temperament between us," he wrote to Van Til. "You prefer a direct frontal assault, and I appreciate the reason for it—so much danger that the true issue will be obscured. On the other hand, I parry for a hearing. . . ." He ended with a call to unite in common cause. "I wish somehow you, Jellema, Clark, Carnell, and I, and possibly Buswell, might sometime get together on the matter of religious epistemology." Henry later added his sympathy to Van Til for the "quite untempered" treatment accorded Van Til by J. Oliver Buswell, and hopefully suggested that if rhetorical restraint would prevail, "we shall find our positions converging."[72]

Henry's appreciation for Van Til was certainly genuine, even if his hopes for apologetic consensus were naïve. As noted, Henry was joined by other neo-evangelicals in his esteem for Van Til's critique of Barth. In this sense, Van Til was regarded much like Calvin Seminary's Louis Berkhof. Berkhof was admired for his firm antimodernism but generally ignored or politely tolerated for his confessional Calvinism. Van Til received a similar reception.

If Van Til was unable to return the words of encouragement and hope, he did express his admiration for Carnell and Henry's written productivity. "Henry writes very rapidly," Van Til observed, "I envy his ability."[73] Writing for a popular audience was excruciatingly difficult for Van Til. He was especially embarrassed at the ease with which Carnell could generate polished prose. Carnell "makes me despair of myself," he confessed. "If he can write a book on apologetics at 28 and I cannot even do it at 52 it is hopeless."[74] Van Til believed that he lacked both the power of expression and the physical stamina to write as others did, and he frequently mocked his lack of productivity as "a lot of noise and no results."[75] He even found himself envying the focus and drive of his colleague Ned Stonehouse when the New Testament scholar set out to write his biography of Machen in 1951.

One reason Van Til was so eager to write on a popular level was to preempt the efforts of others. When Van Til heard that his colleague E. J. Young was contemplating a primer on apologetics, he privately doubted whether Young was equal to the task. "Young feels that I can't write something that is popular enough," he confided to Henry Van Til. "That is true but it does not prove that he can write something that is sufficiently guarded against modern philosophy."[76]

That Van Til's writing style seemed to some too far removed from the popular reader was due in part to his respect for the theologically informed laity in the church. He wrote in 1967, "I am glad that I have never unlearned the ability to speak the simple person's language. I am deeply convinced that there are many laymen who understand the gospel better than many ministers and theologians."[77] Chief among his examples was his older brother. Though lacking a college education, Reinder Van Til was steeped in the knowledge of Reformed theology, and he raised two sons, Henry and Nick, who went on to academic careers. Reinder encouraged his younger brother to set high expectations of his readers, and Van Til's prose never treated his readers condescendingly.

In expressing his literary frustrations, Van Til was being too hard on himself. Despite his struggles he was able to compose a relentless and devastatingly consistent criticism of neo-orthodoxy. It is impossible to overemphasize the role that Van Til served in the early American evangelical reaction to Barth. He succeeded in characterizing neo-orthodoxy as a more subtle form of modernism, and this analysis carried far beyond the Reformed churches. Many evangelicals were quick to note Barth's weaknesses in the doctrine of Scripture, but Van Til went much further. His competency in reading Barth in the original German rendered his 1946 assessment the first full-scale English-language appraisal. His philosophical training enabled him to study the complexities of Barth's and Brunner's dialectical approaches, and he ably identified the Kantian sources of their formulations.

In the decades that followed, American evangelicals would take a different stand on Barth and begin to appropriate certain features more appreciatively. Younger evangelical scholars began to suspect that Van Til had poisoned American evangelicals on Barth, prompting their blindness to elements of genuine orthodoxy in Barth. Bernard Ramm wrote in frustration that "no fundamentalist could use more explicit language than Barth in affirming a bodily resurrection."[78] Much of the reaction of evangelical Barthians to Van Til was remarkably thin-skinned. In contrast, Van Til's polemics against Roman Catholicism and liberal Methodism earned him the esteem of opponents, who were able to recognize both the depth of his insights and the principled character of his approach. William M. Shea recently wrote that Van Til's anti-Catholic apologetics "struck cleanly" and "without insult." Van Til "disagreed in the strongest possible terms with the Roman Catholic position, yet he did not demean it."[79] This academic respect was glaringly absent among the Barthians, who continually harped on their sense of foul play.

Appreciation for Van Til would continue to linger among more conservative and fundamentalist expressions of evangelicalism. While this connection does not render him a fundamentalist, it does point out a common interest in maintaining a tone of militance against modern theology. For both Van Til and the fundamentalists, opposition to Barth remained a crucial litmus test in their efforts at boundary maintenance. For this reason, many expressed lasting appreciation for Van Til. Progressive evangelicals, especially at Fuller, increasingly bristled at Van Til's generalizations. Virtually every evangelical reappraisal of Barth that warmed up to his insights included a stinging indictment of the pernicious role that Van Til played in corrupting a fair evangelical assessment.

In the end, Van Til's polite distance from evangelicalism served, as did his disdain for Barth, the "interest of plain intellectual honesty."[80] This, he reminded the readers of *The New Modernism*, was the same cause that had motivated Machen's earlier defense of historic Christianity. Van Til's efforts to emulate his mentor could be measured as a partial success. He failed to communicate the threat of Barthianism in the plain language that Machen had mastered. To be fair, Machen himself felt that Barth was a difficult read, and that his beguiling rhetoric sounded "like John Bunyan and John Calvin and the Shorter Catechism." Moreover, Machen ultimately agreed with Van Til's assessment that neo-orthodoxy represented "an extension rather than a repudiation of liberal Protestantism."[81]

Enemies and Allies in the Old World

If criticism from Barth and his English translators was expected, Dutch Reformed criticism struck too close to home for Van Til. I. A. Diepenhorst, writing in the *Free University Quarterly*, charged Van Til's *Intellectual Challenge* with superficial treatment of Barth. "Van Til treats all those whom he criticizes in too much the same way," ignoring the vast differences that separate thinkers such as Barth and Bultmann.[82] Van Til was devastated to read this, confessing to Henry Van Til that it left him "down in the dumps about writing anything" and "losing confidence in himself."[83]

Far worse was the antagonism from a former Dutch ally. Van Til had frequently praised the early work of theologian G. C. Berkouwer of the Free University. In Berkouwer, "Reformed theology has found an exponent worthy of its glory," Van Til wrote, and he borrowed heavily from Berkouwer's early criticism of Barth, especially Berkouwer's insights into Barth's nominalism, which Berkouwer pronounced as "opposite of a Scriptural dogmatics."[84] As previously noted, one of Van Til's favorite lines about Barth was borrowed from Berkouwer: there could be found "no transition from wrath to grace in history" in Barth's *Dogmatics*. Regarding that phrase, Van Til later remarked, "No more basic criticism of Barth's theology can be made."[85]

When Van Til reviewed Berkouwer's *De Tromf der Genade in de Theologie van Karl Barth* in the 1955 *Westminster Theological Journal,* he noted that Berkouwer sounded "quite a different note," and he was disappointed in Berkouwer's new take on Barth. Berkouwer was now eager to speak of Barth's theology as a theology of grace, finding "it to be in line with Reformation theology," though Van Til found no evidence that Barth was any less activistic or more committed to historic orthodoxy. According to Van Til, there was no theology of grace in Barth, "not if what Luther and Calvin meant by grace has any validity." Van Til was led to suspect less evidence for a new Barth than for an early and a later Berkouwer, especially on the doctrine of Scripture. Years later, Van Til described Berkouwer as seeking incoherently to combine Barth and Bavinck, and "Barth is gaining on Bavinck."[86]

When Berkouwer's book was translated into English in 1956, it prepared the way for a more hospitable reception of Barth in North America, and a new level of criticism toward Van Til. The English translation even included an appendix that directly attacked Van Til's assessment of Barth. Van Til's methodological approach of studying Barth's philosophical background produced some "very audacious utterances," as Van Til drew conclusions that Barth himself opposed at great length. Van Til simply lacked an appreciation for the critical nuances of Barth's theology, and his obsession with the "earlier Barth" did not do justice to the "deepest interests of Barth's theology." The result was a "onesidedness of critique" that failed to perceive where "in many places the light of the truth of the word breaks through" in Barth's work.[87]

Van Til's polemical exchange with Berkouwer would serve to lower his standing in Dutch-American circles, the focus of the next chapter.

If Van Til felt a growing sense of isolation in the development of his Reformed apologetic, he was simultaneously heartened by corroborating work taking place in the Netherlands. Nearly three decades earlier, during a post-graduation tour of the Netherlands in 1928, Van Til had met Herman Dooyeweerd, a young member of the Free University of Amsterdam faculty. Van Til followed Dooyeweerd's work in the next decade, and he lauded the Dutch scholar (along with D. H. Th. Vollenhoven, also at the Free University, and Hendrik Stoker of South Africa) for the promise of developing a truly Reformed philosophy in the footsteps of Augustine, Calvin, and Kuyper. Dooyeweerd stressed the radical character of the Christian faith as he forged a transcendental argument against the self-sufficiency of the immanence philosophy found in non-Christian thought. Vollenhoven's *Calvinism and the Reformation of Philosophy* (Amsterdam, 1933) contrasted the "ground motives" of biblical and non-biblical philosophy. These insights resonated strongly with what Van Til advanced by his argument from presuppositions. In 1936, Van Til eagerly accepted the invitation to join these philosophers on the masthead of *Philosophia Reformata*. He would serve in collaboration with them for forty-two years (although he was not an active editor, and he contributed only one article for the journal).

Van Til never claimed to be a Christian philosopher, and when asked how his work would take philosophical shape, he referred students to the work of these scholars. In the light of Van Til's sustained polemics against evangelicals, Barth, and Berkouwer, it was a welcomed change of pace for him to commend so highly the scholarship of these men. In Van Til's judgment, both Dooyeweerd and Vollenhoven were firmly rooted in the doctrine of the antithesis, and only from this radical starting point could genuine Calvinistic philosophy emerge.

So appreciative was Van Til of the work of Dooyeweerd and Vollenhoven that he tended to exaggerate their early influence on him. In deference to their accomplishments, Van Til corrected anyone who regarded his own work as revolutionary by observing that he was merely writing for the English speaking world what they had already produced in Dutch. Strictly speaking, however, Van Til was no disciple of Dooyeweerd and Vollenhoven. In the early part of their careers, Van

Til and the Free University scholars were pursuing similar questions and reaching common conclusions though working independently. The more he read of their works, the more encouraged he became. Early on, his enthusiasm was unrestrained. "I rejoice in the work of Christian Philosophers like Vollenhoven, Dooyeweerd and Stoker."[88] Their "cosmonomic philosophy" provided reinforcement and support for his emerging apologetic distinctives. Van Til's writings became bolder, and he felt the freedom to write more explicitly from a presuppositional point of view. No doubt he was thinking autobiographically in 1951 when he described Vollenhoven's contribution in this way: "the Reformed apologete is gradually beginning to see more of the resources that are at his disposal," and is "better able than ever before to cut himself loose from every form of Scholasticism and Arminianism."[89]

Armed with reinforcement from these colleagues, Van Til was emboldened to express his approach in the language of radical confrontation with unbelief. "The Reformed apologete will seek for a head-on collision with all those who interpret reality with man himself as a final reference point. Only then can he make a real point of contact."[90] This, for Van Til, represented genuine progress for the Reformed faith, and not the naiveté of Henry Beets.

6

Through the Fires of Criticism

an Til maintained close ties with the church of his youth after he joined the Orthodox Presbyterian Church in 1936. His extended family in Indiana was still in the Christian Reformed Church, and he hoped that its testimony of Reformed piety might guide the younger church, especially as Orthodox Presbyterians struggled with the temptation to align with the cause of American evangelicalism. In letters to friends he regretted his sense of exile from his former denomination. He was especially disheartened over his son's unhappiness at Calvin College; Earl Van Til struggled to fit in with the Dutch community. Moreover, Van Til complained that as an "outsider" he had to pay full tuition for his son, despite his annual contribution as an alumnus. In 1949 he wrote that "I am at heart as much a member of the Christian Reformed Church as I have ever been."[1] That sentiment would be put to the test during an extended confrontation with parties in the Christian Reformed Church. A decade later, after Van Til found himself in the center of controversies, and still another decade

149

later, after his apologetic views were subjected to intense criticism, he would have been hard-pressed to express loyalty to his former church in such terms.

In 1946 the Orthodox Presbyterian Church commissioned Van Til to serve as its fraternal delegate to the Christian Reformed Synod for the third time in the church's first ten years. Van Til reported that the Orthodox Presbyterian Church had established a "beachhead for the Reformed Faith" and he urged that the bond between the two churches be strengthened.[2] (As noted in chapter 4, Van Til also described Westminster Seminary as a "beachhead for the Reformed faith." His employment of the phrase for both institutions reveals the extent to which he saw the church and seminary working in tandem for the Reformed cause.)

Van Til's old church had held his new church at arm's length during its early years, particularly concerned to see that the OPC take a strong stand against freemasonry. Moreover, a conflict developed between Rochester, New York, congregations of each denomination when some former CRC members left for the OPC in what the Christian Reformed Classis of Hudson judged to be a schismatic manner. Although the OPC's Presbytery of New York and New England apologized for its failure to scrutinize the terms of those transfers, tensions continued for a time. Christian Reformed confidence in the OPC grew from Van Til's address, and in response, the 1946 Synod voted to send its first representative to the OPC General Assembly in the following year.

Van Til himself could sense that he was addressing a church in transition. Dutch Americans were undergoing a process of assimilation after World War II with a new wave of immigration and a desire on the part of "Positive Calvinists" to join the American Protestant mainstream. Van Til's Synod address contrasted the Reformed faith with a "false traditionalism," and he hoped to convert the ethnic separatism of the earlier generation into a zeal for Reformed orthodoxy.[3]

The post-war character of the CRC found expression in the periodical *The Calvin Forum*, edited by Clarence Bouma, which called for a more open embrace of American culture and learning. Bouma sensed that the church stood to gain little from Van Til, who seemed to have left his Dutch roots for a still smaller religious enclave just as distant from the American religious mainstream. When Van Til sparred with Bouma on these matters, the lively exchange between the two came to be known as the "Clarence and Casey Show."

Van Til considered the influence of his former professor William Henry Jellema to be an even greater threat to the denomination's Reformed character. Jellema created the philosophy department at Calvin College from 1920 to 1935, when he left on a self-imposed exile at Indiana University for thirteen years. He returned in 1948 to what he regarded as a different college in a changed church, and over the course of the next fifteen years he shaped a generation of Reformed philosophers, including Nicholas Wolterstorff and Alvin Plantinga. Throughout his long career, Jellema distinguished himself as a classical philosopher who taught a deep respect for the Western cultural tradition. While he followed Kuyper's call for the transformation of culture, he minimized the Kuyperian teaching on the antithesis, and he pursued philosophical common ground with non-Christians.

Van Til could not fathom Jellema's appeal for classical education, which could yield, in Van Til's judgment, an education that was at best half-Christian and half-pagan. "It seems to me," he wrote to Henry Van Til, "that in all educational philosophy that pretends to be Reformed the choice is simply between covenant keepers and covenant breakers . . . the ancient and modern mind both worship and serve the creature."[4] This pedagogical principle was lacking in Jellema's approach. Nor was Jellema's idealism of any service to a Reformed approach to education, because "for idealism there is no Creator-creature distinction. The idealists were and are covenant breakers as much as are the pragmatists."[5]

Jellema thus was compromising Calvin College's pedagogy by failing to establish a thoroughly Reformed basis for education. While Van Til expressed a personal fondness and appreciation for Jellema, he wrote that "Calvin will never get on its feet philosophically as long as his views and policies prevail."[6] Van Til also feared the educational monopoly that Calvin College held over the Christian Reformed Church, and as early as 1950 he yearned for the rise of other educational options in the church.

Debating Common Grace

In the most general terms, Van Til's dispute with Jellema centered on the proper interpretation of father Abraham. As theologian John Bolt noted, "The lasting impact of the antithetical strand in Kuyper's thought found less fertile ground in the CRC more broadly than it did in one of its famous but departed sons, Cornelius Van Til."[7] Christian Reformed progressives challenged Van Til's rigorous adherence to the antithesis, especially when he provided an opening for them in 1947 with the publication of his second book, *Common Grace*. Originally appearing as three articles in the *Westminster Theological Journal*, this short book was not an exegetical exposition of the doctrine (which John Murray had written for the *WTJ* in 1942) but an effort to locate common grace within a Reformed philosophy of history. The book also served as an occasion for Van Til to extend his case that the defense of the Reformed faith must be aligned with the character of the Reformed faith. Van Til conceded that neither Kuyper nor Bavinck was altogether consistent in the way each advanced common grace, and he believed that their ambiguities led to the 1924 deliverance of the Kalamazoo Synod that forced Herman Hoeksema out of the church. Van Til's own evaluation of that Synod was qualified and subject to misinterpretation. While he affirmed the actual formulation of the 1924 Synod, he argued that the thinking in Reformed circles was "swinging back and forth between the two extremes of a total denial of common grace (difference without sameness) and a scholastic affirmation of common grace (sameness without difference)." Neither extreme integrated common grace "with the genius of Calvinism."[8]

In Van Til's judgment, Reformed theology had three options after the 1924 deliverance. One was to continue in the line of thought of Kuyper and Bavinck. As tempting as this was, Van Til warned against defending Kuyper "at all costs." Van Til described this tendency as Dutch traditionalism, found in varying degrees in J. H. Bavinck, V. Hepp, and even L. Berkhof, and it threatened the church's ability "to deal effectively with current heresies such as that of Barthianism."[9] Van Til also refused to jettison common grace in the manner of Herman Hoeksema. The third option left for him was to subject the doctrine to "reconstruction." This direction, he noted, would complement the Dutch labors of Dooyeweerd and Vollenhoven and lean also on the work of Klaas Schilder (1890–1952). Schilder was a Dutch Reformed minister who led an exodus out of the Gereformeerde Kerken in Nederland, and he formed the Gereformeerde Kerken (Vrijgemaakt) in 1944. From 1920 to 1940, he edited *De Reformatie*, a Dutch newspaper for which Van Til wrote two dozen "Letters from America," beginning in 1924.

In his work of reconstruction, Van Til faulted Kuyper for allowing areas of relative agreement between Christians and non-Christians in certain fields that amounted to zones of neutrality (such as mathematics). Van Til's corrective was to place common grace onto a better foundation, centered in the work of Christ, and rooted in the antithesis.

Van Til proceeded to connect Kuyper and Bavinck's ambiguity over common ground to contemporary confusion over the role of formal logic and natural revelation in apologetics. He underscored the importance of a distinctively Reformed and covenantal understanding of logic and natural theology. (Van Til made his most profound expression of this point in his contribution to the 1946 Westminster faculty symposium on *The Infallible Word*. There he defended a peculiarly Reformed doctrine of natural theology, and he rejected any concept of natural theology that could be attained without reference to special revelation.) Van Til went on to construct a Reformed doctrine of common grace on the basis of the antithesis. Common grace, as God's restraining grace, prevented the absolute expression of human depravity throughout history.

As with Van Til's first book, Louis Berkhof treated it to a friendly review in *The Banner*, though he wished for more biblical exegesis. Robert Churchill commended the book to Orthodox Presbyterians in the *Presbyterian Guardian*: "For centuries the preacher of the gospel and the professor of apologetics have had a different message and a different approach. Here, for the first time, evangelist and preacher are one."[10] Henry Stob's mildly favorable treatment in the *Calvin Forum* did not foreshadow that journal's future treatment of Van Til.

Christianity and Culture

Part of Van Til's difference with Kuyper had to do with his more circumscribed agenda. Van Til was not a Christian philosopher; he rarely strayed beyond theology in his writings or in the classroom. His interest in this book was narrowly apologetic, and he focused on the epistemological scope of common grace and the nature of the real commonness that the apologist and preacher could draw upon. While Kuyper's reflections served the ambitious agenda of establishing a Christian approach to culture, Van Til for the most part shied away from the larger cultural consequences in his work. He was especially cautious with respect to politics. Although he was a life-long Republican, he declined to draw political conclusions from his theology, and he refused the bait of many letter writers to pontificate on current events in American politics.

On one occasion Van Til tried his hand at cultural analysis, without satisfactory results. In a 1949 article on Calvinism and art published in the *Presbyterian Guardian,* Van Til posed the question of whether or not one could articulate a Reformed approach to art, with principles that went beyond the generalities found in Abraham Kuyper's *Lectures on Calvinism.* Stylistically, the article was uncharacteristically tentative for Van Til, as it included as many questions as statements. It was apparent that Van Til was out of his field, and the *Guardian* subsequently published withering criticism from two of his Westminster colleagues. Paul Woolley asserted that Calvinistic art made as much sense as Calvinistic medicine, and John Murray dismissed the particular object of Van Til's reflections as an idolatrous portrayal of the incarnate Christ.[11]

Van Til retreated from cultural analysis after this unsuccessful foray, though he frequently encouraged his students to take up the challenge. He was particularly eager to commend the study by his nephew Henry Van Til. In *The Calvinistic Concept of Culture* (published in 1959) the son of Reinder Van Til summoned Reformed Christians to resist both "the pietistic withdrawal from the world and the Anabaptistic denial of the Christian's cultural calling." Henry's broad historical survey began with Augustine and Calvin, and continued through Kuyper, though tempered by Schilder's qualifications. Henry joined his uncle in rejecting Kuyper's doctrine of common grace as "common terrain," which inevitably reduced it to a zone of neutrality and thus a denial of the antithesis.[12] Drawing a sharper distinction between this world and the world to come, Henry also underscored the transience of common grace. He borrowed from Schilder the dissent against Kuyper's argument that the New Jerusalem of the consummated state would receive into the heavenly kingdom even some works of reprobate culture through God's work of common grace.

Since Henry Van Til had joined the faculty of the religion department at Calvin College in 1946, he was a loyal disciple of his uncle. He faithfully followed in Cornelius's assessment of Barth and thus he steadfastly refused to acknowledge any Barthian contributions to the Christ and culture question. He defined the antithesis in the categories of the older Van Til, which identified the metaphysical as the common and the epistemological as the antithetical.[13]

Van Til also came to depend on the wisdom and advice of his nephew. When Cornelius was invited to speak on the sociology of religion at Alma College in Michigan in 1954, he was inclined to accept, even though he knew little technically about the subject. Henry prevailed upon him to turn down the offer by convincing him that he was out of his field and warning against the danger of spreading himself too thin.[14]

Van Til also developed a close bond with another nephew, Fred Klooster, who served in the religion department of Calvin College for three years before joining the Calvin Seminary faculty in 1956. Klooster wrote several critical articles on Karl Barth in the pages of the *Westminster Theological Journal*, and both he and Henry were trustworthy sources of information for their uncle in the unfolding developments at Calvin and in the Christian Reformed Church.

"The Seminary Situation"

The progressive and conservative camps within the Christian Reformed Church both gained a voice with the advent of two Grand Rapids–based popular magazines in 1951. In March, the *Reformed*

Journal made its debut, seeking to promote "fruitful discussion of the many problems and interests which engage us as a church," under the editorial oversight of Harry Boer, James Daane, George Stob, Henry Stob, and Henry Zylstra.[15] A month later, the Reformed Fellowship began to publish the *Torch and Trumpet* with the purpose "to arouse those of like mind with us to a more serious study of the Word of God and the Reformed heritage, that we may all put on the whole armor of God and be better equipped to fight the good fight of faith."[16] Henry Van Til served on its editorial committee, and Cornelius Van Til contributed to the inaugural issue with an article on "Defending the Faith." Although the *Torch and Trumpet* (whose polemical tone earned it the nickname *TNT*) denied that it was formed in response to the *Reformed Journal*, Henry Stob dismissed it as an ultra-conservative journal that valued "safety above advancement and militancy above engagement."[17] Throughout the next several decades, both journals became vehicles for warring sides in the Christian Reformed Church.

When these tensions spread within Calvin Seminary, they provoked shouting matches at faculty meetings, and the CRC Synod determined to resolve the conflict that became euphemistically known as "the Seminary Situation." A 1951 Synod advisory committee expressed the fear that Barthianism had seeped into the instruction of the school, and the Synod's remedy included an invitation for Van Til to join the faculty. The Calvin board had firsthand experience with Van Til's views on Barth because in the previous fall he had been the first guest in the new college-seminary lecture series. He delivered five lectures on the new modernism to a large audience that received them appreciatively.

Van Til was "overwhelmed" at this latest invitation, and he feared that friends "have put me on a pedestal." He expressed his reservations in a letter to Clarence Bouma, who was a senior member of the faculty. Calvin Seminary was expecting too much from him, he demurred: "I have neither the physical energy nor the mental and spiritual strength. The result would be sad disappointment after a year or two. It might mean the breakdown in my health, which is none too robust."[18] These words were ironic, because in the next year Bouma himself suffered a nervous breakdown in the midst of the civil war within the faculty.

Synod granted Van Til the luxury of deliberating for a full year on its offer, and Van Til used all of that time. In the midst of his decision making on a permanent appointment, he was invited to serve as a guest lecturer. In 1952, he took a semester's leave from Westminster Seminary and moved with Rena to Grand Rapids, where he served as visiting professor of apologetics at Calvin Seminary (filling the spring apologetics and ethics courses for the ailing Clarence Bouma).

This fourth invitation for Van Til to return to Grand Rapids prompted the most agonizing process of decision making for him. The recommendation before the Synod underscored Van Til's gifts in teaching contemporary theology, especially the theology of crisis. Westminster acted quickly to dissuade Van Til. On September 22, 1951, the faculty of Westminster unanimously approved a resolution that Paul Woolley, faculty secretary, forwarded to Van Til:

> In view of the invitation to our colleague, Cornelius Van Til, to accept appointment to a professorial chair in Calvin Theological Seminary, the faculty wishes to express to him our most earnest and heartfelt hope that he may see his way clear under the providence of God to remain at Westminster in the continuance of the happy association which has characterized our twenty-two years together to this time.
>
> We recognize the great importance of the work at Calvin Seminary and wish great success for it. We believe that the fruitful collaboration of various streams of Reformed tradition in developing the implications of the faith is mandatory. Thus far, Westminster has been the scene of such collaboration in a happy and useful fellowship which has enjoyed a measure of success and has been largely unique, both in this country and abroad. We earnestly desire that we may see still greater victories for this hope in the future and we are confident that Professor Van Til's remaining with us would be a powerful contribution to that end.
>
> We, therefore, urge him, in all due respect, to consider the grave consequences which would, we fear, result from his failure to continue with us in the full exercise of his exceptional powers for good in our midst.[19]

The Westminster board also passed a resolution at its October meeting, stating that Van Til's departure would do "incalculable harm to Westminster Seminary" and that "it is the conviction of the Board that Dr. Van Til can serve the worldwide interests of the Reformed Faith more effectively by continuing at Westminster." In his letter to Van Til that enclosed the board resolution, Robert Marsden, Executive Secretary of the Seminary, added a personal note that Van Til's departure, coupled with R. B. Kuiper's forthcoming retirement from Westminster, would discourage both prospective students and donors about the future of the school. Finally, he warned Van Til that the stress of the ongoing controversy at Calvin would have an adverse effect on his precarious health.[20]

The Westminster faculty kept the pressure on Van Til with personal appeals for him to stay. When Van Til had expressed the thought that Calvin would demand a lighter teaching load that would free him with more time to write, Ned Stonehouse countered that the affairs of the school and the church would demand more, not less of his time. "My own impression is that you would, even if your teaching load were lightened, be far busier than you have ever been in your life. And I am frankly doubtful that you would have the physical stamina to make the kind of fight that the situation seems to me to require."[21]

For every letter he received from Philadelphia, voices from Grand Rapids offered countervailing pleas. George Gritter, writing on behalf of the committee dealing with the "seminary situation," conveyed the unanimous sentiment of the committee that Van Til accept Calvin's offer.

> Your influence has been deeply felt during the past semester and has been most gratifying. Calvin Seminary today needs men who are of mature judgment and who are able to impart to the students a thorough understanding of and a glowing enthusiasm for the Reformed faith. You have been blessed with ability and personality which would make your services highly desirable at any time, but in view of the critical situation which now prevails it is our conviction that your presence at our seminary would be a godsend, not only for our school but for the future of our denomination and for the Reformed witness which we seek to propagate.[22]

Finally, E. J. Young took one last shot in a letter of April 6. He pointed out to Van Til that even under a best-case scenario at Calvin,

> you would be cutting yourself off from the general American scene. American boys will not come to Calvin as things now are. Your influence—through disciples—would be practically limited to the Christian Reformed Church. It would be giving a green light to Clark, Buswell, Carnell, and the rest to go on and capture the American churches. You simply cannot oppose these men effectively from Calvin Seminary.[23]

For both Cornelius and Rena, the temptation to move to Grand Rapids was great. Van Til confided that they both still felt much more at home with "'our own people' than we do in 'American' circles."[24] Moreover, his teaching at Calvin was popular and well received. At the end of the semester the junior class at Calvin Seminary presented him with an "A" grade in a mock exam book, signed by his thirty-three appreciative students.[25]

Meanwhile, Synod continued to monitor the crisis, and in 1952 it cleaned house by removing a large portion of the Calvin faculty, terminating the services of two progressive professors (George Stob and Harry Boer) and not reappointing two conservatives (William Rutgers and William Hendriksen). With the eventual emeritization of two others (Clarence Bouma and Samuel Volbeda), only one faculty member remained.

At last, by the end of his spring semester at Calvin, Van Til determined to remain at Westminster. His decision ultimately rested on personal terms. He had asked his son, Earl, a recent graduate of Calvin College, now married with an infant daughter and living nearby, whether he and his family would be willing to move to Grand Rapids with them. Earl's answer was a certain and unambiguous no, and that was all that his father needed to hear. Van Til was not willing to put Rena through another separation from her family.[26]

Altogether, there were four efforts by Calvin College and Seminary to recruit Van Til. In 1936, the board invited him to replace W. H. Jellema, Van Til's former philosophy professor, who left Calvin for a time before returning in 1948. In 1943, Van Til declined the invitation to succeed Louis Berkhof as professor of dogmatic theology. (The Synod eventually appointed William Rutgers.) Four years later, Van Til turned down William Hendriksen's suggestion that he consider a post in historical theology. The apologetic post in 1952 was the closest fit and in that sense the most tempting, but by this time Westminster had become a more stable institution, and the differences between Van Til and his potential Calvin colleagues were far more pronounced. Had he accepted any of these invitations, he would have been the first of Machen's young faculty to leave Westminster. Instead, Van Til served the longest tenure there.

After Van Til's decision, Calvin sought to recruit another Calvin alumnus at Westminster, Ned Stonehouse (for New Testament), but this effort also failed. Westminster, however, did not leave Calvin completely empty-handed in its crisis. R. B. Kuiper agreed to postpone his planned retirement, and he served as acting president for four years. With a firm and steady administrative hand, Kuiper helped to rebuild the school, although his Reformed militance did not have lasting effect. The eventual replacement for Clarence Bouma's post was Henry Stob, who began his long tenure at Calvin Seminary when the 1952 Synod elected him over Fred Klooster.

Calvin's Atom Bomb

Van Til's return to Westminster reunited him with colleagues who were closer to him ideologically and an environment that was friendlier. But it hardly ended his warfare with the progressives in the Christian Reformed Church. In fact, he left Grand Rapids with a metaphorical bang.

In May of 1952, near the end of his semester at Calvin, Van Til participated in a public debate in the seminary chapel with William Masselink of the Reformed Bible Institute. Before a packed audience, Masselink repeated the charge that Van Til denied the Reformed doctrine of common grace. The rhetoric of the exchange quickly heated up, and Van Til finally responded in exasperation that if one held to Masselink's formulation, "one might as well blow up the science building with an atom bomb!"[27]

The infelicitous statement shocked and offended many listeners. Van Til regretted the statement as soon as he uttered it, but the damage could not be undone. It was unwise and undiplomatic, he later reflected, but it was "absolutely true." Henry Stob remembered that Van Til's statement was "echoed in following days by certain partisans who tended to think that truth was held in custody by the orthodox at Westminster Seminary."[28] In George Stob's words, the science building withstood Van Til's presence but "harmful irradiation" spread throughout the school's constituency.[29]

The furor that his "atom bomb" statement had provoked haunted Van Til for months. Several friends, equally embarrassed by the comment, encouraged him to publish an explanation in the *Torch and Trumpet*. He tried to secure his actual words, but an audio recording of the debate had ceased before capturing his remark. R. B. Kuiper urged him to do nothing about it, warning that a public comment might do further damage. Because of the notoriety that accompanied his departure from Calvin Seminary, it was common for many to associate Van Til with the school's antagonistic atmosphere. James Bratt went so far as to write that Van Til "shatter[ed] the delicate settlement of 1924."[30] This was hardly a fair assessment, however, given the volatility of the seminary situation that preceded Van Til's coming.

There was at least one important silver lining in Van Til's experience at Calvin. It provided the occasion for his meeting Dr. Gilbert den Dulk, a medical doctor who was attending a conference in Grand Rapids. Van Til immediately struck up a close friendship with den Dulk and his wife, Jessie, and their son, Robert (who would eventually become president of Westminster Seminary California). At the den Dulks' invitation he began a pattern of summering in their home in Ripon, California, while Rena extended her stay with her family in Munster, Indiana. Van Til traveled to the West Coast every year during this decade, until Jessie den Dulk's sudden and unexpected death in 1960. He accomplished a good deal of writing then, and he also referred to the recuperative benefits of these California sojourns. (A testimony to Van Til's intimate friendship with the den Dulks is found in the dedication of his 1963 book *Christianity and Barthianism*, "To the memory of Jessie den Dulk.")

Calvin Forum

The communication between Bouma and Van Til generally remained cordial, but the same could not be said for other relationships. His Calvin debating partner, William Masselink, wrote an extended critique of Van Til's "reconstructionist" views of common grace in his 1953 book *General Revelation and Common Grace*. (The term referred to Van Til's desire to "reconstruct" common grace beyond the work of Kuyper and is not related to the subsequent movement known as "Christian Reconstruction.") Although Masselink was quicker than other critics to acknowledge Van Til's scholarship, the book was a harsh broadside against alleged innovations in Van Til's teaching. Labeling it "the new apologetic," Masselink dismissed Van Til's claim that he was reaching beyond Kuyper and Bavinck and further into the tradition by reclaiming Calvin. Masselink also overlooked the way Van Til followed the lead of Geerhardus Vos by locating the commonness of common grace in the federal headship of Adam. While Van Til might have followed John Murray's biblical construction of the doctrine more carefully, his work was not, as Masselink alleged, a speculative argument that was distant from the biblical text.

Masselink's main charge was that Van Til failed to distinguish absolute depravity from total depravity, thus rendering an extreme version of the antithesis. Van Til reiterated that the absoluteness of the antithesis exists in principle, when the unbeliever is reasoning with complete epistemological self-consciousness. Non-Christians are successful in science and other cultural enterprises, he argued, because of "borrowed capital."

Masselink's desperate opposition to Van Til led him to claim that there was a basic agreement between old Princeton and Amsterdam that Van Til was threatening to destroy. Van Til countered that his qualms with both schools were in the interest of protecting their best insights. "In short, because I hold to the appeal to reason as autonomous to be both illegitimate and destructive from the point of view of [the] Reformed faith that I am bound to reject [Valentine] Hepp's position as well as that of old-Princeton apologetics. But happily I can do so in view of the theology that I learned from old Princeton and Amsterdam."[31]

Edwin Palmer (the pastor of Van Til's former Spring Lake Christian Reformed Church) cried foul in the *Calvin Forum* in a 1954 article that exposed the caricatures by William Masselink.[32] Although Van Til responded to Masselink in his pamphlet *Letter on Common Grace*, he considered Masselink an incompetent reader, and he did not take the book seriously. Masselink, moreover, was an occasional contributor to the *Torch and Trumpet* and was not numbered among the progressive critics of Van Til within the CRC. Masselink's broader concern was to discourage the discussion of union between the two denominations. In particular, he feared the OPC's tolerance of membership in oath-bound secret societies.

But Masselink was far from the worst of Van Til's critics. After Cecil De Boer succeeded Clarence Bouma as editor of the *Calvin Forum*, he declared a full-scale war against Van Til. As Van Til wrote to his nephew, Henry, "Cecil is trying to do expertly what Masselink tried to do blunderingly, namely discredit me."[33] At first, some of Van Til's friends welcomed the vigorous debate in the magazine. Robert Churchill, for example, described the value of De Boer's evaluation: "Van Til's method of apologetics is bound to be attacked, it must go through the fires of criticism. It is in a sense new, and it must be tried."[34] When De Boer enlisted others in his sustained attack over the course of several months, the tone of the debate changed, as extreme and absurd charges were leveled against Van Til.

The most virulent of the critics was Jesse De Boer (no relation to Cecil), a philosophy professor at the University of Kentucky. His three-part series was the fiercest attack on Van Til's scholarship, as he joined other *Calvin Forum* critics in accusing Van Til of "substituting idealism for Christianity."[35] The concluding paragraph to this third article was a crescendo of vitriol against Van Til's reputation:

> I am convinced, not only that Van Til's apologetics is riddled with glaring ambiguities, with bald fallacies, and with misinterpretations of the thought of other men, but also that his writings are capable of damaging the intellectual habits of those who read them.

163

Indeed, I have witnessed the existence of that effect in certain young theological students. Scholarship suffers when great texts are distorted. The Reformed scholar is in peril of presumption if it is hinted and alleged that now for the first time a purely Reformed theology is being developed. And to cap it off, the purist version is impure, tainted not only with fallacious reasoning, but, what is still worse, with the logical and metaphysical legerdemain of absolute idealism.[36]

Calvin Professor John Bratt, "grieved and disturbed" over this rhetoric, apologized to Van Til for the uncharitable tone of the *Calvin Forum*. "You have done pioneering work in the field of Reformed Apologetics, and even though pioneering efforts have from the very nature of the case some deficiencies and shortcomings, your contributions deserve to be recognized and gratefully acknowledged."[37] Nicholas Monsma, minister of Second Christian Reformed Church in Paterson, New Jersey, expressed similar sentiments about the *Calvin Forum*'s hatchet job. "They sling mud and use abusive language, belittling your capacity. Do not fall into the temptation of responding to them in like manner. I feel that they show their weakness in using such tactics. You will show your strength in remaining calm and 'waardig' [dignified]."[38]

Philip Edgcumbe Hughes (secretary of the Church Society, Dean Wace House, in London) canceled his subscription to the *Calvin Forum* after reading "with much distaste" its broadside on Van Til. "You may be assured that your own friends remain thoroughly loyal to you," he wrote to Val Til two years later:

> What I want you to know is that your labours are, I believe, by God's grace, bearing fruit in my life and thinking. I am convinced that your thesis is fundamentally *right*, that is, *scriptural*. The task is to convince others of this, and the main difficulty of this task is the *unwillingness* of other Christians to think so deeply and radically. But we must strive in faith for a new reformation of thinking amongst Christians. Do not doubt that God will prosper us in this purpose. As for the criticisms and misconceptions of those who oppose you, they are for the most part superficial and at times despicable.[39]

Jesse De Boer supplemented his published criticism with a personal letter to Van Til that was unrepentant. De Boer began by way of a condescending metaphor that likened his criticism of Van Til to that of a professor flunking an incompetent student. He went on to belittle Van Til's work in stronger language than he had employed in print: "I have concluded that a good deal of what you say is vague, ambiguous, inconsistent, or meaningless, with the result that the pious tone of your expressions is all the more a barrier to our understanding you and a cause of ignorant misunderstandings." Claiming that his focus was strictly on Van Til's arguments, he continued, "I cannot avoid saying that many times you misinterpret other writers, you reason in a contrived and artificial manner, that you make up fantastic puzzles and difficulties, and that you unconsciously forsake Reformed doctrine due to habituation in idealistic modes of talk."[40]

Meanwhile, Henry Stob quietly urged Cecil De Boer to keep the heat up. In a letter that Stob specified was not meant for publication in the *Calvin Forum*, he thanked the editor for its sustained critique of Van Til. "The presentations help the attentive reader to make a responsible judgment concerning an apologetic which, one suspects, has suffered more in the past from over-zealous sponsorship than from critical appraisal."[41]

De Boer gladly obliged Stob. In the April 1955 issue of the *Calvin Forum,* Leonard Verduin mocked Van Til's stubborn isolation as that of a man at war against the modern spirit. "Anyone conversant with Van Til's thought habits," Verduin wrote, "will have detected in him a veritable phobia for that-which-men-of-all-categories-have-in-common."[42] In the same issue, James Daane argued that Van Til had established an "orthodoxy by reputation," which thereby enjoyed the unearned confidence of the Christian Reformed Church. Incredibly, after all of the criticism heaped on Van Til in the pages of the *Calvin Forum*, Daane still was bold enough to claim that there remained in the CRC "a strange reluctance to face the issues of Professor C. Van Til's theology."[43]

A crucial point of Van Til's that was universally ignored by *Calvin Forum* writers was his distinction between the epistemological and psychological consciousness of unbelievers. "I do not deny," he wrote Henry Van Til,

> that [unbelievers] can and do know God. I have only maintained that they could not do so in terms of their epistemological and metaphysical principles. It terms of their principles there would be no possible identification of one fact from another. . . . So it is in spite of their principles and they still have to work with our principles, albeit against their will, that they can know as much as they do.[44]

Despite the pains he took to clarify himself, Van Til was subjected to ruthless caricature that bordered on mockery. One critic claimed that if he took up Van Til's doctrine of common grace, he would dare not use toothpaste made by non-Christians. A chemist at Calvin College, Thedford Dirkse, argued that Van Til's doctrine of the antithesis insisted that a child of the covenant would be breaking the covenant if he or she agreed with a non-Christian about the color of a particular object.[45]

To add insult to injury, Van Til felt betrayed even by his friends. He was furious when Cornelius Jaarsma of the Calvin education faculty published essays of his that expressed the antithesis in extreme and unvarnished terms. Jaarsma's 1953 anthology, *Fundamentals in Christian Education*, contained four addresses that Van Til delivered, from 1930 to 1932, at conventions of the National Union of Christian Schools. In those early works Van Til, in his mid-thirties, described Reformed pedagogical principles in basic and unqualified ways. "The principles upon which believers live," he wrote, "are squarely opposed to the principles by which unbelievers live. . . . The whole Christian church is based upon the antithesis idea," he told his audience.[46]

Characteristically, Van Til vented his frustration to his nephew. "I do not recall that he consulted me about republishing my articles," Van Til complained to Henry Van Til. "I would have liked to have had a chance to revise them, especially in the light of the present controversy."[47] To Van Til's embarrassment, reviewers extracted comments from his work out of context, including his claim that "no teaching of any sort is possible except in Christian schools."[48]

Even in these early essays, Van Til qualified his absolute ethical antithesis with a nuanced expression of common grace, which is useful to quote at length:

> At this point I may interject that when I thus emphasize the absolute antithesis, I am not denying or even for a moment forgetting the doctrine of common grace. That doctrine does not militate against the doctrine of the absolute antithesis, but here as elsewhere confirms it. Common grace does not overlook ultimate differences. Nor does it, when correctly understood, in any way tone down those ultimate differences. On the contrary, common grace helps to point out that things which look alike are not ultimately alike. Common grace points specifically to the fact that similarities between the people of God and the people of this world are but proximate similarities and that these proximate similarities play before the background of ultimate differences. If people do not believe in common grace or do not know what it means, they are likely to raise proximate similarities to ultimate similarities or to raise proximate differences to ultimate differences with the result that the absolute differences are toned down. It is this which has often taken place in non-Reformed churches. There it has been thought that religion is a condiment that may be added to the otherwise neutral territories of life. Because they did not understand the doctrine of common grace these churches took it for granted that no ultimate difference could be hidden behind the statement of a Christian that two times two are four and a statement of a non-Christian that two times two are four.
>
> Now the fact that two times two are four does not mean the same thing to you as a believer and to someone else as an unbeliever. When you think of two times two as four, you connect this fact with numerical law. And when you connect this fact with numerical law, you must connect numerical law with all law. The question you face, then, is whether law exists in its own right or is an expression of the will and nature of God. Thus the fact that two times two are four enables you to implicate yourself more deeply into the nature and will of God. On the other hand, when an unbeliever says that two times two are four, he will also be led to connect this fact with the whole idea of law; but he will regard this law as independent of God. Thus the fact that two times two are four enables him, so he thinks, to get farther away from God. That fact will place the

unbeliever before a whole sea of open possibilities in which he may seek to realize his life away from God. And it is this basic difference between what "two times two are four" means to the believer and what it means to the unbeliever that the doctrine of common grace has helped us to see. It has enabled us to focus our attention upon the antithesis without fearing that we are doing injustice to any of the facts that surround us.[49]

Yet these qualifications were largely ignored, and Van Til was shocked at the animosity that was stirred up. Reflecting on his Grand Rapids experience, he wondered how he "came out of Grand Rapids alive."[50] He heeded the advice of friends to remain quiet throughout his *Calvin Forum* ordeal. He was careful never to describe his Christian Reformed opponents as "liberal." The strongest language that he employed was "inconsistently Reformed." (Although the friendly connection that he drew between Calvin and Princeton Seminary encouraged his readers to draw stronger conclusions.)

Among close friends he maintained his sense of humor. After John DeWaard brought to his attention the motto that Charles "Engine Charlie" Wilson, the Secretary of Defense, displayed on his desk, "Nulli bastardo carburundo," Van Til was fond of invoking the [fractured?] Latin expression to summarize his attitude toward his critics. (Roughly translated "Don't let the bastards wear you down," the phrase is found in several of his letters to Henry Van Til.)

The controversy affected his ability to write, and it took its toll on his health. He spoke to his closest friends of insomnia, heart pain, and attacks on his nerves, while pleading with them to keep it quiet. By 1952 he was receiving weekly liver injections, and he complained of frequent sinus headaches and struggles with his eyesight.

The best remedy for his health proved to be a return to Westminster—to friendly colleagues and to healthy routines. His garden continued to provide a peaceful pastime and bountiful harvests, and he delighted in handing out pumpkins to neighborhood children in the fall. He resumed his Sunday afternoon visits to the nearby Chestnut Hill Hospital, and of course, he looked forward to his annual August sojourn to the den Dulk farm in Ripon, California, to write and enjoy rest.

Upon his return, Van Til picked up his pace at Westminster. He took on the task of delivering the charge to Westminster's graduates, inheriting an assignment that R. B. Kuiper had regularly filled. These addresses, which he delivered regularly for nearly a decade, were time-consuming and burdensome to write, he confided to Henry.[51] They were also stirring messages that called graduates to faith and courage as they set out as ministers of the gospel. They were often accompanied by Van Til's pledge to support them in their work. "Do not feel that you are alone. . . . We as a faculty shall continue to bear witness *with* you, as we have in these few years borne witness *to* you."[52]

Following the example of E. J. Young (and before him, J. Gresham Machen), Van Til also began to teach at Winona Lake School of Theology in Indiana in 1955. Van Til claimed that the four-week summer school was a good opportunity to reach fundamentalists. However, the grueling schedule was hardly conducive to his health (four hours of teaching, six days a week, was taxing on his strength), and he likely took on the task for several years to allow Rena more time with her family in nearby Munster.

Defense of the Faith

The failure of *Calvin Forum* writers to understand Van Til was a constant source of frustration. By 1954 he concluded that "Cecil De Boer must be raging mad."[53] Yet he still kept public silence. After he read the August–September 1953 issue of the *Calvin Forum,* he wrote in his journal: "I hope I shall be kept by the Spirit of God from expressing bitterness. The misrepresentation seems to be inexcusable, but I must aim to express myself more clearly."[54]

The *Calvin Forum* criticism stood in sharp contrast to the ease with which many outsiders seemed to comprehend and even appreciate his writings. In 1950, when Van Til returned home aboard the Queen Mary from the Tyndale Lectures in England, he met John H. Ramsey, a Roman Catholic priest from Kentucky, with whom he struck up a friendship. Van Til sent Ramsey several books, which Ramsey found "a most pleasant experience." Van Til critiqued Catholicism on a "highly intellectual and dispassionate plane" that has "practically disappeared from Protestant writings," Ramsey noted. He applauded Van Til's "painstaking study," his "unbiased appraisal" that lacked the "bitter denunciation" that generally characterized Protestant critics. He allowed that other priests in his school were "glued" to Van Til's work and "impressed with his erudition."[55]

Van Til encountered a similar experience several years later when, in March 1956, he delivered lectures on Boston Personalism at the Boston University School of Theology. As vast as their theological differences were, Van Til left greatly impressed at the "courteous and generous" attitude of his liberal Methodist hosts, who listened to his analysis with great interest. He found the week's experience "very rewarding," and a sharp contrast to the relentless satirizing he was receiving from critics in Grand Rapids.[56]

Van Til decided against responding point-by-point to his *Calvin Forum* critics. For one, there were too many of them. Also, he did not want to descend into mud-slinging, and he questioned whether he could respond directly in a way that "Christian charity demands."[57] Instead, he took the magazine's relentless assault as a challenge to express himself more clearly on the subject of Christian apologetics. In 1954 he wrote a popular tract, *Paul at Athens*, in which he claimed to take his apologetic cue from the apostle Paul. Van Til may also have hinted at some biographical similarity to Paul who would "rather be stoned to death than flattered."[58]

A fuller statement of his expression of Reformed apologetics took shape in his 1955 book *The Defense of the Faith*. This book was the first full-length exposition of his views on the proper method of encountering modern unbelief. The 400-page book contained extensive references to his Christian Reformed critics, including James Daane, the De Boers, and Masselink. It is here that Van Til constructed his famous apologetic trialogue among Messrs. Black, White, and Grey. In addition, Van Til expressed his "atom bomb" point in a more restrained form: "Is there then no such thing as a Reformed philosophy of fact, of logic, in short, of science that differs from the scholastic view? How would you justify the erection of a science building on the campus of Calvin College, or on the campus of any other Reformed institution?[59]

The Defense of the Faith contained Van Til's mature reflections on Reformed apologetics, and it was the first lengthy exposition of his apologetics for a general readership. For years, this book served as the most complete introduction to his thought. Much of the book was organized around the Westminster Shorter Catechism, further evidence that Van Til had no difficulty finding himself at home within the Westminster Standards. If there was any adjustment in moving from the continental Reformed confessions, Van Til never expressed a hint. The language of the Westminster Standards was tripping easily off his tongue and spilling effortlessly into print.

Van Til's deference to the strict language of the creeds and confessions of Reformed orthodoxy found only one curious exception in his work, and that was his formulation of the Trinity. In his effort to challenge the impersonalism of much of modern Trinitarian thought, Van Til provocatively proposed that God was one person.[60] This was an uncharacteristic departure from the language of the Nicene Creed (one being, three persons), but it was for an orthodox end. God is, Van Til rightly insisted, a fully personal being. However, his language was confusing for some readers especially as it pertained to the connection between personhood and relationship. As personhood is commonly in relation to other persons, it is a term traditionally limited to the threeness of the Trinity. Van Til's formulation was at least vulnerable to heretical conclusions, and for this reason, Nicea and historic orthodoxy had carefully chosen other terms to describe God's personal oneness.[61]

The recurring charge of philosophical idealism in the *Calvin Forum* was another frustration that baffled Van Til and further revealed the magazine's failure to grant his views a fair hearing. In response to one critic, he wrote: "I cannot think of anything I have written in which I have expressed any sympathy with idealism. On the contrary, beginning with my dissertation, I have sought to expose idealism as being basically hostile to the Christian religion, inasmuch as it destroys even the Creator-creature distinction."[62] In an effort to silence this line of criticism Van Til also published *Christianity and Idealism* in 1955. This was a collection of previously published, mostly scholarly articles and reviews, including "God and the Absolute," a summary of his doctoral dissertation that had appeared in the *Evangelical Quarterly* in 1930. In his preface he sought to put distance between idealism and his position in the clearest possible terms:

> From time to time I have written on the relation of idealist philosophy to Christianity. It is obvious that such philosophies as materialism and pragmatism are foes of Christianity. It is less obvious but no less true that Idealism and Christianity are mutually exclusive. Christianity teaches man to worship and serve God the Creator. Idealism, no less than materialism or pragmatism, teaches man to serve and worship the creature. Idealism has a language which resembles that of Christianity but its thought content leads inevitably toward pragmatism. That is the idea expressed in the articles that are herewith reproduced.[63]

The book was a success as the charge of idealism tended to recede after its publication (though it resurfaced from time to time). Most of Van Til's readers have come to understand that the controlling principle in his philosophy of history is the principle of the covenant, and that his work reveals the influence of Geerhardus Vos far more than of A. A. Bowman. *Calvin Forum*'s failure to appreciate Vos's shaping of Van Til reflected the lack of a covenantal sensibility in his more philosophically oriented critics.

Van Til was eager to see both of these works published. By the spring of 1955 he had just turned sixty, and he wondered how much writing he had left in him. Although he confessed that he scarcely had the energy to reopen "those big white tomes" of Barth's *Kirchliche Dogmatik*, he sensed the burden to write again on Barth, this time a more popular work than *The New Modernism*, which had just gone out of print. For one thing, despite the growing American enthusiasm over the allegedly Reformed orthodoxy of a "later Barth," Van Til was convinced that the subsequent volumes in Barth's dogmatics were more universalist than ever. And so he imagined writing a book patterned after Machen's *Christianity and Liberalism*, though he confessed, "I have nothing like the ability to write that Machen had."[64] Furthermore, Van Til believed that another study of Barth would be the best way to address the defection of G. C. Berkouwer (whose mind was "poisoned by Barth") and the growing naiveté of the Christian Reformed Church.

Meanwhile, the anti–Van Tilian warfare in the *Calvin Forum,* which "rode the issue to death," according to James Bratt,[65] ended abruptly on November 2, 1955, with the sudden passing of Cecil De Boer. When no successor could be found willing to take up the cause, the journal ceased publication. Van Til refused to gloat over the passing of his adversary. A month later he wrote in his journal: "How thankful I now am that I was moderate in expression in reply to his violence. We must always speak as those who may be called to give an account any day."[66] Throughout the controversy, Van Til's tolerance and forbearance with his critics were apparent, at least to disinterested parties.

Van Til's Grand Rapids opponents labored to read him in the worst possible light, the very charge, ironically, that they placed on his treatment of Karl Barth. The tendency to get carried away in their criticism of Van Til was noted by another Dutch Reformed theologian who advocated a more gentlemanly approach. Professor Elton M. Eenigenburg of Western Seminary in Holland, Michigan, observed that throughout the debate "scholarship has been abandoned in favor of personal pique," and that critics, carried away by emotions, have failed to understand Van Til's teaching.[67]

Debating James Daane

The first book-length criticism of Van Til appeared in 1954 with the publication of James Daane's *The Theology of Grace,* subtitled "An Inquiry into and Evaluation of Dr. C. Van Til's Doctrine of Common Grace." Although Daane reviewed *The New Modernism* and *Common Grace* favorably, he came to question the "overstating" of Van Til's case against Barth that located Van Til's nemesis "outside of the Christian Truth." There is, Daane wrote in the *Calvin Forum,* "surely much 'grey' in Barth, but it is not all unrelieved black."[68]

Daane argued that Van Til's common grace was no grace at all, and he claimed to unmask Van Til along with Herman Hoeksema as the twin descendents of the "staticism" of Louis Berkhof. As Daane read him, Van Til differed only in degree from Hoeksema, and both threatened the ability of the CRC to rise beyond its insularity. (Three decades later, Henry Stob continued this line of thought when he connected Van Til and Hoeksema's doctrines of the "antithesis."[69]) If Van Til accepted common grace, argued Daane, he did so by warding off its force. Daane was most offended over Van Til's argument that common grace prompted the non-elect to "crucify the Son of God afresh." This rendered God as the cause of sin, and he concluded that Van Til established an "equal ultimacy" between election and reprobation, and was thus more deterministic than Reformed.

Daane scored some points against Van Til. It was true, for example, that Van Til was not completely satisfied with the language of the 1924 Synod statement, and he tried to stake some territory between Hoeksema and Hoeksema's critics. Moreover, common grace as "earlier grace" was an awkward formulation that Van Til developed inadequately. But readers generally dismissed Daane's book as an angry analysis that missed its target. Even Herman Hoeksema, no friend of common grace, commented that he "could easily defend Van Til" against Daane's criticisms.[70]

William Young noted the ironic nature of Daane's attack. Daane faulted the often polemical Van Til for what seemed to be an irenic effort by Van Til to mediate between Hoeksema, Klaas Schilder, and other Reformed theologians on common grace. Writing in the *Banner*, John H. Stek lamented the "large element of confusion" that Daane introduced by his "unfortunate and unnecessary reading of Van Til." In particular Stek cited Daane's characterization of Van Til as "a compound of Hegelian rationalism and modern existentialism." In S. J. Ridderbos's review in the *Reformed Journal* he dismissed Daane as one who did not make his case and whose tone of petty bickering unfortunately characterized too much recent Dutch theological debate.[71]

Van Til responded in kind to Daane with a book-length plea of innocence to the charges. "The structure of my thought is simply Biblical in the orthodox sense of the term. Daane has not produced and can produce no evidence to the contrary."[72] He quickly went from the defensive to the offensive. He charged Daane with resurrecting the old Pighius-Calvin debate. Daane represented the former, with a dash of existentialism that he had picked up from Princeton Seminary, where he had earned a graduate degree in 1945. Van Til claimed to follow Calvin in observing the distinction between God as the ultimate cause and man as a derived and yet genuine cause. "Equal ultimacy," Van Til argued, still observed the distinction between God's passing by of the reprobate, and his wrathful punishment of them (the latter on account of their sin). In a Calvinistic understanding of causation, the perdition of the unbeliever owes both to God's counsel as the ultimate cause and to human sin as the proximate cause.

Meanwhile, a second book-length treatment of Van Til was in the works, this one by Rousas J. Rushdoony, a California scholar who established a literary relationship with Van Til during this decade. Although Van Til was impressed with Rushdoony's grasp of his thought, he expressed two concerns about the book. Van Til believed that early drafts were so complimentary that the adulation of Rushdoony's prose would prove embarrassing. He also requested Rushdoony to tone down his criticism of Berkouwer and to reduce his criticism to Berkouwer's treatment of Barth.

Like Daane, Berkouwer was strongly opposed to Van Til's notion of the "equal ultimacy" of election and reprobation, and he claimed that the Synod of Dort itself emphatically rejected this formulation and its accompanying theological determinism. Yet Van Til never equated "ultimacy" with "symmetry," as Berkouwer seemed to read. When Van Til's former Westminster student, Norman Shepherd, studying at the time under Berkouwer at the Free University of Amsterdam, reported Berkouwer's fierce attack, Van Til responded with a long open letter to Berkouwer on "equal ultimacy." Along the way he turned the charge around by claiming that Berkouwer's misreading of Dort affirmed its own equal ultimacy, between the counsel of God and human responsibility.[73]

Herman Dooyeweerd in North America

Before the decade ended, Van Til came to an even greater awareness of the unsoundness of contemporary Dutch Reformed theology. As noted, for decades Van Til had been greatly encouraged by the prolific output from Herman Dooyeweerd's pen, which was, in Van Til's words, "a marvelously beautiful sight to behold."[74] Van Til credited him with plumbing deeper insights from Kuyper, avoiding all dualisms, whether the form-matter of the Greeks, the nature-grace of the medievalists, or the nature-freedom dialectic that beset modern thought. Only the presupposition of the Christian faith (what Dooyeweerd referred to as ground-motive) could avoid the bankruptcy of autonomous thought.

Van Til actively promoted Dooyeweerd's four-volume work when it first appeared in English translation in 1953. He encouraged its wide reading in North America, and even subsidized the purchase of the work for seminarians struggling with the high price tag. For this reason, Van Til was quick to demur from the credit of originality. He claimed the more modest role of introducing to the English-speaking world what Dooyeweerd and others were doing in Europe, that is, deepening and applying the work of Calvin and Kuyper in the development of a truly Calvinistic philosophy. It came as a great shock to Van Til, therefore, to see Dooyeweerd's work greeted with Dutch Reformed hostility. Van Til exerted great effort to defend Dooyeweerd from Christian Reformed critics who had misunderstood him, and he was particularly frustrated by W. H. Jellema's quick dismissal of Dooyeweerd.

It came as a deeper disappointment for Van Til eventually to develop his own suspicions about Dooyeweerd. In 1958 Dooyeweerd traveled to North America and his itinerary included lectures at the University of Pennsylvania. Van Til hosted Dooyeweerd where he learned that Dooyeweerd had come to reject the full inerrancy of the Bible. Dooyeweerd told Van Til "point-blank that he did not believe in a historical Adam."[75]

Dooyeweerd's defection was heartbreaking. "My big worry," Van Til wrote to H. J. Kuiper of the *Torch and Trumpet*, "is that his own view of Scripture seems to be of a compromising nature."[76] Van Til kept his concerns private for a time, refusing to write about Dooyeweerd's visit for the *Torch and Trumpet*, eager instead to devote more time to reflect on it. But he was no longer prepared to give an unqualified defense of Dooyeweerd's philosophy.

Despite his suspicions, Van Til's respect ran deep until Dooyeweerd's death in 1977. Dooyeweerd was regularly included, along with Calvin and Kuyper, in Van Til's short list of Reformed giants who had made his work easier. In his memorial to Dooyeweerd in the *Westminster*

Theological Journal, Van Til observed that in any account of the development of Reformed philosophy in the twentieth century, Dooyeweerd was the "first among equals."

By the end of this decade-long warfare with progressive elements of the church of his youth, Van Til still displayed his love and appreciation for the Dutch Reformed tradition. He maintained his interest in continental Reformed thought, and he devoured the studies on the Heidelberg Catechism by Herman Hoeksema and Klaas Schilder. "Both are great theologians," he wrote to Henry Van Til.[77] In 1958, at the request of several Reformed Church in the U.S. students at Westminster Seminary, he offered an elective course on the Heidelberg Catechism. This course, like much of Van Til's work, performed double duty. In his classroom syllabus on the Heidelberg Catechism, Van Til noted that today's preaching from the catechism must be as familiar with modernism as Zachary Ursinus (the author of the catechism) was with Romanism. Much of this syllabus was a polemic against Barth, and its very title was a none-too-subtle reaction to Berkouwer's sympathetic reassessment of Barth.[78]

Still, Van Til's ties to the Christian Reformed Church were loosening. In a sense, Van Til did not leave the CRC so much as it left him. The robust Calvinism that he was so eager to see the OPC emulate was waning, and the antithesis had vanished from its authors. In a letter to William Hendriksen, he identified a broadening movement at Calvin College: "It is getting clearer by the day that there is a determined group in the church, centering at Calvin, that means to follow a broader way than our fathers trod." The common grace debate was a means toward that end, and at the heart of the movement was his former professor Jellema. Worse yet, the Calvin faculty was following Berkouwer in warming up to Barth.[79]

Van Til likened many of his opponents in the *Calvin Forum* to his earlier foes among American evangelicalism. In a revealing letter, he wrote,

> We went through the same sort of struggle in the Orthodox Presbyterian Church with Dr. Clark. He insisted that there was exact identity of content in the mind of man with the content of the mind

of God in his knowledge. Over against this view we argued that man as the creature of God is analogical of God in his knowledge. And we stressed the fact that this meant a one way dependence of man on God. Clark argued that such a view led to equivocism in knowledge. In the same way the De Boers and [C. J.] Orlebeke and Jellema (so far as he has expressed himself) tend to stress that there must be a reality out there that is what it is independently of God and the "mind." They oppose modern idealism but fall into Platonic realism which is the mother of modern idealism.[80]

In some respects the protracted Calvin episode of the 1950s was for Van Til the equivalent of Machen's Princeton experience. The *Torch and Trumpet* itself drew a comparison with Machen's treatment by the Presbyterian Church in the U.S.A.[81] The analogy is not far-fetched, given the comments of Van Til's critics. Some of them wondered whether the exodus from Princeton had been unwarranted, and they even questioned the propriety of Westminster's existence.

In the judgment of the Grand Rapids progressives, Van Til had broken the peace of the 1924 common grace settlement with atomic weaponry, and his departure served to restore that peace. The progressives in the CRC feared Van Til mostly for the prospect that he would continue its parochial ways. Ironically, they shared a similar agenda with Van Til. Both parties recognized that the CRC could not survive as a sustainable religious community merely on ethnic identity after World War II. Van Til sought to cultivate within the Dutch Reformed a deeper sense of Reformed identity. This required the church to venture beyond the tradition of Kuyper and to dig deeper into its heritage by recovering the insights of Calvin.

For the progressives, Van Til's apologetic was a formula for greater insularity and isolation. Yet they were unable to see how parochial they were in their own ways by their naïve embrace of the American Protestant mainstream. In comparison, Van Til, for all his emphasis on the antithesis and Reformed particularism, may have been in far greater contact with international Calvinism.

Presbyterian Patriarch

On Sunday morning, August 9, 1959, the Rev. John J. DeWaard died in his sleep. Van Til's closest friend since college days had retired the previous January from his pastorate at Memorial Orthodox Presbyterian Church in Rochester, New York. Van Til traveled to Rochester to preach the funeral sermon, where he recalled how the Presbytery of the PCUSA had dissolved DeWaard's ministerial relationship with his Cedar Grove, Wisconsin, church in 1936 because DeWaard refused to promise loyalty to the denomination's official boards that were riddled with modernism. Van Til always admired DeWaard as one who counted the cost of faithfulness to the Reformed faith. It amazed Van Til that DeWaard never complained about this miscarriage of justice, and he eulogized his friend as "one whose life was absorbed in the service of his Savior."[1]

Soon thereafter Van Til was shaken by the passing of other friends and loved ones. He conducted the funeral service for Robert Marsden, longtime executive secretary for Westminster Seminary, in 1960. Jessie den Dulk, wife of Dr. Gilbert den Dulk, passed away suddenly in that same year, and Van Til was especially shocked at the unexpected death in 1961 of his nephew, Henry Van Til, who succumbed to a heart attack in his office at Calvin College. Ned B. Stonehouse's death in November 1962 brought to an abrupt end the long collective tenure of the founding Westminster faculty, and it marked the beginning of significant changes on the faculty throughout the next several years.

As Van Til began to outlive his friends and colleagues, he transitioned into the patriarch for the seminary and the church, and he reveled in this role. Van Til was at the height of his influence, and the new decade ushered in a period of ambitious travel, expanded opportunities, and heightened productivity. In 1960 he approached his sixty-fifth birthday in his writing prime. The previous decade's "fires of criticism" prompted no sense of retreat, and unlike DeWaard, Van Til gave no thought to retirement. It was symbolic of his plans for the years before him that when Van Til posed for his Westminster faculty portrait in 1961, the artist did not capture him seated in academic regalia, like his colleagues. Instead he was pictured in the classroom, standing at a lectern before a chalk-filled blackboard.

Van Til's reputation extended far beyond Westminster Seminary and the Orthodox Presbyterian Church. He lectured frequently at Inter-Varsity chapters and other campus ministries throughout the Northeast, where he impressed students and faculty by speaking intelligently about Christian orthodoxy. He became something of a mentor to a rising generation of Reformed and evangelical leaders. J. R. DeWitt, Os Guinness, Richard Mouw, Ronald Nash, and David Wells were among the dozens of young scholars who wrote to him. He readily dispensed graduate school advice as well as his books, which he sent either for free or with the request that the inquirer pay whatever he could afford. (The requests came often because of the difficulty of obtaining his syllabi, and he freely distributed $500–$1000 worth of books per year throughout the decade.) Clark Pinnock, then a Calvinist on the faculty of New Orleans Baptist Seminary, expressed "enthusiasm" for Van Til's work, leading Van Til to anticipate the publication of Pinnock's apologetics book *Set Forth Your Case*. Van Til was disappointed to discover that Pinnock fell "right back into Butler's analogy."[2]

Whether any of these future scholars of American evangelicalism realized it or not, Van Til's work may have triggered a significant transition in their thinking. His reasoning by presupposition was a radical challenge to the foundationalism of mid-century evangelical thought that was generally following in the train of Enlightenment rationality. Van Til's early and penetrating critique of evangelical apologetics (classical or evidential) anticipated the collapse of Cartesianism and the rise of the role of interpretation, even though the writings of self-styled post-foundational evangelicals a half-century later rarely documents any acknowledgment of Van Til's influence.

On the eve of his sixty-fifth birthday, Van Til took a long-anticipated trip to the Far East. He originally planned an ambitious seven-week itinerary, but it was shortened and nearly canceled altogether when he developed a bronchial infection a month before his departure. (A side trip to Australia was eliminated, much to his dismay.) At the last minute, Dr. Gilbert den Dulk, recently widowed, decided to accompany him, and Van Til was grateful for the medical doctor's attention to his health needs. The pair visited Orthodox Presbyterian missionaries in Taiwan, Japan, and Korea, all of whom had implored Van Til for years to visit them. He delighted to reacquaint himself with several Westminster alumni, especially Goji Tanaka in Japan, who had enrolled at Westminster in its second year. Van Til preached and lectured before attentive audiences wherever he went, including before many students in universities in Taipei and Seoul.

Van Til returned home physically exhausted but spiritually enriched. He confessed a greater appreciation for the sacrifices of the denomination's missionaries and a firmer resolve to encourage more international students to come to Westminster and return to their native lands. He was also further troubled by the evidence that Barth reigned supreme in many quarters of the Far East.

A similar impression followed his visit to Mexico in 1964, during which he spoke at the Synod of the Presbyterian Church of Mexico and at a couple of Reformed seminaries in Mexico City. Accompanied by missionaries of the Christian Reformed Church, he was struck by the Roman Catholic grip on the Mexican culture and also by several encounters with Barthians.

Throughout the decade, Van Til also traveled and spoke at several new Reformed colleges and seminaries, and it pleased him to see the rise of challengers to Calvin College's monopoly on Christian higher education. He traveled to Dordt College, in Sioux Center, Iowa, in 1965 (where his nephew, Nick Van Til, taught in the philosophy department), and he often commended Dordt and Trinity Christian College in Palos Heights, Illinois, to inquirers. In 1967 he visited Covenant College in Lookout Mountain, Georgia, and he left the school impressed that the faculty "meant business with the Reformed faith."[3] He welcomed the formation of Reformed Theological Seminary in 1966. Several of his former students served on the faculty there, and he traveled to Jackson, Mississippi, as a visiting lecturer in the spring of the seminary's second year.

The New Evangelicalism

These Reformed institutions were encouraging because Van Til was expressing ever-widening doubts about the viability of American evangelicalism, especially the phenomenon he described as the "new evangelicalism." He first employed the phrase in a 1957 address to entering students at Westminster, where he warned them of voices they would encounter who would challenge their confidence in the Word of God. This was "new evangelicalism," and it had "nothing basically in common with historic Christianity." By denying the infallibility of the Bible and substituting a human-centered approach to interpreting God's Word, it had "no help to offer to modern man in his hopelessness and loneliness."[4]

In the next month, perhaps in response to Van Til's address, Harold Ockenga preached a sermon from his Park Street Church pulpit in Boston, defending neo-evangelicalism, which, he countered, was faithfully applying the historic Christian faith to contemporary social issues. Founder of the National Association of Evangelicals, former president of Fuller Theological Seminary, and one-time editor of *Christianity Today*, Ockenga carried an impressive evangelical résumé. He was eager to correct Van Til because he claimed to have coined the term *neo-evangelicalism* in a 1948 address at Fuller Seminary. Although fundamentalism and evangelicalism were largely synonymous terms in the first half of the twentieth century, Ockenga labored to distance

American evangelicals from the extremes of fundamentalist separatism. Neo-evangelicalism, he asserted, represented the best of orthodox Christianity while applying it to the social and political issues of its time: "the neo-evangelical is willing to face the intellectual problems and meet them in the framework of modern learning."[5] The expanding network of institutions that Ockenga helped to create offered the prospect of irenic dialogue as an alternative to militant polemics. Under his prodding, evangelicals sought to be diplomats and infiltrators instead of warriors and separatists.

Van Til could not share Ockenga's enthusiasm, and part of his skepticism was etymological. Contrary to Ockenga's claim, the term *neo-evangelicalism* had been employed three years earlier by John Mackay, president of Princeton Seminary. After returning from the World Council of Churches meeting in Amsterdam, Mackay called for an ecumenical gathering of denominations in America, including Roman Catholics and Greek Orthodox. "We are going to need the evangelicals," he added. "There must be a neo-evangelicalism."[6] Van Til interpreted Mackay's invitation as evidence that Ockenga was playing right into the hands of the liberal ecumenical movement.

Still, if Ockenga objected to Van Til's characterization of evangelicalism in his RTS address, he had a point. Whether Van Til's 1957 audience of young theologians understood him or not, his address conflated neo-orthodoxy and contemporary evangelicalism. None of the so-called new evangelicals (including the faculty at Fuller Seminary) were denying biblical infallibility by this point. Van Til later described "new evangelicalism" in more cautious terms when he delivered lectures on "The New Evangelicalism" for an OPC Ministerial Institute in May 1961.

The result of his presentation was a seventy-five-page syllabus in which he observed that the fundamentalist-modernist battle had evolved into a neo-orthodox and neo-evangelical dialogue. His analysis of contemporary evangelicalism fell under three categories: theology, journalism, and evangelism. The first category focused on the chief theologians of the movement, E. J. Carnell and Bernard Ramm, whom he scored for defending the Christian faith on the neutral terrain of human autonomy. Van Til charged that by this concession evangelical theologians battled modern unbelief with less than the full armor of God.

Incoherence was also found in the principal voice of evangelicalism, *Christianity Today*. Since its founding in 1956, the magazine had deliberately avoided ecclesiastical issues, which reduced it to "a cacophony of different voices" in Van Til's judgment. "The result of this policy," Van Til wrote, "was an amalgam of Calvinism and Arminianism." And where the two are combined, "more often Arminianism wins."[7]

Van Til charged that Billy Graham embodied the cooperative spirit of evangelism and that Graham's popular crusades also undermined the doctrine of the church. For Graham, church membership was "no more important than the style of hats." Consequently, Graham "softened the offense" of the cross. Defending a Reformed view of missions, Van Til turned the standard criticism of Reformed indifference to evangelism on its head. Ultimately the theological indifferentism of evangelicalism tended toward an impoverishment of biblical evangelism.[8]

Van Til feared that evangelicalism was softening its message in hopes of a more fruitful encounter with neo-orthodoxy. These bridge-building efforts with mainline Protestantism, he warned, came at too great a price. While the evangelical movement may not itself have forsaken the Bible, its entangling alliances established compromises with movements that had rejected the Word of God.

This critique naturally flowed from the wellspring of the antithesis. The both-and strategy of the new evangelicals was a fatal concession that failed to express "the full gospel of the grace of God."[9] In a desire to reach more souls for Christ, evangelicals lowered the claims of the gospel. At times, however, Van Til's "New Evangelicalism" was an overstated broadside, and his appeal to the antithesis smacked of fundamentalist separatism in the eyes of many readers. Charles J. Woodbridge (a former minister of the Orthodox Presbyterian Church and former professor at Fuller Seminary who was settled into fundamentalist independency by this point) enthusiastically commended the work in his travels as a masterpiece, prompting fundamentalists to write to request a copy from Van Til.

In responding to these requests, Van Til stressed that "The New Evangelicalism" was a tentative work, which he hoped to refine for publication. Van Til never achieved this goal, perhaps because others beat him to it. He was irked that Ronald Nash stole his title and quoted much of his material without permission in Nash's hastily published book by the same name. Harold Ockenga plugged Nash's upbeat assessment of evangelicalism, and it was sold through the Evangelical Book Club. Nash may well have had Van Til in mind when he wrote in a letter to D. A. Wait, "I believe I have provided documented evidence that neo-evangelicalism does not deserve the slanderous attacks many uninformed and ill-mannered fundamentalists have made upon it."[10] In 1969 Woodbridge himself published a book by the same title, exposing "new evangelicalism" for its toleration, accommodation, and capitulation to error, without citing Van Til by name.

The failure of Van Til's reflections on contemporary American evangelicalism to reach published form also owed to his career-long struggle to achieve definitional precision on evangelicalism. As previously noted, he went so far as to identify at least more progressive forms of evangelicalism with neo-orthodoxy. Most often he likened evangelicalism to Arminianism; on other occasions the term was even more broadly employed as a synonym for all non-Reformed Protestantism (and thus also inclusive of Lutherans). On yet other occasions he borrowed B. B. Warfield's taxonomy to argue that Calvinism was a subset of evangelicalism that embodied its most biblically consistent expression.

In the many contexts in which he contrasted the Reformed faith with more broadly evangelical forms of Christianity, Van Til was eager to distinguish between theology (ideas considered in principle and their consequences) and practice (which accounted for inconsistency in both camps). In this way Van Til sought to strip his critique of pride or chauvinism. "We are not wiser than others," he frequently reminded his students. And though reluctant to cooperate with evangelicals, he readily observed that "many Evangelicals are no doubt better Calvinists in practice than other men who are officially known as Calvinists."[11]

Although he failed to express a succinct Reformed response to evangelicalism, "The New Evangelicalism" was a revealing glimpse into Van Til's deepest concerns for the church. All of his usual suspects were present—Arminianism, Barthianism, ecumenism, and theological indifferentism—and all of them, he feared, were active ingredients in the emerging theology and practice of evangelicalism. This syllabus recalls his zeal for the integrity of the visible church, and it reminds readers that reducing Van Til's interests to apologetic methodology fails to acknowledge his passion as a churchman.

Van Til's struggles with evangelicals were further complicated by their increasing expressions of indebtedness to and respect for him even as he turned a sharper critical eye in their direction. In November 1959, he was honored in the heartland of evangelicalism when the sixth annual Wheaton Philosophy Conference bestowed a citation of gratitude upon Van Til "in warm appreciation of his signal contributions to evangelical thought in the twentieth century, of the stimulation he has afforded to younger scholars, [and] of his unstinting service in philosophy classes and conferences." Wheaton Professor Kenneth Kantzer highlighted Van Til's "standing in the gap for conservative Christians" in his defense of the Bible. For all of the ambivalence on Van Til's part, American evangelicals continued to recognize the value of his work and solicited his instruction.[12]

Carl Henry felt stung by Van Til's attack in "The New Evangelicalism." "You rather take me to task," he wrote to Van Til in 1961.[13] Nevertheless, under Henry's editorship, *Christianity Today* regularly cited Van Til as a respected senior voice. For five years, beginning in 1959, Van Til joined a panel of twenty-five contemporary theologians that commented annually on contemporary theological trends. Van Til used the platform to warn evangelicals of the ecumenical movement, and he took constant aim at Barthians and Roman Catholics. Despite his reservations, Van Til was regularly associated with the evangelical movement. Any differences between Van Til and Henry were lost in a 1963 *Time* magazine article that described the two as among American evangelicals' "best-known writers" who "strive for consistent, logical theology."[14]

The goal behind Van Til's dissent was to highlight the distinctiveness of the Reformed faith that yielded not only a Reformed system of doctrine but also a Reformed doctrine of Scripture and a Reformed defense of the faith. These were of a whole cloth; they were not exchangeable features, and thus Van Til would accept no substitutes. Hence Van Til would not concede that separatism belonged to the fundamentalists. There was a Reformed separatism that was grounded in Kuyper's doctrine of the antithesis, and it was modeled courageously by Machen. Van Til even admired the separatism of Gordon Clark, who left the United Presbyterian Church in 1958 after its merger with the northern mainline church. For that reason Van Til refused to number Clark among the new evangelicals.[15]

And yet, the distance he carved and the isolation he expressed was ultimately for genuinely ecumenical purposes, even for the evangelical cause. In the introduction to his *Christian Theory of Knowledge* (1969), Van Til wrote that evangelicalism "is bound to profit from a defense of the Reformed faith" because "a defense of the Reformed faith is a Reformed method of the defense of Christianity."[16] Reformed particularism, Van Til argued, is ultimately in service of the whole church. Thus Reformed separatism was always accompanied by a Reformed ecumenism: the particularity of the Reformed faith was the key to its genuine universality. Van Til constantly lobbied for Orthodox Presbyterian fellowship with all Christians of like faith and practice. His 1963 Reformation Day address in Baltimore was a call for such a joint undertaking: "Our task . . . is to unite in a common effort of carrying forth the gospel as proclaimed by the Reformers to a world that is lost in sin today. Let us not compromise the gospel of God by cooperating with those who proclaim the gospel of man."[17] Only Reformed ecumenism could raise high the banner of the Reformed faith. In contrast, American evangelicalism was prone to compromise with unbelief.

Ein Menschenfresser

One measure of Van Til's own sense of his widening influence can be found in the publication of the second edition of *Defense of the Faith* in 1963. This considerably smaller reprint omitted references to his Christian Reformed opponents of the previous decade. According to the introduction, these edits rendered his argument "more readily available" to seminaries, Bible schools, and university philosophy departments. Whether or not that claim was true, the abridgement was at least an indication of how far the Christian Reformed Church fell from his chief concerns.

Another barometer was the attention that Van Til received in connection with Karl Barth's famous American tour in 1962. Over the course of the previous decade, many American evangelicals had begun to warm up to Barth, a growing affection that revealed methodological differences between Van Til and Barth's evangelical sympathizers. Critics of Van Til contended that by exposing the deep philosophical roots of Barth's system, Van Til pushed Barth into conclusions that the Swiss theologian did not intend. Some interpreters searched the *Church Dogmatics* for proof-texts that vindicated Barth's orthodoxy. Van Til conceded that plenty of them existed, but he warned that these superficial similarities to historic Protestantism rendered Barth's work all the more pernicious. Van Til was particularly dismayed by the attitude of Donald Grey Barnhouse of Tenth Presbyterian Church in Philadelphia. Barnhouse's *Eternity* magazine chastised Van Til for criticizing Barth in print before confronting him personally and privately.[18] As early as 1954, Barnhouse tried to arrange a meeting between Van Til and Barth. "I have felt [Barth to be] amazingly approachable and ready to accept the strongest statements of faith on all major principles," he wrote to Van Til.[19]

Van Til scoffed at this suggestion in the classroom, and he laughed at his students' playful offer to subsidize the encounter if it involved a one-way ticket for Van Til to Basel. The truth is that Van Til made at least two efforts, during travels to Europe, to meet Barth, including a special trip to Basel. He telephoned Barth's home to make an appointment but learned that the Swiss theologian was away on travel.[20]

Had they met, Barth was not likely to receive Van Til warmly. As indicated in chapter 5, Barth had identified Van Til as his most vicious English-language critic, especially for Van Til's suggestion that no heresy was as "deeply and ultimately destructive of [the] gospel" as the theology of Barth. Barth lumped Van Til among the "butchers and cannibals" of American fundamentalism.[21]

Van Til wrote *Christianity and Barthianism* quickly to coincide with Barth's visit to America. Updating the argument of *The New Modernism* and continuing his assault on Barth's activism, Van Til concluded that "Barthianism, using the language of Reformation theology, is still only a higher humanism."[22] What was particularly new in this book was his attack on G. C. Berkouwer, who by this point had become fully sympathetic with Barth. Throughout the book Van Til cited with approval Berkouwer's earlier assessment of Barth, to the effect that Barth could not account for a "transition from wrath to grace" in history.[23] Van Til made clear that unlike his Dutch counterpart there was no change in his own evaluation of Barth. Rather than conceding a shift from an earlier to a later Barth, Van Til identified a difference between an earlier and a later Berkouwer. (In his 1969 book *The Sovereignty of Grace*, Van Til drew this distinction explicitly.)

Evangelicals were less receptive to Van Til's second book on Barth. Carl Henry was more critical, perhaps still reeling from the treatment he had received in Van Til's "The New Evangelicalism." "Barth's modifications of his system are considered quite inconsequential," wrote Henry, and the "surviving biblical elements" in Barth should be "welcomed."[24] In the *Reformed Journal* James Daane scolded Van Til for what he described as an unfair use of Berkouwer (and for good measure he linked Van Til again to the fatalism of Herman Hoeksema).[25]

Van Til's title for the book, which intentionally resembled Machen's *Christianity and Liberalism*, exposed him to further criticism by the comparison he invited especially in his conclusion:

> The late J. Gresham Machen was confronted with the Christ of the higher humanism of his day. . . . Speaking as objectively as we can, we must say, as in Machen's time "Liberalism," while propagated in the church as though it were the gospel, was in reality a man-made religion, so Barthianism, using the language of Reformation theology, is still only a higher humanism.[26]

Many readers struggled to appreciate the analogy. Van Til's obscure philosophical references and dense writing style hardly resembled the direct prose of Machen's book. Machen made his argument in fewer than two hundred pages, and Van Til stretched to well over four hundred, with more references to Kant, Kierkegaard, and

Schleiermacher than to Jesus or Paul. If Van Til sought to demolish Barth in the manner of Machen on modernism, he failed in the judgment of most readers.

Barth's much publicized tour of America was the seventy-five-year-old's only visit to the United States after retirement from his post at the University of Basel. America, he had observed, was a land where even the Barthians "misrepresent me."[27] His visit provided the occasion for the one very brief encounter between him and Van Til. Several versions of this meeting have circulated, and many involve a significant embellishing of the facts. (One popular account involved the two men ministering together in Chicago's Cook County jail.) What actually transpired was far less dramatic.

The stage was set on April 20, 1962, when *Time* magazine ran a story on Barth. The cover featured a portrait of Barth against the background of an empty tomb, and the article quoted Van Til along with Reinhold Niebuhr. The latter dismissed Barth for offering an "irrelevant theology to America," and Van Til, representing a "host of U.S. fundamentalists," thundered that "Barthianism is even more hostile to the theology of Luther and Calvin than Romanism." The reporter's intent seemed clear. The cover illustrated Barth's orthodoxy, and the visceral reaction he received from both the religious left and the religious right in America was proof that he resided safely in the religious mainstream.[28]

Barth's American itinerary included an engagement at Princeton Seminary as part of the seminary's sesquicentennial celebration. Van Til attempted to arrange a private audience with Barth through the seminary, but the Princeton administration denied his request. Instead, Van Til traveled to Princeton with Arthur Kuschke, the librarian at Westminster Seminary, to hear Barth at the Princeton University Chapel. They hurried out of the packed gothic cathedral after the lecture and caught up with Barth as he was being ushered out of a side door. Van Til quickly introduced himself, and the two longtime antagonists shook hands. "You are Van Til?" Barth asked. "You said some bad things about me, but I forgive you, I forgive you." Van Til was too overwhelmed to reply. Nor did he have an opportunity after collecting his thoughts because Barth was quickly whisked away into a waiting car.[29]

Van Til tried to follow up through correspondence. Edward Geehan, a Westminster graduate studying in the Netherlands, broke the ice by writing to Barth on Van Til's behalf. Barth's brief response, dated November 14, 1965, indicated no interest in reconciliation. Van Til, he charged, "seems to have understood *not a single word* from all I have written." Furthermore, Barth added, "certainly I myself have *not* understood *a single word* of his critique." He suggested that a meeting of the minds must await the future, when Van Til and he would enjoy a "more fruitful encounter" not in this world but in the world to come, "humbly and even laughing" together.[30]

That Barth even responded to Geehan emboldened Van Til to write. "I have always admired you greatly," Van Til wrote to Barth. Although Van Til had spent much of his career elaborating their differences, he insisted that he had never called Barth "the greatest heretic" in the history of the church, nor had he ever judged Barth's personal Christian faith. The latter was certainly true, the former was harder to reconcile with Van Til's acerbic characterization in the previous decade. Van Til went on to ask for forgiveness wherever he had misunderstood or misrepresented Barth, and he too expressed his hope that the two might eventually meet in heaven. The letter was self-effacingly signed, "C. Van Til, Ein Menschenfresser" (cannibal).[31]

Apparently, Barth did not write back to Van Til. Three years later, after Barth died on December 10, 1968, Van Til traveled to Princeton Seminary with John Frame, Richard Gaffin, and Norman Shepherd from Westminster Seminary to attend a memorial service for Barth, where two of Van Til's old antagonists, E. G. Homrighausen and George Hendry, spoke. Van Til restricted his reflections to an appreciation for the dignity of the service, and declined to use the occasion for further analysis of Barth.[32]

Barth's American tour marked the final break between Van Til and his former prize student, E. J. Carnell. Carnell had suffered a series of nervous breakdowns, and his teaching at Fuller was interrupted by bouts of severe depression. He was well enough to attend Barth's presentation at his other American venue at the University of Chicago, and he served on a panel that posed questions to Barth. In reporting on his encounter in the *Christian Century*, Carnell gushed that Barth "radiated irresistible charm," and what the Swiss theologian "may lack in the way of doctrinal consistency he compensates by his Christian graciousness." In his conclusion he lashed out at Van Til: "I am utterly ashamed of the manner in which extreme fundamentalists in America continue to attack Barth." In particular, Van Til's quotes in *Time* magazine prompted "actual physical pain" when Carnell read them. "I propose that Van Til ask God to forgive him for such an irresponsible judgment. Barth's Thursday lecture, for instance, could have been given at Moody Bible Institute, without offense, so rich was it in evangelical content." [33]

While outraged friends of Van Til's rushed to defend him in print, Van Til himself seemed less concerned. "Carnell is not well," he wrote to William Gray, "and we should not take some of his extreme statements too seriously." [34] After a final exchange of brief and cordial letters in 1964, Carnell died under mysterious circumstances, and Van Til declined any public comment.

Carnell's failing health afforded another publishing opportunity for Van Til. In 1959, Westminster Press published Carnell's *The Case for Orthodox Theology* in a series with two other books, *The Case for Theology from a Liberal Perspective* by L. Harold DeWolf and *The Case for a New Reformation Theology* by William Hordern. Van Til lectured on these three books in March of 1962 in Berkeley, California, as he prepared his book-length response, *The Case for Calvinism.* Eighteen months later, substituting for an ailing Carnell, Van Til joined DeWolf and Hordern for a symposium at the Boston University Philosophical Club.

In 1964 Presbyterian and Reformed published Van Til's book, which was mostly an extended review of the three-book Macmillan series. Predictably, Van Til asserted little difference between DeWolf's modernism and Hordern's neo-orthodoxy. He dwelt at greater length on Carnell's failure to represent the historic Protestant alternative. Carnell's approach was flawed in appealing to the rational man in judging the trustworthiness of Scripture, which the Fuller professor expressed flamboyantly in his *Introduction to Christian Apologetics*: "Bring on your revelations! Let them make peace with the law of contradiction and the facts of history, and they will deserve a rational man's assent."[35] This was precisely the fatal strategy of appeasement that Van Til warned was a key component of the new evangelicalism.[36]

The Confession of 1967

When Van Til turned seventy in 1965, R. B. Kuiper wrote him a congratulatory note and urged him not to retire. Van Til replied that he had no plans to do so.[37]

Retirement would have to wait because there were more battles to face and the Orthodox Presbyterian Church was eager to employ his services.

Four years earlier James McCord, the president of Princeton Seminary, invited the Orthodox Presbyterian Church to participate with other Presbyterian and Lutheran churches in Reformed-Lutheran conversations. The OPC General Assembly debated the propriety of participation, and when it was satisfied that church union was not a goal of the talks, it asked Van Til to be its representative. Van Til agreed, and he attended meetings for three years, from 1963 to 1965, seizing an opportunity to testify to genuinely Reformed principles.

Sounding a familiar theme, Van Til reported to the General Assembly that although the participants claimed to be descendents of Luther and Calvin, a modernist agenda lay behind their orthodox rhetoric: "It would not do much good," he told the Assembly, "if the Reformation understanding of the gospel was tested ever and again by the regulative principle of the Word, if this Word itself is nothing more than an expression of the ever-changing understanding of an unknowable something such as it is in Tillich's theology."[38] The heirs of the Reformation were united most significantly in their allegiance to Kant.

Van Til saw little value in the ongoing participation in this modernist consultation, nor did he enjoy acting as a "nuisance" throughout the discussions. And so the OPC's ecumenicity committee thanked him for his "faithful witness" and released him from the obligation of attending the 1966 conversation.

Van Til was particularly disappointed with the representatives from the Lutheran Church, Missouri Synod, a denomination that was on the verge of strident debates on biblical infallibility. Most of the

Missouri Synod delegation seemed to minimize their differences with liberal Lutherans, and Van Til regretfully suggested that they were digging their own grave. At the same time, the experience exposed Van Til to other Missouri Synod Lutherans who would command his respect. He struck up a particular friendship with Herman Otten, the editor of the *Lutheran News*. At Otten's urging, Van Til wrote a long assessment of Martin Marty in a 1964 issue of *Lutheran News*. Though only thirty-six years old at the time, Marty was already an influential voice of the liberal movement of the Missouri Synod. His reputation was established as a professor of church history at the University of Chicago and a popular columnist in the *Christian Century*. Van Til subjected Marty to a withering critique, charging that Marty was committed to "an unknown and unknowable Christ." Marty rejected classical Lutheranism and unconditionally surrendered to the modern world, to which Marty's theology had no grace to offer. Otten was appreciative of Van Til's work, but he later reported that Marty dismissed Van Til as a critic who was "either completely ignorant or demon possessed."[39]

The Reformed-Lutheran conversations were a precursor to the biggest battle of the decade, the passage of the Confession of 1967 in the United Presbyterian Church in the U.S.A. (northern Presbyterian church). In anticipation of a confessional crisis that would attend the adoption of the new confession and a possible windfall of conservative congregations seeking to affiliate with the Orthodox Presbyterian Church, Van Til wrote *The Confession of 1967: Its Theological Background and Ecumenical Significance*. The den Dulk Christian Foundation underwrote a wide distribution of this book, including copies to the members of the newly formed conservative Presbyterian Lay Committee. In a cover letter Van Til warned that the new confession "was calculated to destroy everything for which the Westminster Confession stands."[40]

Van Til claimed that Karl Barth was the father of the Confession of 1967 and that the actualized version of the "Christ-Event" was the central principle around which it organized its theme of reconciliation. Thus the Confession of 1967 was a vindication of his thirty-year war against the theology of Barth. In fact, Van Til argued that neo-orthodoxy proved to be more triumphant in the mainline Presbyterian church than had liberalism; after all, liberalism had undermined the church's confidence in the Westminster Standards, but never to the point of crafting a new confession.

Beyond a new confession, mainline Presbyterians took the additional step of uniting several confessions into a book of confessions, in order to remind the church of the cloud of witnesses from its past and also to teach the church that every confession was a product of its particular historical circumstances and that no single one could capture the fullness of the Christian faith. Van Til charged that this *Book of Confessions* was a book of discord and a collection of mutually exclusive gospels.[41]

This generally overlooked book by Van Til was important because it revealed his sensibilities as a churchman. Along with Edmund Clowney, who wrote a widely distributed tract on the Confession of 1967, Van Til desperately sought to alert remaining conservatives in the mainline Presbyterian church of the consequences of the steps they were taking. The changes of 1967 would signal the end of the UPCUSA as a confessional church. In Clowney's terms, the Confession of 1967 created a "creedal museum,"[42] and Van Til added that mainline Presbyterians would from this point recognize the Westminster Standards just as modern highways would tolerate the horse-drawn buggies of the Amish.[43]

Orthodox Presbyterian hopes were dashed when most conservatives in the church accepted the new confession, especially after John Gerstner changed his mind and pronounced his imprimatur on the confessional changes. And so a mainline confessional crisis did not result. Nevertheless, Clowney and Van Til may actually have underestimated the effects of the actions of 1967. When the Orthodox Presbyterian Church perceived modernism (old or new) as the greatest threat to Reformed faith and practice, it regarded confessional fidelity as the most important indicator of ecclesiastical health. In sparring with the mainline Presbyterian church for the first thirty years of its life, the OPC maintained a consistent tone of Reformed militancy. But 1967 ushered the OPC into its own confessional crisis. Absent the mainline church and its counterfeit claims to confessionalism as a backdrop, the

OPC looked less at its chief adversary to construct its identity. Instead, it compared itself increasingly with other conservative and evangelical Presbyterian churches, and sought to emphasize the features they had in common. The result was a gradual decline of Reformed militancy in the OPC, the effects of which will be explored in the next chapter.

Barthianism in the UPCUSA was short-lived. The fragile theological consensus it yielded fragmented into many contextual theologies soon after the Confession of 1967. As the winds of American theology shifted from Barth to Bultmann and beyond, Van Til realized that Barth was becoming passé in mainline Protestant circles. He devoted his attention to more current theological trends in a series of shorter works that he published quickly. These included *Pierre Teilhard De Chardin—Christ or Evolution?* (1966), *Is God Dead?* (1966), and *Christ and the Jews* (1968). Beyond Barth, he wrote on Bonhoeffer, Bultmann, Heidegger, and the "new hermeneutic" of Fuchs and Ebeling. His ongoing interest in Dutch-Reformed theology produced *The Sovereignty of Grace* (1970) and *The New Synthesis Theology of the Netherlands* (1975). By this point Van Til had overcome his reluctance to write, and he was publishing at great frequency. If these works lacked the precision he had devoted to previous developments, they testified to his active and attentive theological mind.

A constant feature in these works was the growing momentum of the ecumenical movement. Van Til's study on the Confession of 1967 ended with his fanciful imagination of subsequent confessions that the events from 1967 would ignite. A Confession of 1977 would unite Reformed and Lutherans, a Confession of 1987 would bring Catholics and Protestants together, and finally a Confession of 1997 would witness the union of Christians and Jews. Van Til and his generation may have placed more stock than was warranted in the effectiveness of the institutions that promoted these causes, such as the Consultation on Church Union and the World Council of Churches. Yet the rise of other ecumenical efforts (e.g., the "Joint Declaration on the Doctrine of Justification" of 1997 by the Vatican and the Lutheran World Federation, and the statement "Evangelicals and Catholics Together" in 1994) might prompt today's reader to credit Van Til with considerable prescience.

Francis Schaeffer: Van Til Popularized?

As previously noted, Van Til generally retreated from cultural analysis. While his work was suggestive for the task of cultural apologetics, he reckoned that he had lacked the gifts to take up the task himself. By the end of the decade, many American Calvinists began to think that this calling might fall to his former student, Francis Schaeffer.

In 1937, Francis Schaeffer withdrew from Westminster Seminary and followed Carl McIntire to Faith Seminary and the Bible Presbyterian Church. While serving later as a Bible Presbyterian missionary in Switzerland, Schaeffer broke away from the extreme separatism of McIntire to join the Evangelical Presbyterian Church in 1956 and eventually (after a 1965 merger), the Reformed Presbyterian Church, Evangelical Synod. For several decades, Schaeffer's L'Abri ministry in Switzerland had a remarkable influence on the Christian development of many college students, especially counter-cultural pilgrims from America. Some of them later enrolled at Westminster Seminary, where they found affinities between the ministry of Schaeffer and the teaching of Cornelius Van Til.

Schaeffer himself claimed that his survey of Western thought was based on the work of Herman Dooyeweerd and that he was in essential agreement with his former Westminster professor. Indeed, Schaeffer argued that presuppositional thinking was the only cogent defense of the Christian faith in response to the challenge of Kant, and that Van Til's work laid the foundation for all future apologetics. However, Van Til found fewer signs of his influence in Schaeffer's writings than he wished.

In 1968 Schaeffer published two books that gained a wide hearing, *Escape from Reason* and *The God Who Is There*, and large portions of them sounded Van Tilian. For example, Schaeffer argued that classical apologetics failed to take into account the role of presuppositions, both in Christian and non-Christian thought, and that "historic Christianity stands on the basis of the antithesis."[44] Even when he veered into a different vocabulary, many readers believed that Schaeffer was effectively translating Van Til's denser prose into straightforward language that was more accessible to a broader audience.

Though Van Til remained unconvinced, he had difficulty pinpointing his grievance with Schaeffer, until Schaeffer wrote *Death in the City* in 1969. With this book, Van Til believed he discovered a point of departure. He frequently cited the "orange analogy" in its last chapter as a "very defective way" of describing the differences between Christians and unbelievers. Schaeffer's analogy involves a Christian telling an atheist that a naturalistic approach to the universe was deficient and unbalanced because it ignored its supernatural character. "It's as if you had taken an orange, sliced it in half, and only concerned yourself with one of the halves," Schaeffer wrote. "To really understand reality in our universe, you need to consider both halves—both the seen and the unseen."[45]

Van Til focused on this reductionism as a particularly un-Reformed element in Schaeffer's thought. He wrote a twenty-page open letter to Schaeffer on March 11, 1969. While careful to express his "greatest admiration" for Schaeffer's ministry at L'Abri, Van Til raised his doubts about Schaeffer's books, and he pointed out the apologetic inadequacies that owed to Schaeffer's employment of the "traditional method of apologetics." Three years later, miffed that Schaeffer "could find no time to reply" and concerned that two of his Westminster colleagues (Edmund Clowney and C. John Miller) were coming to Schaeffer's defense against criticism aired in the *Presbyterian Guardian*, Van Til wrote a longer analysis of Schaeffer. The privately printed typescript on "The Apologetic Methodology of Francis A. Schaeffer" (a collection of Van Til's reviews of Schaeffer's works) cut to the chase on the very first page. "For all of Schaeffer's claim to use a presuppositional or biblical approach," Van Til charged, "his method is still basically similar to that of the traditional Aquinas-Butler approach."[46]

"True truth" was Schaeffer's term for describing the need to return to older epistemological ideals. Christian apologetics had to recover an objective notion of truth to effectively reach a generation that did not believe in truth. Focusing on the Enlightenment as a point of departure, Schaeffer sought to rescue Western thought from its Hegelian "escape from reason." Van Til countered that this was a futile enterprise that placed false trust in a premodern unregenerate consciousness, which was just as autonomous as modern unbelief.

Thus Schaeffer turned the antithesis into relativism, and he reduced autonomy to secularism. This stripped Van Til's apologetics of the radical character of its critique. Van Til pressed upon Schaeffer the need to dig deeper, to go beneath the surface and to expose human autonomy that lurked beneath both the modern skeptic or the premodern pagan. For Van Til, then, Schaeffer represented little advance from the apologetics of evangelicalism that he had devoted his career to opposing. Schaeffer's presuppositions were hypotheses to be verified by logic or empirical evidence. In William Edgar's words, Schaeffer was a "hybrid-presuppositional evangelist" and not fully consistent with Van Til's approach. Van Til's transcendental approach looked beyond the inconsistencies and contradictions and sought to expose the rebelliousness of modern unbelief.[47]

Still, Schaeffer's work was remarkably effective in promoting a Reformed enthusiasm for influencing culture. His book and film series "How Shall We Then Live?" (1976) galvanized a growing coalition of Christian social activists. Many fundamentalists and conservative evangelicals who latched onto Van Til in the 1960s were quoting Schaeffer a decade later. Later still, Schaeffer's *Christian Manifesto* (1981) was especially popular among culturally and politically ambitious conservative Protestants, but this was a cause to which Van Til was never engaged.

Suaviter in Modo, Fortiter in Re

As Orthodox Presbyterians initiated merger talks with the Reformed Presbyterian Church, Evangelical Synod, Van Til's criticism of Schaeffer fuelled frustration with some readers over his Reformed militancy. It seemed that no other Reformed apologist could earn his commendation, and it appeared that the circle of theologians that he embraced was ever narrowing.

Van Til often joked at his own expense about the impression that his apologetic methodology had become a litmus test for Orthodox Presbyterian ministers. When former student John Gerstner's anti-Van Tilian *Reasons for Faith* was published in 1960, the author wrote a gracious letter to acknowledge his indebtedness to Van Til. "I hasten to assure you that, in spite of any appearances to the contrary, I appreciate you, your work, and your impact on my life—though I am unable to share your apologetic views." Van Til thundered back to Gerstner in mock indignation: "You may have heard that it is a great sin to differ with Van Til on his views of apologetics. You may also have heard that anyone who does and comes in striking distance of Philadelphia would have his head cut off. So I would advise not to come near my office!"[48]

Behind the humor lay a vexing question for which Van Til lacked a simple answer. Critics of the Orthodox Presbyterian Church have sometimes chafed at the misconception that Van Til's apologetics had become the standard of orthodoxy for OPC ministers. Strictly speaking, Van Til's views did not hold confessional status, and thus adherence to them was not required of office-bearers in the church. Still, Van Til was fully convinced that his views were most consistent with Scripture and the confession, and he urged the church to settle for nothing less than the best defense of the Reformed faith.

Generally, the Orthodox Presbyterian Church agreed, and Van Tilian apologetics became the majority report in the church. In 1987 (the year of Van Til's death), the General Assembly added to its Book of Church Order a "Recommended Curriculum" for its ministerial candidates. Included in that curriculum was mastery of "the school of Van Tillian presuppositionalism as the most biblically faithful expression of Reformed apologetics, and a survey of positions held by other Reformed apologists." The Assembly's stamp of approval did not entail constitutional status, but it indicated the high esteem for Van Til's approach within the denomination.[49]

Van Til's push for methodological consistency provoked his constant dissent from other Reformed approaches. After harboring private reservations about the philosophical work of Herman Dooyeweerd for nearly a decade, Van Til publicly criticized him in 1962 in his three-volume syllabus, "Christianity in Conflict" (produced for a seminary course on the history of apologetics). The "hopeful beginning" of Dooyeweerd's work collapsed when he drew a distinction between transcendental criticism and transcendent criticism. Van Til subscribed to the former, which he defined as setting "the state of affairs from a Christian framework" and demonstrating "negatively that unless we accept this framework on the authority of Christ there is no meaning to human dialogue." He charged that Dooyeweerd's approach abandoned a particularly Christian foundation and sought to make contact with the unbeliever on a neutral basis.[50]

Van Til regretted the need to go public on Dooyeweerd. He despaired to Fred Klooster that this dispute was, from a personal perspective, the "worst one" of his life.[51] Van Til continued to defend Dooyeweerd against his American critics "who could not understand let alone do justice to Dooyeweerd." He was incredulous that Ronald Nash published a critique of Dooyeweerd without learning Dutch. Van Til had urged Nash to study more Dooyeweerd before he rushed his book into print, but Nash disregarded the advice.[52]

Often Van Til complained about the loss of militancy in other conservative voices. To his dismay the *Torch and Trumpet* softened its message and was no longer "giving forth a very clear sound." Long gone were the days of Henry Van Til's "fearlessness," Van Til regretted.[53]

Van Til also worried about his other nephew, when Fred Klooster participated in a Christian Reformed study committee to revisit the nature and extent of biblical authority. Van Til had strong misgivings about this report, and his initial attacks on it in its preliminary form were "painful" to Klooster. In extensive correspondence Klooster urged his uncle to read the report "carefully and sympathetically." (James Daane did Klooster's cause no service by throwing his support behind the report and claiming that it vindicated his view of predestination and the new theology emerging from the Netherlands.) Although he never brought himself to endorse it, Van Til generally kept his silence when the final report was issued, out of respect for his nephew.[54]

To the casual observer it appeared that there was no pleasing Van Til, who seemed to find fault with everyone. Yet a closer look yields a better appreciation for the distinctions that he was able to draw. For example, Van Til continued to express appreciation for his longtime antagonist, Gordon Clark, whom he refused to link with the "new evangelicals." "Clark has stood absolutely faithful to the Scriptures and to the Reformed faith," he wrote to R. J. Rushdoony.[55] In truth, Van Til hardly employed an all-or-nothing approach to critics of his work. He was even gentle in the exercise of polemics, as former student Grady Spires observed: "I recall his debating liberal and neo-orthodox champions at Boston University. He graciously, respectfully, but incisively told them that they were going to hell."[56]

Transitions at Westminster

In 1968, Harold Lindsell, editor of *Christianity Today*, invited Van Til to participate in a series with other elder statesmen to reflect on their life and work. Van Til declined because he could not imagine that his retractions would be beneficial to readers. "I have made plenty of mistakes," he wrote to Lindsell, "but just to make a list of them would not help much."[57]

Although Van Til demurred from Lindsell's opportunity for self-reflection, he willingly participated in the Festschrift that appeared in 1971, *Jerusalem and Athens*, which provided the occasion for a broad assessment of Van Til's work. The editor, E. R. Geehan, ambitiously gathered a wide range of contributors, some of whom were far beyond the pale of Reformed orthodoxy. The response by Van Til to the contributions made at times for a lively exchange and a fresh expression of his views. For example, when Paul King Jewett faulted Van Til's criticism of Martin Buber for failing to articulate a *Christian* "I-Thou relationship," Van Til replied to his former student and longtime Fuller Seminary professor that the human relationship with God was sufficiently comprehended in terms of the covenant and required no supplement from the inwardness of modern phenomenology.[58]

But *Jerusalem and Athens* was an uneven work and at times the exchanges were less effective. When Herman Dooyeweerd responded to Van Til's criticism of his "Christianity in Conflict" syllabus with the counter-charge that Van Til's "transcendent" critique was more rationalistic than Reformational, Van Til felt constrained, now that his differences with Dooyeweerd had gone public, to render a full reply. And so Dooyeweerd's fifteen-page assessment received a thirty-seven-page response. Van Til was so consumed in its composition that he hoped that G. C. Berkouwer would not contribute to the Festschrift, thereby sparing Van Til the burden of another lengthy response.[59] To

Van Til's chagrin, Berkouwer did write and Van Til, too exhausted to reply in detail, wrote a brief (one-page) response. Unfortunately, it contained a polite concession to Berkouwer ("The lack of detailed scriptural exegesis is a lack in all of my writings") that has been used to unfair advantage by Van Til's critics ever since. Fred Klooster expressed strong exception to Berkouwer's false charge and his uncle's unnecessary confession, and he argued that Berkouwer's own work was bereft of "decent exegesis."[60]

Van Til's apologetic distinctiveness made for delicate moments at Westminster Seminary as the school contemplated his retirement. Through the decade, Van Til was actively engaged in the life of the seminary as other founding faculty began to pass from the scene. He was insistent on finding Van Tilians among their replacements. When E. J. Young died on February 22, 1968, Van Til lobbied Meredith G. Kline (a former member of the faculty who had moved to Gordon Divinity School in 1965) to return to Philadelphia. Although Kline's framework interpretation of the days of Genesis 1 had generated a measure of controversy, Van Til had no doubt about Kline's orthodoxy and assured him that the issue would not impede his candidacy.[61]

In 1971 the Westminster faculty interviewed Harold O. J. Brown as a possible successor to Paul Woolley in church history. Van Til wrote to the search committee with concerns that Brown was too Schaefferian in his approach. He especially cited Brown's curious notion of the Enlightenment as a "second fall." While Brown was warning other culturally sensitive Christians about the rise of secularization in American society, Van Til argued that such analysis failed to come to adequate terms with the deeper problem of apostasy.

For all of his attention to these faculty searches at Westminster, it was surprising that Van Til devoted less time to identifying and cultivating his own successor. The challenge was complicated by the strain in Van Til's relationship with his junior colleague, Robert Knudsen. Knudsen was hired in 1958 in anticipation of the expansion of the doctoral program and in order to lighten Van Til's course load. Beyond their theological differences (Knudsen was a more sympathetic reader of Dooyeweerd), Van Til was not convinced that Knudsen was an effective teacher and thus not eager to promote him. For his part, Knudsen felt that Van Til unfairly barred him from promotion. Despite his ambivalence, Van Til delicately dissuaded some board members who sought Knudsen's dismissal for his ineffectiveness.[62]

Van Til eventually expressed his despair to a colleague: "When I retire, who else is available?"[63] Van Til's own choice was T. Grady Spires, a Westminster graduate who taught philosophy at Gordon College. "I personally would like nothing better than to have you take over the junior class," Van Til begged Spires, convinced that Spires understood Van Til's work and could teach it competently.[64] In 1972 Westminster offered Spires a permanent appointment, and he considered the matter seriously, but his Gordon colleagues prevailed upon him to stay.

Seminary President Edmund Clowney, meanwhile, came to the conclusion that no one man could replace Van Til, and so Van Til's succession involved expanding the department. Clowney wrote: "We do not therefore seek to replace a man like Dr. Van Til when he reaches the time of retirement. His shoes are a little too large. Rather, we are working toward a team of teachers with a Scriptural apologetic."[65] Eventually Van Til's courses would be covered by Harvie Conn and John Frame. Van Til described Frame as an "extraordinary brilliant and accomplished young man," though Frame admits that the two had temperamental and methodological differences.[66]

In all of his dealings within the seminary and beyond, Van Til held out for himself the goal of *suaviter in modo, fortiter in re*: "gentle in persuasion, powerful in substance." The seminary's board of trustees captured these virtues in a tribute it presented to Van Til on the fortieth anniversary of the seminary in 1969, which read in part:

> To salute his competency as a scholar and his congeniality as a mentor, however, is an empty gesture unless from the heart acknowledgement is made of the vital force that made Cornelius Van Til the kind of person he is. Never a man of boastful pride, he has given evidence in countless ways of his humble faith in the triune God, the Creator of the world, the Redeemer of man, and the Sanctifier of sinners reborn by sovereign grace. Every word he spoke made plain that he realized his wisdom and ability were not his own, but were learned from the

Holy Scriptures and impressed upon him constantly by the renewing and enlightening of the Holy Spirit through the saving merits of Jesus, the Son of God.[67]

By his own admission Van Til did not always live up to the slogan that his disciples have associated with his work. Although his rhetoric often was overheated, Van Til gave indications, especially in the classroom, that his criticisms were pleas toward less-consistent brothers in the faith.

As Richard Gaffin has observed, Van Til at his best argued that the "Reformed faith could not be negotiated away because it was held in trust for all believers as that which they hold at their deepest disposition as believers." Van Til was unrelenting in his defense of the faith, he was consistently biblical in his approach, and he steadfastly resisted any compromise with unbelief. Moreover, he did not succumb to the allure of counterfeit movements that presented themselves as new Protestantism or new orthodoxy. Beyond the Orthodox Presbyterian Church, Van Til guarded these truths to safeguard the integrity of the gospel, and his ultimate interest, in Gaffin's words, was "for believers in any place for whom these truths are really their truth."[68]

This may have rendered Van Til too suspicious of his contemporaries, such as J. Oliver Buswell, Herman Dooyeweerd, Carl Henry, or Francis Schaeffer. He singled out competing messages as regressive tendencies and obstacles toward that goal. To follow the path of inconsistency was to abandon the church's calling. Van Til expected much of others, but it was no less than he demanded of himself. He directed the seminary and the church to ever-deepening appreciations for the Reformed witness of God's sovereign grace, fully convinced that faithfulness in this cause would reap clearer expressions of the gospel.

Meanwhile, changes were taking place in the church and the seminary that Van Til himself did not fully anticipate. New faculty would come to terms with evangelical theologians and denominations in different ways from Van Til, and this led to his eventual estrangement from the school that he had served for over four decades.

8

Steadfast, Unmovable, and Abounding

ornelius Van Til preached before the Orthodox Presbyterian General Assembly for the last time on May 13, 1968. The Assembly was meeting in Westfield, New Jersey, and Van Til was preaching on fewer occasions, usually close to his Philadelphia home to minimize his travel. (After this Assembly, he served as a commissioner once more in 1971.) The title of his sermon was "Joshua's Appeal to Covenant Consciousness," based on Joshua 23. Like Joshua, Van Til, at the age of seventy-three, looked toward the future, and the sermon revealed much about his hope for the Orthodox Presbyterian Church at the twilight of his career. Van Til noted that both Calvin and Machen, at the very end of their lives, were concerned with covenant faithfulness in the generations that followed them. It is no stretch to imagine that Van Til was filled with the same sense, and as he neared the end of his life, he admonished the next generation in the church to continue in covenant fidelity.

If the Israelites of Joshua's day and the Presbyterians of Machen's day were "rapidly losing their sense of identity," Van Til's hearers were put to an even greater test. "There are more gods today than there were, even in Machen's time," he proclaimed as he surveyed the current landscape of god-is-dead theology and situation ethics. Behind these current trends was Barthianism, which he once again identified as the new modernism: "Dr. Machen said of liberal theologians that they held to *another* religion. The same must be said for the so-called neo-orthodox theologians today."[1]

Like Israel, the Orthodox Presbyterian Church had before it much unconquered territory, and it was surrounded by temptations that threatened her identity. It was a time of covenant renewal for the Orthodox Presbyterian Church. The task for the OPC was to align herself not with an "emaciated" or "fragmented" gospel (perhaps Van Til was alluding to talk of merger with other Reformed churches.) Progress would be measured only by the faithful proclamation of the whole counsel of God. "We are, therefore, as a church, and as Christian people, called upon to present the full significance of the person of Christ as that One through whom alone men must be saved from the wrath to come."[2]

His listeners could not have missed his analogy. If Machen was the Moses of the OPC, Van Til was her Joshua, and he posed to the church Joshua's command, "Choose ye this day whom ye will serve." Characteristically, the sermon ended with what became Van Til's favorite Pauline injunction, from 1 Corinthians 15:58, which Van Til quoted from the King James Version: "Be ye steadfast, immovable, always abounding in the work of the Lord, for as much as ye know that your labor in the Lord is not in vain." Van Til preached often from this text, including the funeral sermons of Robert Marsden and O. T. Allis. Consistent with his apologetic approach, he laid stress on the word "know." Reformed ministry abounds in the work of the Lord because it is grounded in the certainty, not the probability, of faith; that is, in *knowing* that labor in the Lord is not in vain.

In 1970, Cornelius Van Til turned seventy-five. The seminary solicited birthday greetings and tributes poured in from former students and colleagues throughout the world. Meredith Kline hailed Van Til as "the prince of apologists."[3] Testimonials of the catholicity of his influence came from Harold Ockenga and Francis Schaeffer and even from some progressives in the Christian Reformed Church. Lewis Smedes wrote a warm tribute from Fuller Seminary: "You have put a stamp on my own life, more profound and pervasive than you have known." Van Til demonstrated, Smedes went on to add, that "it is possible to be profoundly critical of all compromises with the truth, and yet always *cum suaviter in modo*."[4]

Most impressive were letters from former students now in the pastorate. These were eloquent testimonies to the pastoral significance of Van Til's teaching. They recalled his convicting sermons, long walks with him on the seminary grounds, his generous distribution of his writings, and his untiring patience in the classroom. Orthodox Presbyterian minister Lawrence Eyres wrote: "It was from you I learned that truth and wisdom consist in exceeding simplicities. All that is required is that God be God and that the creature be the creature."[5]

In 1972, Westminster Seminary announced the retirements of Cornelius Van Til and Paul Woolley, marking the end, after forty-three years, of the last of the original faculty. Yet Van Til continued to teach the junior class for several years while the seminary struggled to hire his successor, and he maintained a visible presence on campus. The Westminster board officially emeritized Van Til in 1973, and in May he delivered the commencement address at Westminster Seminary for the last time. Like his General Assembly sermon, it bore evidence of a farewell address, though it may have reminded listeners of his standard classroom lecture, as it recapitulated his life-long concerns. To be an effective minister of the gospel, he told graduates, "one must be *certain* that this gospel is not some cunningly devised fable, but that it is true and that all truth everywhere springs from this gospel." All of the familiar Van Tilian themes were present in this address, including a summary of redemptive history and a survey of church history with the usual heroes (Luther, the Heidelberg Catechism, and Machen) and villains (Greek philosophy, Kant, Princeton Seminary, Barth, and the Confession of 1967). Van Til's focus on the merit of the blood of Christ was lavishly seasoned with familiar Bible verses, including, once again, 1 Corinthians 15:58.[6]

There were other occasions in which Van Til was honored late in life. He was featured on the cover of *Christianity Today* on December 30, 1977, as a "Down-to-Earth Scholar." The interview by David Kucharsky was a respectful tribute that captured Van Til's contribution to conservative Protestantism, along with his humble and gracious demeanor (though omitting any reference to the Orthodox Presbyterian Church). Van Til's responses were of a decidedly reconciling character. He referred to Gordon Clark as his "good friend" and to evangelicals as his "brethren," even while rejecting their reliance on traditional defenses of the faith based on human autonomy. He demurred from opportunities to reengage in old wars, even when the interviewer seemed eager to bait him. For example, few of Van Til's friends and former students could have believed his claim that he knew "too little about dispensationalism to make a fair judgment of it."[7]

In another interview for a Dutch magazine (translated and reprinted in the *Outlook* in 1978) Van Til demonstrated the same restraint, as he reflected on his life's work. Several questions presented an opportunity for vindication for Van Til, but he showed no interest in evening any scores. When his interviewer suggested that Calvin Seminary was failing to defend the Scriptures and the Reformed faith as it had in the past, Van Til cautioned, "You should not overemphasize that." When asked to reflect on the developments within the Christian Reformed Church, he preferred to respond introspectively: "The only thing that can save us is holding fast to the gospel. . . . We are all dependent on grace. He who stands, beware, lest he fall."[8]

The Theological Seminary of the Reformed Episcopal Church conferred an honorary doctorate upon Van Til in 1968, as did Potchefstroom University in South Africa fourteen years later. Calvin College produced a long-overdue recognition of Van Til's accomplishments in 1979 when it honored him with the Distinguished Alumni Award on May 23, 1979. The plaque read:

> For more than half a century as a theologian you have been an ardent defender of the faith, renowned at home and abroad for your unflinching dedication to your calling.

As professor of Apologetics at Westminster Theological Seminary since the inception of that institution of Reformed learning you have been an inestimable influence in shaping the thought of twentieth-century Western theology. As a mentor of numerous Calvin College and Seminary faculty members you have instilled some of your zeal for the Kingdom in generations of Christian scholars. In the manner of the Old Testament prophets, you "have been very jealous for the Lord," and your trumpet has never given an uncertain sound in the battle against liberalism.

Van Til referred at times in letters to an autobiography he hoped to compose, but which never came about. Nor did he spend time in his retirement penning any Augustinian retractions. The closest he came to reflecting on his life's work was a pamphlet he published in 1972 entitled *Toward a Reformed Apologetics*. He introduced his self-assessment in this way:

> Throughout, my aim has been to show that it is the historic Reformed Faith alone that can in any adequate way present the claims of Christ to men for their salvation. The Reformed Faith alone does anything like full justice to the cultural and missionary mandates of Christ. The Reformed Faith alone has anything like an adequately stated view of God, of man, and of Christ as the mediator between God and man. It is because the Reformed Faith alone has an essentially sound, because biblical, theology, that it alone has anything like a sound, that is biblical method of challenging the world of unbelief to repentance and faith.[9]

The five "alones" in that paragraph underscored Van Til's sense of isolation. The Reformed faith was to set itself against liberalism, neo-orthodoxy, Roman Catholicism, Arminianism, and evangelicalism, old or new. And these were the distinctive characteristics that Van Til sought to cultivate in the seminary and the church. Though evangelicalism was mired in traditional apologetics and Reformed progressives were "slouching toward Basel,"[10] Van Til remained steadfast.

These convictions were kept remarkably undisturbed throughout his long life. "Van Til has not changed his method or the substance of it at any point in his career," observed Scott Oliphint. While he steadily elaborated on his system of apologetics, Van Til "never wavered from his fundamental conviction that God is the presupposition behind all thought and all life."[11]

Deaths of Friends and Foes

Retirement was marked by the passing of many friends. In March of 1975, when John Murray (who had retired from Westminster and returned to Scotland in 1967) was on his death bed, Van Til wrote him a note that expressed his appreciative memories of Murray's love for the psalms and the eloquence of his public prayers. "Nothing has helped me more, John, than to hear you pour out your heart in prayer for the church of Jesus Christ as a whole and for individuals in particular." When Murray passed away two months later, Van Til paid particular tribute to the "humble boldness" of the "conscience" of Westminster Seminary.[12]

Van Til's wife, Rena, also suffered from ill health for several years. She broke her hip after a fall in 1973, and she was hospitalized again in the next year for surgery to remove her spleen. Though she made significant recoveries, she suffered a stroke in January 1978.

Van Til recorded in his journal his last visit to her room at the Chestnut Hill Hospital. He asked her several questions: "Do you see Jesus your Savior all glorified now? Do you see your own mother and dad with Jesus in glory? Are you anxious to occupy one of the many mansions which Jesus promised his disciples and, through them, promised to all who believe in Him?" He prayed for her and sang her favorite hymns, in Dutch and English. He recalled her countenance as smiling, and when he promised to join her soon, with a nod of her head and a squeeze of his hand "she was trying ever so hard to tell me—of course you must, of course I want you to come."[13] On January 11, Van Til's wife of fifty-two years passed away. Westminster's John Skilton conducted the funeral service, and Rena Van Til was buried in Hillcrest Cemetery in Roslyn, Pennsylvania.

Rena Van Til was a shy and retiring woman; she did not drive nor did she like to fly. She struggled all her life to adjust to suburban

Philadelphia, and she always preferred the quieter pace of Munster, Indiana. Still, she stood faithfully by her husband's side and she modeled Christian hospitality for generations of students. Van Til's devotion to his wife was not lost on his colleagues. Paul Woolley's respect for Van Til's intellectual accomplishments was exceeded by his admiration for Van Til's loving care for his wife. The day after Rena's death Woolley wrote a note to Van Til:

> You have been, and are, probably the most remarkable husband I have seen. No one else could have given Rena the care, support, and admiration which you have given her over the years. Time has not dulled your patience and steadfastness. You have thought of her and her welfare over the years and under all possible conditions and have done everything you could to make life possible for her. It has been a most remarkable demonstration of Christian love and tenderness and is a pattern that I am sure no one will equal for uncounted time.[14]

After Rena died, Van Til insisted on remaining in his home on Rich Avenue in Erdenheim. His son and daughter-in-law, Earl and Thelma Van Til, arranged for seminary students to live with him, providing him meals and transportation, which enabled Van Til to maintain his walking regimen on the Westminster campus. Three years later, Van Til was grief-struck by the unexpected death of his son, who suffered an aneurism in 1983 at the age of fifty-three. Perhaps no death since Machen's was harder for him, and he consoled himself and his friends with the same Scripture he cited with Machen's passing: "The Lord giveth, and the Lord taketh away."[15]

With former antagonists Van Til spent his last years pursuing reconciliation. In 1976 he joined ten other Reformed elder statesmen to express words of appreciation for J. Oliver Buswell in Covenant Theological Seminary's journal *Presbyterion*. Van Til saluted Buswell for having "fought the good fight" throughout his "long and brilliant career."[16] When Van Til's former professor William Henry Jellema was in failing health, Van Til paid him a visit in Grand Rapids and thanked him for his influence on his life. Jellema responded, "Yes, but Kees, it was you who at times kept us from going too far." In 1981, when Van

Til learned that James Daane was dying of cancer, he wrote a note of consolation, to which Daane replied with a letter of gratitude.[17]

In 1977, Herman Dooyeweerd died of lung cancer at age eighty-three. Publicly, wherever he felt he could, Van Til continued to express his high regard for Dooyeweerd and was reluctant to describe himself as an opponent. In the *Westminster Theological Journal*, Van Til saluted Dooyeweerd for his distinguished career at the Free University. Muting the criticism of his later years, and putting aside the differences that found expression in *Jerusalem and Athens*, Van Til declared that Dooyeweerd's project to deepen the Kuyperian pursuit of a Reformed world-and-life view was "a marvelous sight to behold." Of all the men associated with the efforts to create a Calvinistic philosophy, including Vollenhoven, Stoker, and Van Til himself, Dooyeweerd remained, in Van Til's assessment, *"primus inter pares."*[18]

Finally, Van Til saw his last colleague among the early faculty of Westminster, Paul Woolley, succumb to Parkinson's disease on March 17, 1984. If Van Til was the most visible name among the original faculty, Woolley, in his estimate, was the key to the seminary's success as he labored behind the scenes, unsurpassed in his integrity and honor. "The good name of Westminster, academically and otherwise, is largely due to his tireless efforts," Van Til wrote.[19]

Preacher and Parishioner

A complete assessment of the life of Van Til must take into account his active churchmanship. Van Til trained for the pastoral ministry and would have been content to have spent his life in that calling. He and Rena were at home in the parsonage, and they referred to that blissful year longingly. Although a pastor for but one year, Van Til spent his entire career in the gospel ministry, and he loved its work. Throughout his time at Westminster, he maintained an active role in his local church, trusting in the Christ he met weekly through the means of grace. Van Til gave attention to the little as well as the great. He doted on children, he visited the sick, he counseled those in need. His witness to the grace of the gospel even brought him to occasional street-corner preaching. One former student found particular inspiration watching Van Til listen to a sermon "because he was receiving the Word like a little child."[20]

When Henry Coray pastored Calvary Orthodox Presbyterian Church in Glenside, Pennsylvania (from 1967 to 1971), he leaned so much on Van Til's labors that he came to refer to his former professor as his "assistant pastor." Van Til accompanied Coray on his hospital visitations, where Coray especially remembered Van Til's prayers. "I was always impressed by his gentle and sympathetic bedside manner, was edified by his fervent prayers and was struck with his zeal that others in the sickroom might also come to know and love the Savior of the world."[21] A typical Sunday for Van Til involved church in the morning, a visit to Chestnut Hill hospital between three and four in the afternoon, followed by a walk, a quick supper with students, and then evening service.[22] Van Til's diligent habits provided a steadying model of Reformed piety that left a deep impression among seminary students, and even those who were not privileged to have Van Til in the classroom witnessed his example of godliness, humility, and generosity.

Throughout his teaching career, Van Til freely offered advice about preaching. A letter written to a young preacher in 1972 is indicative of his passion. While acknowledging this young man's gifts, Van Til suggested three areas of improvement. First, he advocated preaching in a "biblical-theological way." Though Van Til did not define what he meant, clearly he referred to the insights of Geerhardus Vos. Second, preaching to "meet needs" is proper, so long as the preacher addresses his listeners' ultimate needs, which are "an ever increasing ability to give witness to our faith to a world of unbelief and to an apostate church." Third, be sure to cultivate covenantal self-consciousness: "How marvelous it would be if you used the Confession and the Shorter Catechism as a help."[23]

If Van Til the Presbyterian came to regret anything about leaving the Christian Reformed Church, it was one difference in polity that frustrated him nearly his entire life as a Presbyterian churchman. In the Presbyterian tradition, ministers are not members of congregations; instead, their membership resides in Presbyteries. Van Til always expressed his preference for the continental Reformed tradition that puts ministers under the authority of the local church, and he believed that Rena Van Til's pastor should have been his pastor too. Van Til lobbied for decades for change in the Orthodox Presbyterian Book of Church Order, and his wish was finally granted in 1978, when a revision in the church order presented ministers with the option of coming under the pastoral care of a local session. Sadly, the session records of Calvary Orthodox Presbyterian Church in Glenside, Pennsylvania, added his name to the church roll only after it deleted his wife's name, because Rena had passed away earlier that year.

Van Til and Theonomy

Controversy followed Van Til well into retirement. Since he had first made the acquaintance (in the mid 1950s) of R. J. Rushdoony, Van Til maintained a close friendship with the Californian, who was one of his greatest admirers (though never his student). Rushdoony helped to edit several of Van Til's books for publication, including *Christianity and Barthianism.* Van Til appreciated Rushdoony's primer on his teachings, *By What Standard* (1959), and he commended it as an accurate (if overly congratulatory) representation of his views. For two decades Rushdoony was an active correspondent who buoyed Van Til with frequent letters of encouragement. "Students should not complain about Van Til being difficult to read," Rushdoony wrote in 1967. "I believe that the problem your readers have can be summed up under two heads, first sin, and second, laziness."[24]

Rushdoony contributed to the 1971 Festschrift, *Jerusalem and Athens*, but he was disappointed with the overall quality of that work. He thought the editor, E. R. Geehan (a Westminster graduate and a doctoral student at Utrecht) was too inexperienced for the task; consequently, several of the contributions, especially those from Dooyeweerd, J. W. Montgomery, and Clark Pinnock, combined to paint too negative an assessment of Van Til.[25] Rushdoony's disappointment was shared by Gary North, who was briefly a Westminster student in the mid 1960s. North further complained that Geehan declined to include his essay on Max Weber that was submitted for the Festschrift.[26]

Eager to defend Van Til against the disrespect from his critics, Rushdoony persuaded North to prepare a second Festschrift in Van Til's honor. Van Til was embarrassed about this project, and he argued that *Jerusalem and Athens* was "more than enough."[27] In the course of the production of the new book, Van Til became more fully aware of North and Rushdoony's commitment to postmillennialism, their right-wing politics, and their distinctive views of the ongoing validity of the Old Testament civil law. The school of theonomy or "Christian Reconstruction" burst into Reformed circles with the publication of Rushdoony's *Institutes of Biblical Law* in 1973 (three years after Rushdoony left the Orthodox Presbyterian Church). Though Rushdoony's *Institutes* made only passing reference to Van Til, Rushdoony generally claimed that his ambitious and comprehensive program for transforming American culture through the application of the Old Testament civil code was firmly based on Van Til's radical presuppositional apologetics.

As theonomy garnered attention in Orthodox Presbyterian circles, Van Til wrote letters expressing his hope that readers would dissociate him from the distinctive features of theonomy. "My only point is that I would hope and expect that they would not claim that such views are inherent in principles which I hold."[28] Despite Van Til's efforts, a popular association between Van Til and theonomy developed after the release of the second Festschrift, *Foundations of Christian Scholarship*, which included mild to strongly theonomic perspectives. Gary North went so far as to describe Van Til as the "patron philosopher" of the Christian Reconstructionist movement.[29] Another former student of Van Til's, Greg Bahnsen, provided a proof-text for North's claim. In Bahnsen's *Theonomy in Christian Ethics* (1977), the epigraph page included a quote from Van Til's *Christian Theistic Ethics*: "There is no alternative but that of theonomy and autonomy."[30]

Others rose to challenge a theonomic connection to Van Til. Meredith Kline of Gordon-Conwell Seminary, a close friend of Van Til's, dismissed Bahnsen's quote as disingenuous: "We are all for theonomy in that general sense."[31] Another former student, T. David Gordon, has noted that in the particular context that Bahnsen quoted, Van Til was deliberately claiming theonomy as general ethical commitment apart from any claims about the Old Testament law.[32] Kline and Gordon's vigorous opposition to theonomy was equally premised on Van Tilian principles and revealed greater sensitivity to Van Til's dependence upon

Vos. Theonomy's insensitivity to the redemptive-historical uniqueness of Israel's holiness, Kline went on to point out, forced theonomists into the non–Van Tilian consequence of denying the reality of common grace.[33] Rushdoony preferred "creation grace" for "common grace," conceding that in his system "common grace needs to be abandoned as a bastard term."[34] Gary North expressed reservations about Van Til's formulations and ultimately dismissed Van Til's treatment of the doctrine as "the worst book he ever wrote."[35]

Theonomists had even greater difficulty reconciling their thought with Van Til's explicit disavowal of postmillennialism. The Dutch immigrant found no abiding home in American culture, and in his life and his work he embodied a pilgrim theology for the church. Van Til wrote little about millennialism because he regarded the matter as settled. The eschatological focus of Geerhardus Vos, implicit in much of Van Til's work, pointed to a covenant relationship with God, a story of life that was hid in Christ in the heavenlies, not seeking cultural advancement in this present evil age. Van Til wrote to an inquirer, "I am of the opinion that careful exegesis favors the amillennial position." He went on to recommend Vos's *The Pauline Eschatology*, adding that "I really do not see how I can say anything that has not already been said many times over in defense of amillennialism."[36]

Greg Bahnsen remained unconvinced and was unwilling to concede that Van Til was amillennial, although he acknowledged that Van Til's millennial position went largely undeveloped. In Bahnsen's own work on Van Til, he largely avoided the matter of theonomy, although he claimed in a footnote that Van Til "certainly had the spirit of reconstruction."[37]

Van Til's personal political views were a matter of speculation for his disciples. His Chicago-area upbringing indoctrinated him in conservative politics, where Dutch Calvinists were "Republicans almost to a man."[38] He was a life-long Republican who opposed the Great Society of Lyndon Johnson with as much zeal as he disdained the New Deal of Franklin Roosevelt, but the Republican Party represented the lesser of two evils for him. He shied away from cultural and political applications of his apologetic system, and he generally kept his political views private, rarely considering that he possessed wisdom to share, despite efforts of friends and associates to draw him out. His silence on church-state matters left his largely undeveloped Kuyperianism at least vulnerable to a theonomic reading and a popular association between him and Christian Reconstruction continued. Among his disciples, John Frame expanded some Van Tilian themes to develop a theonomic-friendly view of the state, although Edmund Clowney expressed them in the more classically Augustinian doctrine of two cities.[39]

If Van Til was no theonomist, his Reconstructionist followers at least deserved credit for carrying the torch for Van Til when others seemed less willing. By the time Van Til reached seventy, he feared that a generation in the church did not understand him, and few quarters in the church beyond the Reconstructionist camp unabashedly championed the Reformed faith as Van Til expressed it. He had very high regard for Bahnsen and regretted the publication of Bahnsen's theonomy book, wishing instead that Bahnsen's early work had focused more on apologetics. If the theonomists drove Van Til's antithesis into excessively this-worldly extremes, they did not abandon the militance that the Reformed faith demanded.

Despite the theonomic connections, Van Til's influence began to wane even among Reformed conservatives, whose attention was increasingly directed to America's culture wars in the 1980s. Van Til's cultural detachment rendered his work less accessible than the writings of Francis Schaeffer. Van Til had little sympathy for the social activism and political conservatism that characterized Schaeffer's final works. Schaeffer's focus on secular humanism (which placed blame on the Enlightenment) slighted the greater problem of human autonomy (resulting from the fall). His *Christian Manifesto* (1981) forged a Christian America argument that both echoed back to an earlier association with Carl McIntire and the Bible Presbyterian Church and rang vaguely of a theonomic reconstuctionism. (Indeed, Schaeffer, who never fully forsook the label of a fundamentalist, was generally wary of expressing his views in the narrowly Reformed vocabulary that Van Til employed. By the end of his life, Schaeffer seemed as comfortable in the company of Jerry Falwell as he had earlier with McIntire.[40])

Estrangement from Westminster

By the time of his retirement, Van Til had joined his younger colleagues on the faculty in yearning for an extension of the seminary's influence. That petition formed the basis of his prayer at a groundbreaking ceremony for a badly needed classroom building at Westminster in 1973. When the new building was dedicated two years later, the seminary surprised him by announcing that it would be named Van Til Hall. Ironically this honor became a symbol of Van Til's increasing estrangement from the seminary. With enlarged facilities, President Edmund Clowney was able to recruit more students, and the student body more than doubled from the time of Van Til's retirement to the end of the decade. Beyond the growth of the Philadelphia campus, the seminary announced the establishment of extension sites in Miami, Florida, and Southern California in 1979. While all this seemed an answer to Van Til's prayer, the growth of the seminary proved unsettling to him.

Van Til feared that expansion watered down the strength of the faculty, and he did not warm up to Clowney's ecumenical ambitions both for the school and for the Orthodox Presbyterian Church. In 1975 the OPC considered a merger with the Reformed Presbyterian Church, Evangelical Synod. Van Til opposed the plan of union because he believed that J. Oliver Buswell still exercised considerable influence among the Reformed Presbyterians, and it was little comfort to observe that Francis Schaeffer had become a chief spokesman for that denomination. To be sure, there were solid men in the denomination, Van Til told an interviewer. "But there is also a lot of chaff among the grain."[41]

"I am not trying to make heretics out of people," Van Til responded to an inquiry about his position on the proposed ecclesiastical merger. "I am just anxious that anything that is being done by way of union or non-union shall operate to put the banner of the full counsel of God on top of the highest mountain." The burden of proof fell on the proponents of ecclesiastical union, Van Til insisted, and only if they could demonstrate that it furthered the Reformed faith would it earn his support.[42] Eventually Van Til's fears were averted when the RPCES surprisingly voted against the plan of union, dissuaded by an eleventh-hour address by Francis Schaeffer himself, who had come to similar reservations as Van Til about the danger of renewing the skirmishes that had led to the division of 1937.

Meanwhile, the Westminster faculty, which formerly was made up entirely of members of the Orthodox Presbyterian Church, had expanded to include ministerial members of the RPCES as well as the Presbyterian Church in America (formed in 1973 when conservatives left the southern Presbyterian church). Almost all of them had publicly embraced a plan to unite the PCA, RPCES, and OPC together in 1981, leaving Van Til further isolated from his former employer.

Greater estrangement from Westminster resulted from another controversy to which Van Til's name was associated in retirement. Van Til came to the defense of embattled Westminster professor Norman Shepherd during the justification controversy that beset Westminster Seminary from 1975 to 1982.

Norman Shepherd was a popular professor of systematic theology who had joined the Westminster faculty in 1963. In 1975, the faculty began intense debates over his views on the relationship between justification and works. Shepherd sought to counter the easy-believism of American evangelicalism by stressing the obedience of faith, even to the point of affirming the role of works as an instrument of justification, while claiming to be loyal to the teaching of the Westminster Standards by assigning a unique role to faith.

The faculty and board of the seminary (as well as the Presbytery of Philadelphia of the OPC) were divided in their assessment of Shepherd's views. A majority supported him (though not necessarily defending his distinctive approach), and he was exonerated by the board on three occasions during the long discussions that lasted until 1981. By that point, opposition to Shepherd had grown in the Reformed community beyond Westminster Seminary, and the controversy surrounding Shepherd's teaching became a key factor in frustrating the merger of the OPC with the PCA in 1981. In the fall of that year, stung by the PCA's rejection of the OPC, President Edmund Clowney came to a reassessment of Shepherd's views and drew the conclusion that they differed from the seminary's confessional standards. Under Clowney's influence, the board of Westminster terminated Shepherd from the faculty in November 1981, after eighteen years of service, for the good of the seminary, citing irresolvable conflicts in his views, while claiming that no doctrinal reasons were involved.

Van Til was deeply disturbed by the action taken against his former student and colleague, and he wrote a five-page letter of protest to the board. However, Van Til's participation in the debate was minimal, and it is unclear to what extent his protest involved a close familiarity with the doctrinal issues. Robert Strimple, for example, recalled "that Van Til attended none of the faculty discussions about the controversy."[43]

Subsequent analyses have offered a variety of explanations for the controversy. Some have argued that the debate divided American and continental Reformed interpretations of justification. If this was true, it would suggest that the Shepherd controversy was a throwback to the American Presbyterian debate of the 1930s, in which Van Til stared down the nativist opposition of MacRae and Buswell. However, opposition to Shepherd's formulations came from Christian Reformed as much as American Presbyterian circles, and this debate could not be reduced to a Reformed-fundamentalist wrestling match.

Others have charged that the firing of Shepherd demonstrated that the Presbyterian Church in America had come to domination and control of the Westminster Seminary board. The expedient action was necessary in order to remove an obstacle many had in the PCA to receiving the OPC. Clowney himself felt the pressure to accommodate PCA voices. He was a passionate advocate of merger and would himself join the PCA after his retirement from Westminster in 1984. Van Til shared the suspicions of others about Clowney's ambition for the OPC and Westminster Seminary, but it is anachronistic to suggest that there was PCA hegemony on the seminary's board at the time of the vote to terminate Shepherd, however that might describe Westminster in the years that followed.[44]

Whether or not Shepherd was a victim of Clowney's vision for the seminary, it seems that Van Til viewed the debate in those terms. Shepherd's termination was regarded by many as a pragmatic solution to the controversy. Van Til's strong reaction owed to his growing dissatisfaction with Clowney's non-militant direction as much as his loyalty to his friend and former colleague. For his part, Clowney was given to express his weariness of Van Til's polemics.

Van Til's judgment on the substance of Shepherd's views is less clear. There is no evidence that Van Til himself weighed in on the specifics of the debate, and at the age of eighty-six by the time of Shepherd's dismissal, he showed little evidence that he understood the full significance of the issues debated. It is certainly unfair to suggest, as some have, that Van Til was senile at the time of Shepherd's termination. But he did confess that he was not equal to handling the exegetical issues involved. He never challenged the forensic character of justification, nor did he suggest, as Shepherd had, that it needed to be reconsidered. Moreover, Van Til maintained close friendships with strong partisans on both sides of the debate.

In the middle of this debate Westminster Seminary celebrated its jubilee in 1979, and much of its commemoration centered on the influence of Van Til in the school's fifty-year history. The seminary made claims that biblical theology and presuppositional apologetics pervaded the seminary's curriculum. According to Jay Adams, the "nouthetic school" of biblical counseling rested on a firm Van Tilian foundation. Harvie Conn sought to apply Van Til's method to cultural analysis. Presuppositional apologetics, Conn argued, served to reveal the "philosophical and theological preunderstandings," including the "personal, class and social agendas," that shaped one's understanding of the world.[45] John Frame expanded presuppositionalism into his own apologetic approach, which he described as "multi-perspectivalism." The extent to which any of these developments was genuinely Van Tilian was contestable, and for his part Van Til rarely offered his own judgment.

Van Til's successors at Westminster only appeared to be following his example. Van Til always claimed that his heroes, Kuyper, Bavinck, Warfield, Machen, and Vos, were deepening the "Reformation principle." He honored their memory by doing the same and digging even deeper into the riches of the Reformed faith. Every generation must take up this challenge anew, he added.[46] Yet Van Til may have seemed less willing to encourage Westminster's second generation in the opportunity to expand his views. In a sense, Van Til's struggles could be expressed in terms of the Kuyperian dilemma of harnessing common grace with the antithesis. What may have spelled the difference for him was the suggestion on the part of some of the faculty at Westminster that their calling was to lean less on the antithesis than Van Til had, and to express more fully a positive affirmation of common grace. No one was more symbolic of Westminster's less bellicose image than Edmund Clowney, about whose leadership of the seminary Van Til grew to develop deep suspicions.

What was missing in the Westminster Jubilee rhetoric was Reformed militance. In its place was Clowney's vision for a broader seminary that would serve a larger, united national Presbyterian church. As the rhetoric of antithesis to the world, which had shaped the founding of the seminary and the OPC, was in steady decline, so Van Til felt, was his standing. By 1979 Van Til regretfully described the student population at the seminary as "a generation that knows not Van Til."[47] Symbolic of this decline, the *Presbyterian Guardian* ceased publication in that year after nearly forty-four years and was absorbed by the *Presbyterian Journal*, whose readership largely consisted of members of the Presbyterian Church in America. This was yet another indication, Van Til feared, that the OPC was losing its militant edge.

The Isolation of Orthodox Presbyterianism

To be sure, Van Til understood Westminster's role in the spread of international Calvinism. For all his loyalty to the Orthodox Presbyterian Church, he was never a denominational chauvinist. When students from other churches came to the seminary and took interest in the OPC, Van Til often advised them to return and serve the denominations from which they came.

Still, he was eager to protect the Orthodox Presbyterian Church from inconsistency in its testimony of the Reformed faith and life. One of his last pieces to appear in the *Presbyterian Guardian* was a November 1976 letter entitled "More Catechism Needed." Van Til contrasted the enthusiasm for the Westminster Shorter Catechism among Orthodox Presbyterian missionaries, who regarded it as their "best evangelistic instrument," with his perception of its waning influence

224

within the congregations of the denomination. The Reformed world was divided into "Shorter Catechism Christians and non–Shorter Catechism Christians," and he urged pastors and parents in the church to rediscover the catechism's benefits.[48]

In the Christian Reformed *Banner*, Van Til submitted short articles on a variety of subjects at the prodding of editor Lester DeKoster, who extended an open invitation for Van Til to write for the magazine. These were placed in the letters column, and they included a broadside against I. John Hesselink, the president of Western Seminary in Holland, Michigan, and a brief critique of Bill Bright and Campus Crusade for Christ. Van Til's charge of Barthian activism in Hesselink invited a rebuttal with more Western Michigan anti–Van Tilianism. Against Bright, Van Til argued that the "gospel was conspicuous by its absence in the Four Spiritual Laws." If these were not Van Til's finest literary achievements, they were at least noteworthy for their testimony to his concern for rigorous consistency in the expression of the Reformed faith. Van Til never flagged in his zeal to distinguish the Reformed faith from what he considered to be its modern counterfeits.[49]

In June 1986, a year before Van Til's death, the Orthodox Presbyterian Church observed its fiftieth anniversary during its General Assembly outside of Philadelphia. Weakened by age at ninety-one, Van Til attended the banquet with the aid of a walker, and it was his last major public appearance. Scores of former students greeted him with words of appreciation. At that General Assembly, the Orthodox Presbyterian Church, no doubt influenced by a semi-centennial consciousness, narrowly voted to decline another invitation to merge with the Presbyterian Church in America. Critics of the OPC's vote, some of whom would voluntarily realign with the PCA along with their congregations within the next several years, decried the vote as another manifestation of Orthodox Presbyterian isolationism.

The language of isolation that the celebration prompted surely gladdened Van Til's heart. The semi-centennial was a fitting parallel to the fiftieth anniversary celebration of the Christian Reformed Church in 1907, two years after he had begun his American experience. There he heard the refrain, "in our isolation is our strength."[50] As the OPC banquet speaker, John Galbraith, himself a longtime minister of the denomination (ordained in 1937), recalled the distinctive Reformed characteristics of the OPC, Van Til the confessional antithetical was pleased to hear the banner of the Reformed faith raised high once again.

Death of Van Til

Near the end of his life, Van Til yearned for friends to read to him from the Psalms. When he realized he was dying, he called upon his pastor, Steven Miller, to read from the last chapters of the book of Revelation. Shortly before his death, the Session of his church gathered around his bedside after morning worship and sang hymns. Miller recalled how Van Til delighted in the imagery of the healing of the nations gathered at the tree of life, the finished work of Christ having reversed the curse. He observed enthusiastically, as if making a first-time discovery, the connection between the beginning and end of the Bible. "You see," he told his pastor, "it comes full circle."[51]

After an illness of several months, Van Til died in his sleep at his Erdenheim home on April 17, 1987, three weeks shy of his ninety-second birthday. In accordance with his wishes, John Skilton conducted a memorial service at Calvary Orthodox Presbyterian Church in Glenside, and Steven Miller performed the graveside service. The last of the original faculty members of Westminster Seminary was buried on April 22 in Hillside Cemetery, in nearby Roslyn, Pennsylvania, beside his wife and son. (Van Til chose not to be buried in the Van Til family plot in the Ridgelawn Cemetery at Gary, Indiana, because he had expected to predecease Rena, and he did not want to burden her with the task of transporting his body to Indiana.)

Two months later, the OPC General Assembly approved a memorial minute to Cornelius Van Til. It read in part:

> His uniquely Biblical apologetics, and his godly militance against unbelief in all its current forms, awakened generations of his students and fellow-ministers to the radical challenge of Christian truth, to bring every thought into captivity to Jesus Christ. Faithful in the lowliest of duties, tireless in teaching and writing among us and also

to far nations, in his preaching he always drove home the gospel that only in Christ do we know true rest and true life.[52]

Curiously, Van Til's death garnered minimal attention. A brief obituary in *New Horizons* (the denominational magazine of the OPC) by his colleague Robert Knudsen exhorted the church to carry on Van Til's work with the same zeal that he had poured into it.[53] The *Reformed Journal* made no reference to his death (in contrast to the extensive attention it had given to the passing of Francis Schaeffer three years earlier). Even *Philosophia Reformata*, the journal for which Van Til had served as contributing editor for forty-two years, treated his passing with silence.

A month later, Richard B. Gaffin Jr. preached in a memorial service in Van Til Hall at Westminster Seminary on "The Scandal of the Cross," from 1 Corinthians 1:18–25. Gaffin remembered Van Til, who "resolved to know nothing except Jesus Christ, and him crucified," and he took the opportunity to reflect further on the theme of isolation in the work of Van Til. As one of the few members of the Westminster faculty who remained in the Orthodox Presbyterian Church, Gaffin conceded that Van Til's reveling in Reformed isolation left him vulnerable to misunderstanding. "But we should not miss his intention," Gaffin urged his listeners.

> His desire is not to turn the Reformed tradition into a sect, nor a ghetto mentality that wants to cut off Reformed believers from other believers and churches. The point is not that the Reformed tradition has found some kind of perfection and can no longer grow. Nor that Reformed Christians have nothing to learn from other Christians and other traditions. Rather, he is concerned for what by God's grace the Reformed tradition has received, and the burden and the responsibility that it places upon us.[54]

Van Til, Gaffin continued, understood that he had inherited the Reformed faith as a steward. He felt the burden to defend and propagate the whole counsel of God for the whole people of God. Van Til understood how Machen found the Reformed faith grand, and he would not rest in his pursuit to proclaim that faith in its fullness. Accordingly, Van

Til's message to the church, Gaffin summarized, was this: "Don't allow anything to deprive you of the riches of your Reformed inheritance. Do not permit that commitment to be undermined in any way."[55]

The seminary itself issued an awkward obituary for public release that failed as an adequate assessment of Van Til's life (and included only passing reference to his membership in the Orthodox Presbyterian Church). By 1995, John Frame admitted that interest in Van Til had declined since his death. Confirming Frame's assessment, apologetics has played a far less foundational role in the Westminster curriculum since Van Til's time, being replaced by greater interest in hermeneutical issues.[56]

The death of Van Til was the close of a remarkable story in twentieth-century American Calvinism. His was a life devoted to the message he had heard upon his arrival in America. There is no area of neutrality in this present evil age, and the covenant community must diligently maintain its militant antithesis with the world. Van Til was a pilgrim for over eighty years in the new world. He was never fully at home in American culture, nor did he ever yearn to return to the old world. His apologetic taught the church to confess that she had no abiding city on earth but was to seek the heavenly city to come. It was a homelessness that rendered Van Til steadfast, immovable, and always abounding in the work of the Lord.

Conclusion:
Against the World,
for the Church

In a letter to John DeWaard, Cornelius Van Til described a suit that he inherited after the death of Machen. He was honored to receive the gift, but it was an ill-fit because it was tailored to the five-foot-eight Machen, and Van Til rose to a full six feet.[1] Similarly, though Van Til was ever conscious of his calling to fill Machen's leadership role after the latter's sudden death, Van Til's succession seemed an awkward fit. Still, Van Til worked tirelessly at continuing Machen's task of maintaining confessional consistency and pure practice within the Reformed faith. And though he lacked Machen's eloquence, Van Til generally succeeded in Machen's mission by consistently warning the church about threats to her testimony from without and about corrosion of her heritage from within. Those who seek to inherit the fruits of Van Til's mind should do so from within the full harvest of his heart and life.

Van Til and Machen

Van Til was called to lead a movement that was embodied in two institutions, Westminster Seminary and the Orthodox Presbyterian

Church. In the judgment of Charles G. Dennison, Van Til's leadership restored hope in these institutions as they recovered from the shock of Machen's premature death. Beyond them, many graduates of other schools and ministers in other churches appreciated Van Til for guiding them into greater biblical fidelity and confessional consistency, especially by underscoring the necessity of a Reformed apologetic for Reformed theology.

Not everyone saw it that way, however. For his fundamentalist and evangelical opponents, Van Til represented a derailing of the Machen-led effort to form a spiritual successor to the Presbyterian Church in the U.S.A. With his Dutch vocabulary and his seemingly obscure references to continental Reformed thought, Van Til, in their view, hijacked the OPC into non-American directions. For his followers, however, Van Til succeeded in the very point that his opponents read as a failure. Machen wanted a consistently Reformed church and seminary, and Van Til delivered. He led a generation after Machen into a Reformed self-consciousness, especially enriching its understanding of its Reformed tradition. Despite his humility and aversion to attention, Van Til came over time to accept this role. Certainly the title of his magnum opus, *Christianity and Barthianism*, was a self-conscious claim that he labored in Machen's steps.

The biographical similarities between Machen and Van Til go far to explain Van Til's devotion to his mentor. Each man forsook the church of his youth, with its stability and its reputation, and cast his lot with a small upstart denomination. Like Machen, who left the south to serve in the northern Presbyterian church, Van Til embarked on what might be considered a cross-cultural missions experience in leaving the comfort and familiarity of the Christian Reformed Church. To be sure, Van Til's sacrifices were not as costly as Machen's. Indeed, Van Til's pilgrimage resembled the upwardly mobile trajectory of many immigrants seeking to assimilate into American culture. Yet it was costly for him in other respects. By remaining in the church that Machen founded, Van Til resisted several tempting offers to return to Calvin College and Seminary, and the Christian Reformed Church. Ironically, membership in the Orthodox Presbyterian Church served, in effect, to extend his immigrant status. Even while living in suburban Philadelphia, he remained more of an outsider from the American Protestant mainline than he otherwise might have been had he stayed in Dutch Reformed Midwest communities.

Moreover, Machen's exile from Princeton Seminary made a particularly lasting impression in the life of Van Til, encouraging him to stand strong even after Machen's untimely death. Along with Hodge, Warfield, Kuyper, and Bavinck, Machen toiled for an institution that eventually departed from historic Reformed orthodoxy. What transpired suddenly and blatantly at Princeton Seminary evolved more gradually and subtly at Dutch Reformed institutions such as the Free University of Amsterdam and Van Til's alma mater, Calvin College. While both men sought to combat threats to orthodoxy, the chief difference between them was that, unlike Machen, Van Til was granted a long earthly life. Continuing Machen's example, Van Til labored faithfully for over forty years for an impoverished seminary and a tiny denomination, keenly aware of the institutional precariousness of the Reformed faith in the twentieth century. Though plagued with nagging health concerns, Van Til's many years of earthly pilgrimage providentially sustained those institutions that could ill afford the premature death of another leader.

By his own admission, Van Til never attained Machen's standard in communicating his ideas in simple language. Liberalism became "post-Kantian thought" in Van Til's more philosophically precise yet less accessible language. There are fewer expressions by "friendly neutrals" who testified to the value of Van Til's efforts than there are of those who lauded Machen's work (such as H. L. Mencken and Walter Lippmann). Instead, Van Til's writings often proved dense and impenetrable. This idiosyncrasy left him as frustrated as his readers. (Particularly disappointing to him was his failure to complete a simple layperson's guide to Barth. Machen would likely have understood. He too was flummoxed by Barth and wondered whether Barth was capable of such a treatment.)

To be sure, Machen perceived Van Til's gifts, and he appreciated Van Til's willingness to guard the theological heritage of Westminster Seminary and the OPC. But Machen's early death prompted a long-standing debate over the compatibility of his views with Van Til's.

In the eyes of some critics, after Machen's death Van Til directed the school and the church into a Reformed identity more narrow than Machen had intended.

Van Til and Hodge

Much of the challenge in interpreting Van Til centers on locating him with respect to his American Presbyterian antecedents. A common claim is that Van Til represented a departure from the apologetic tradition that was established at "old Princeton." For as much as this question has captured the attention of his followers, Van Til himself seemed ambivalent and even uninterested in answering it. He tended to minimize his differences with B. B. Warfield. Nor was he content merely to be the carrier of Amsterdam into the new world, for he found vestiges of "scholasticism" (i.e., contamination with un-Reformed elements) in Kuyper and Bavinck even while he lavished praise upon their accomplishments. Comparisons to either Warfield or Kuyper were less important to Van Til because he preferred to underscore that he was following Calvin, who had followed Augustine, who had followed Paul. Van Til lauded both the Princeton and the Dutch schools for working, at their best, toward the same goal: neither found contentment in merely restating an older version of Calvinistic orthodoxy; both took on the task of broadening and deepening the Reformed tradition in order to meet the challenge of unbelief in its age. With his appreciation for the breadth of Reformed history, it is inappropriate, then, to interpret Van Til solely by his American Presbyterian precursors.

In a tribute that Van Til paid to Paul Woolley in 1969, he praised his longtime colleague for his "genuine following of and going beyond the old-Princeton method of teaching Church History."[2] Though Van Til did not elaborate on Woolley's approach, his language was telling. As much as Van Til symbolized Westminster's unique testimony, he seemed to understand his work no differently from that of the other faculty at Westminster with whom he enjoyed a long collaboration. All of them were building upon their common Reformed heritage by correcting its weaknesses and advancing its strengths.

For this reason it is beneficial to compare the career of Cornelius Van Til with that of Charles Hodge (1797–1878). Living nearly a century apart, both theologians spent remarkably long tenures at a single institution. Van Til's longevity approximates that of Hodge more closely than any other twentieth-century American theologian. According to his biographers, Hodge trained over three thousand Presbyterian ministers in a career that spanned over five decades at Princeton Theological Seminary. Van Til also accumulated impressive figures. He likely educated more than fifteen hundred students in a forty-seven-year teaching career. (Though that number of students is only half of Hodge's, it is still significant, given the humble origins of Westminster and the small sizes of its early classes.) Both professors were active churchmen who witnessed a significant division in American Presbyterianism, and both became symbolic representatives of one side of their respective divisions. Both were opposed to denominational reunions that were proposed late in their lives, fearing the theological corrosion that such reunions would generate. Hodge regretted the Old School–New School reunion of 1869, while Van Til expressed relief that Orthodox Presbyterian union efforts in the 1970s and 1980s were unsuccessful.

In addition to their similarities, the differences in the ways in which their lives have been interpreted are especially worth noting. Princeton Seminary historian John Stewart, in his introduction to a recent symposium on Charles Hodge, quoted an observer of American religious history who quipped that historians "have tended to stress the vigor of innovators and to forget the vigor of the religious orthodox." Stewart lamented that for this reason Hodge had fallen into neglect among American religious historians. Hodge was the maintainer of a tradition, and he is often ridiculed for his misunderstood observation that no new idea originated at Princeton during his tenure.[3] Van Til suffers from the opposite problem: he is frequently misinterpreted and often portrayed as an innovator whose radical redesign of apologetics included a heavy dose of criticism toward Hodge and his old-Princeton colleagues. These short-sighted summaries are unfair to both men; and if such narrowness has yielded a neglect of Hodge, it has also bred a distortion of Van Til.

To focus solely on Van Til's novelty fails to appreciate the many ways in which he tried to preserve his tradition by standing on the shoulders of those who went before him. Furthermore, such a narrow understanding of Van Til is harder to square with his frustration and disappointment over the changes that characterized Westminster Seminary and threatened the Orthodox Presbyterian Church in the last years of his life. Van Til's instinct was to resist theological innovation when he encountered it; thus, a proper assessment must assign greater prominence to his work as a defender of the Reformed tradition, including the best of the Princeton tradition.

Consistency lay at the heart of what it meant for Van Til to be Reformed. When a letter-writer inquired of him to define Calvinism, Van Til responded: "It is not the five points. It is rather the measure of consistency with which it applies all the doctrines of Christianity."[4] If Van Til parted company with the giants of old Princeton, he did so only by following Warfield's lead. Calvinism, Warfield noted, was Christianity come into its own. Like Warfield, Van Til sought the full flowering of Reformed theology and the weeding out of counterfeits. Therefore, where vestiges of non-Christian thought (whether Arminianism or Enlightenment rationality) corrupted even the giants of old Princeton and old Amsterdam, Van Til refined those expressions of "less consistent Calvinism."

Van Til the Controversialist

Controversy followed Van Til throughout his life. He accepted it reluctantly and came to believe that controversy was a means of exercising his calling. "He was not a man to be accused of inconsistency," wrote a Catholic critic, William Shea.[5] Van Til's relentless drive for methodological consistency prompted a "take no prisoner" approach to theological issues, and as John Frame observed, Van Til invited readers to an "all or nothing" reception of his work.[6] He polemicized against fundamentalists and evangelicals, modernists old and new, and Catholics pre– and post–Vatican II. All of his Reformed adversaries were proven inconsistent in some way. Indeed, any one of Van Til's books leaves the reader with the impression that he seemed eager to pick a fight with any adversary, past or present.

Why did Van Til seem so bellicose? The simplest explanation is his Dutch stubbornness. As Gary North colorfully quipped, Van Til "clings to his favorite mistakes with the same fervency that he clings to his favorite truths."[7] To be sure, there were aspects of Van Til's ethnic heritage that he never shed, even after fifty years in the Orthodox Presbyterian Church. In spite of his "Dutchness," however, Van Til was a shy and retiring personality. He was hardly one to seek the limelight of theological controversy, and there were plenty of episodes in his life when he actively sought to avoid controversy.

Others have suggested that the distinctiveness of Van Til's apologetic methodology lent itself to a controversial style of argumentation. There is some truth to this claim. Van Til's exposure to Abraham Kuyper at Calvin College opened him up to see the fundamental antagonism between believers and unbelievers in the world, and Van Til placed this antithesis at the forefront of his apologetic method. The authority for the believer is the Word of God, and there can be no epistemological common ground between the dependent believer and the autonomous unbeliever. Therefore, because he viewed unbelievers as being in fundamental rebellion against God and blind to the truth of the gospel, Van Til rejected general appeals to the reasonableness of the Christian faith on primarily rational or empirical grounds (from either "classical" or "evidential" approaches) that failed to proclaim the specific claims of the gospel.

Yet, to put Van Til's work in exclusively negative terms is unfair, for Van Til followed Calvin in viewing controversy as a necessarily negative means to the positive end of proclaiming the truth. In 1976 Van Til published an article entitled "Calvin as a Controversialist" in a collection of essays in honor of John H. Gerstner. The article was a fitting tribute to Gerstner, himself no stranger to theological controversy and one with whom Van Til had crossed apologetic swords. Van Til appealed to his and Gerstner's common theological ancestor, and he noted that Calvin's life of controversy began when he embraced Protestantism. By definition, being a Protestant left Calvin no option but controversy, for in stating the truth positively he also had to protest errors negatively. In outlining the contours of Calvin's theology, Van Til carefully underscored that throughout his work the Genevan Reformer bore a pastoral and ecclesiastical burden. For Calvin, the Protestant Reformation was the recovery of the true Christian story for the true Christian community. In an earlier essay with the same title, written in 1959, Van Til concluded, with words laced with autobiographical overtones, that controversy inevitably attended the faithful preaching of the Word. As he wrote in a earlier essay on Calvin, "For the Lord hath appointed us ministers of his doctrine with this proviso, that we are to be as firm in defending as faithful in delivering it."[8]

Van Til the Postmodernist?

Van Til's polemical rhetoric has served to further alienate him from many contemporary readers. Controversy does not play well in a winsome age of "generous orthodoxy" and "gracious Christianity." Not surprisingly, a recent book-length plea for "humble apologetics" makes no reference to the work of Van Til.[9]

And yet there are some aspects of his thought which lead interpreters to regard him as a precursor to postmodernism. Van Til's anti-modernism apologetic was an extended critique of Enlightenment notions of rationality. On the one hand, he challenged the positivistic reductionism that pursued epistemological issues while dismissing metaphysical concerns. On the other hand, he scolded evangelicals who took the modernist bait and rested Christianity on the unsure foundation of autonomous rationality, thereby belittling the mystery in God's revelation. In these ways, Van Til anticipated the culture of postmodern interpretation, and he would not countenance the notion of brute facts any more than the staunchest of postmodernists.

In a similar way, Carl Raschke has recently suggested that Van Til influenced American evangelicals to embrace the notion of "worldview" thinking. The "father of presuppositionalism" (as Raschke called him) introduced *weltanschauungen* into the American vocabulary. Raschke claims that Van Til catechized evangelicals to see how their understanding of the created order is shaped by their worldview and that Van Til stressed particularly that all interpretive grids are ultimately religious in character.[10] Raschke may be overstating Van Til's role; Van Til spoke not of "worldviews" but of a "divine system of truth" that made human experience meaningful and intelligible. These terms are more objective (and even hegemonic) than postmoderns would be comfortable employing. At the very least, it is safe to suggest that Van Til anticipated postmodern themes when he spoke of rooting human knowledge in the narrative of redemptive history. "'Logic' and 'fact,'" he wrote, "have meaning only in the 'story.'"[11]

Westminster Seminary's William Edgar has acknowledged that there is a "surface plausibility" to the claim that Van Til's apologetic is friendly to postmodernism. But Van Til was no less prophetic in anticipating the failures of postmodernism, especially in its reduction of theological truth to mere perspective. Van Til's transcendent centering of meaning in the self-attesting Christ of Scripture was no scratching of an imaginary itch, as Richard Rorty would claim. For Van Til, writes Edgar, "there is metanarrative after all, the true story of Christian revelation."[12] Postmodernism evaluated through a Van Tilian grid is not hermeneutical humility but epistemological agnosticism.

If in the years since his death the pendulum has shifted from modernism to postmodernism, Van Til, were he alive, would likely have dismissed that development as but another example of the dialectical character of unbelief. (Perhaps he might have labeled it "new-new modernism.") For him all unbelief awkwardly attempts to reside between immanence and transcendence, Enlightenment and post-Enlightenment, rationality and irrationality. Wherever unbelief arises, the results are the same: apostate autonomy. For Van Til, then, the fire of postmodernism's irrationality was no refuge from the frying pan of modernity's rationalism: in his mind true biblical thinking is antithetical to all autonomous unbelieving thought, old or new.

The Ecumenical Van Til

Assessments of Van Til are plagued not only with hyperbole but also contradiction. If he was a dangerous radical for some interpreters, he was hopelessly obsolete for others. Some evangelical critics classified him as a fideist to the point of being indistinguishable from his arch-enemy, Karl Barth. He was far too static and rationalistic for others, such as his Christian Reformed antagonist James Daane. Still others who knew Van

Til personally tended to contrast his warm and gracious personality with the militance of his pen, as if there were a Jekyll-and-Hyde schizophrenia in the man. In person he was nothing like his writings, former students were quick to point out, as if the human side of Van Til emerged only after one scratched the surface of his militant Calvinism.

This well-meaning effort to defend Van Til fails by unnecessarily conceding that Van Til's militance was at odds with his ecumenism. For Van Til, the Reformed faith yielded the most generous form of orthodoxy because, to a greater degree than other expressions, it highlighted the work of God's saving grace. In a study of the Heidelberg Catechism that Van Til wrote in 1962, he underscored how this catechism was ecumenical precisely in its Reformed, grace-exalting character. In reciting this catechism, the believer speaks his or her personal faith, not in existential isolation, but as a member of the one holy, catholic church. The spirit of the Heidelberg Catechism, he wrote, is the confession of the *whole church*. The triumph of the grace of God in Christ enables the church to be the church.

The Heidelberg Catechism, he went on to point out, along with the other confessions and catechisms of the Reformation, contains Protestant claims, and Van Til sought to restore the militancy of Protestantism. To proclaim fully the work of God's grace required a protest against all those who "fail to proclaim the triumph of the grace of God in Christ."[13] Everywhere the Reformed church confesses Christ, it dissents from the corruptions of Rome, the errors of Arminianism, and the unbelief of modernism.

Moreover, the exaltation of God's grace was the confession of the whole church. Where the church fails in its confession, it weakens its testimony to the world. Van Til's language explicitly invokes Machen's doctrine of the corporate witness of the church. Accordingly, his apologetics was controversial because it was self-consciously ecclesiastical. The faith that he defended was the *Reformed* faith, which was found in the confessions of the Reformed *churches*.

"Gracious" Christianity, in the words of one recent book, ought not to elevate one Christian tradition above others. It must offer a welcoming theology of inclusiveness, content with what C. S. Lewis described as a "mere Christianity." Van Til categorically rejected that approach. Mere

Christianity is not Christianity come into its own; rather, it is less than the whole counsel of God, and it serves an insufficient means of nurturing and sustaining the Christian faith from generation to generation.

Van Til's Reformed particularity, however, did not deny the importance of ecumenicity. Instead he offered a more excellent, albeit paradoxical way. True ecumenicity requires the Reformed not to weaken their identity, but to embrace their distinctiveness and to raise the banner of the Reformed faith on the highest mountain. In the end, that is the kindest and most gracious way for the Reformed to witness to the world and to relate to non-Reformed Christians. The paradox, then, for Van Til was that to be more ecumenical meant being more deeply Reformed, not less.

For this reason the Reformed apologetics of Van Til must be located in its larger context: Reformed militance. The Reformed faith must be satisfied with nothing less than its *best* defense, rid of the inconsistencies and weaknesses that would hamper its witness against unbelief in modern times. Nor can Reformed apologetics be fully applied absent Reformed ecclesiology. The pursuit of obedience to the whole counsel of God, in other words, had apologetic and ecclesiastical consequences. This was *fortiter in re*.

Of course that militance was always accompanied by Van Til's gentleness of approach: *suaviter in modo*. Some of his foes could not see past Barth's cannibal. But others, even some of his opponents, who studied him more thoughtfully and were privileged to know him personally, were able to draw vastly different assessments.

Van Til understood the distinctiveness of the Reformed faith not as an impediment to ecumenicity but as the means whereby the Reformed could exercise true ecumenicity. The Orthodox Presbyterian Church and other Reformed churches held the Reformed faith as stewards of the whole church. The "whole church" included mainline Protestants and evangelicals whom Van Til sought earnestly to win over to the Reformed faith. Van Til served the church catholic only as he was an Orthodox Presbyterian, not despite his ecclesiastical labors. And the gospel he defended needed no adjustment. It was neither reshaped theologically to become more palatable to modern listeners nor altered apologetically to gain a better hearing. Therefore, for the Reformed to abandon its particularism was not only to cheapen the Reformed tradition, but also to impoverish the entire church.

That consistency is an underappreciated testimony for those who have come to regard Van Til's version of Reformed particularism as too narrow for sustaining Reformed identity. Here it is worth observing that recent assessments of American Reformed denominations are not encouraging. The identity crisis that is characterizing the decline in mainline Presbyterian identity is replaying itself in the conservative Reformed and Presbyterian churches, where aging memberships, geographic mobility, and the pursuit of individual forms of spirituality are combining to forge post-denominational sensibilities.

The Christian Reformed Church for a time located the strength and vibrancy of its Reformed identity in the stability of its Dutch subculture. Perhaps the most significant feature of the life and work of this Dutch-American theologian was his testimony to a way of being Reformed that went beyond ethnicity. As Van Til watched the erosion of Reformed identity in formerly stable Dutch enclaves like the one in which he grew up in Munster, Indiana, he yearned for a deeper connection to the Reformed tradition and a more robust expression of its theology, refusing to bargain away its hard edges.

Ultimately, Van Til found a greater following among a mostly non-Dutch audience. His teaching sustained a generation within the Orthodox Presbyterian Church, but even in that communion his views have come under criticism and neglect. A rediscovery of Van Til will not be possible until the bankruptcy of post-denominational "mere Christianity" becomes increasingly evident.

What makes Van Til's life a compelling story and his theology one that merits a hearing is not so much a narrow analysis of his distinctive apologetic methodology. For this reason he is often disagreed with, and perhaps more often misunderstood. Van Til carved out a way to be distinctively Reformed in the twentieth century. To be sure, that way involved apologetics, but it also involved much more. Van Til taught that the defense of the faith must be as Reformed as the exposition of the faith. Thus, to separate the man from his church is an abstract reduction of the richness of his heart and life. This unity of thought and life continues to be Van Til's gift to the whole church of Jesus Christ.

Notes

Abbreviations

CVT   Cornelius Van Til
OPC   Orthodox Presbyterian Church
PCA   Presbyterian Church in America
WTS   Westminster Theological Seminary

Acknowledgments

1. CVT, "Boston Personalism," unpublished manuscript, 1956.
2. Elmer Dortzbach to CVT, April 20, 1970, CVT Archives, WTS.

Introduction: Apologist and Churchman

1. Charles G. Dennison, "Cornelius Van Til and the Identity of the Orthodox Presbyterian Church" in *Perspectives: A Pre-Assembly Conference Commemorating the 60th Anniversary of the OPC* (n.p.: Committee for the Historian of the OPC, 1997), 30.

2. Preeminent among the interpretations of Van Til's apologetics are the works by Greg L. Bahnsen, *Van Til's Apologetic: Readings and Analysis* (Phillipsburg, NJ: P&R, 1998); and John M. Frame, *Cornelius Van Til: An Analysis of His Thought* (Phillipsburg, NJ: P&R, 1995). The bibliographic essay surveys these and other works about Van Til.

3. John M. Frame, review of *Van Til, Defender of the Faith*, by William White Jr., *Westminster Theological Journal* 42 (1979): 202.

Chapter 1: A Child of the *Afscheiding*

1. Robert P. Swierenga, *Dutch Chicago: A History of Hollanders in the Windy City* (Grand Rapids: Eerdmans, 2002), 59.

2. Quoted in Jacob Van Hinte, *Netherlanders in America: A Study of Emigration and Settlement in the Nineteenth and Twentieth Centuries in the United States of America,* ed. Robert P. Swierenga, trans. Adriaan de Wit (Grand Rapids: Baker, 1985), 96.

3. Abraham Kuyper, *Lectures on Calvinism* (Grand Rapids: Eerdmans, 1931), 12.

4. Ibid., 79.

5. Edward E. Ericson Jr., "Remembering the Antithesis," *Perspectives: A Journal of Reformed Thought* 8 (September 1993): 4.

6. James D. Bratt, *Dutch Calvinism in Modern America: A History of a Conservative Subculture* (Grand Rapids: Eerdmans, 1984), 19.

7. See Swierenga, *Dutch Chicago,* chapter 2, who cautions that these were generally very subtle differences within the family of Dutch-American colonists.

8. Kuyper, *Lectures on Calvinism,* 15.

9. B. B. Warfield, "Calvinism," *New Schaff-Herzog Encyclopedia of Religious Knowledge,* ed. Samuel Macauley Jackson, 2 vols. (New York: Funk and Wagnall's, 1908), 2:359.

10. Ibid., 171.

11. Quoted by John Bolt in his introduction to Herman Bavinck, *In the Beginning: Foundations of Creation Theology* (Grand Rapids: Baker, 1999), 12.

12. CVT, "Bavinck the Theologian: A Review Article," *Westminster Theological Journal* 24 (1961): 48–49.

13. CVT, *The New Synthesis Theology of the Netherlands* (Nutley, NJ: Presbyterian and Reformed, 1975), 1.

14. For example, Harry Boonstra, *Our School: Calvin College and the Christian Reformed Church* (Grand Rapids: Eerdmans, 2001), 17.

15. Mrs. Nena Chapman to Bob Cara, June 24, 1990. Thanks to my colleague Bob Cara for showing me this letter. Nena Chapman's mother, Gepke Mulder Schuil, was Van Til's teacher in Grootegast.

16. CVT, *Why I Believe in God* (Philadelphia: Committee on Christian Education of the Orthodox Presbyterian Church, 1948), 5–6.

17. Ibid., 3.

18. Bernardus De Bay, letter in *Provinciale Groninger Courant,* June 8, 1870, quoted in Swierenga, *Dutch Chicago,* 21.

19. Van Hinte, *Netherlanders in America,* 833. Apparently, it was unnecessary by this point to process all European immigrants at Ellis Island, though there are Ellis Island records for Van Til's brother, Reinder.

20. J. Van Bruggen, "An Interview with Prof. C. Van Til," *Outlook* 28 (July 1978): 14.

21. Elton J. Bruins and Robert P. Swierenga, *Family Quarrels in the Dutch Reformed Churches in the Nineteenth Century* (Grand Rapids: Eerdmans, 1999), 6.

22. *Centennial of the First Christian Reformed Church, Munster Indiana* (n.p.: Published by the Centennial Committee, 1970), 99.

23. CVT, undated journal entry, 1979, CVT Archives, WTS.

24. CVT, *Centennial of the First Christian Reformed Church*, 99.

25. *History of the First Christian Reformed Church of Highland, Indiana* (n.p., 1958), 9.

26. CVT, undated journal entry, 1979, CVT Archives, WTS.

27. This is attested to by his grandson, Reinder Van Til; quoted by Richard Mouw in his foreword to Henry R. Van Til, *The Calvinistic Concept of Culture* (Grand Rapids: Baker, 2001), xi.

28. Quoted in Helen Kletzing, "World Acclaim for Dr. Van Til," *The Calumet Press*, January 12, 1978, 1.

29. Van Hinte, *Netherlanders in America*, 881.

30. Quoted in Swierenga, *Dutch Chicago*, 66.

31. Abraham Kuyper, quoted in R. B. Kuiper, *To Be or Not to Be Reformed* (Grand Rapids: Zondervan, 1959), 8.

32. B. K. Kuiper, quoted in Bratt, *Dutch Calvinism in Modern America*, 41.

33. Bratt, *Dutch Calvinism in America*, 59. Bratt particularly cites Foppe Ten Hoor's use of the expression. Ten Hoor and other Dutch Americans used the term *Methodism* loosely, referring to the "easy evangelicalism" of the "American spirit."

34. Henry Beets, quoted in Swierenga, *Dutch Chicago*, 74.

35. Swierenga, *Dutch Chicago*, 491.

Chapter 2: "Fit Modesty and Unreserved Conviction"

1. CVT to Henry Van Til, February 21, 1931, Family Letters from Reinder Van Til.

2. Harry Boonstra, *Our School: Calvin College and the Christian Reformed Church* (Grand Rapids: Eerdmans, 2001), 37.

3. CVT to R. B. Kuiper's widow, Marie Kuiper, undated, quoted in Edward Heerema, *R.B., A Prophet in the Land: Rienk Bouke Kuiper, Preacher, Theologian, Churchman* (Jordan Station, Ontario: Paideia, 1986), 89.

4. CVT to Homer Hoeksema, July 17, 1967, CVT Archives, WTS.

5. John J. Timmerman, *Promises to Keep: A Centennial History of Calvin College* (Grand Rapids: Calvin College and Seminary, 1975), 177.

6. Ibid., 177–78.

7. CVT, "Our Seminary Preparatory Course," *Calvin College Chimes* 15, no. 5 (May 1921): 198–204.

8. CVT, "Our Attitude Toward Modern American Literature," *Calvin College Chimes* 16, no. 2 (February 1922): 49.

9. CVT, "The New Year," *Calvin College Chimes* 16, no. 1 (January 1922): 7.

10. Ibid., 8.

11. CVT, "The Wedding of Faith and Reason," *Calvin College Chimes* 15, no. 6 (September 1921): 239–46.

12. J. Van Bruggen, "An Interview with Prof. C. Van Til," *Outlook* 28 (July 1978): 15.

13. CVT, interview by Joseph Hall, undated (early 1970s), PCA Historical Center, St. Louis, MO.

14. George Stob, "The Christian Reformed Church and Her Schools" (ThD diss., Princeton Theological Seminary, 1955), 443.

15. CVT to John R. DeWitt, February 18, 1965, and December 23, 1974, CVT Archives, WTS.

16. CVT, "Calvinism and the New World," unpublished college paper (January 1922), 20, CVT Archives, WTS.

17. CVT, interview by Charles G. Dennison, December 15, 1982, OPC Archives.

18. CVT, "Students and Controversies," *Calvin College Chimes* 16, no. 3 (March 1922): 88.

19. Ibid., 89, 91.

20. Stob, "The Christian Reformed Church and Her Schools," 340.

21. Case Van Til (Reinder's son), interview by the author, February 2005.

22. CVT, interview by Joseph Hall.

23. CVT, untitled editorial, *Calvin College Chimes* 15, no. 9 (December 1921): 352.

24. Quoted in Ned B. Stonehouse, *J. Gresham Machen, A Biographical Memoir* (Grand Rapids: Eerdmans, 1954), 310.

25. CVT, "Evil and Theodicy," handwritten paper written at Princeton Seminary for C. W. Hodge Jr., 1923, CVT Archives, WTS.

26. Ibid.

27. Ibid.

28. CVT, "The Will in Its Theological Relations," handwritten paper written at Princeton Seminary for C. W. Hodge Jr., 1924, CVT Archives, WTS.

29. Ibid.

30. Ibid.

31. CVT, interview by Joseph Hall.

32. CVT, review of *Studies in the Philosophy of Religion*, by A. A. Bowman, *Westminster Theological Journal* 2 (1939): 62.

33. K. Scott Oliphint, "The Consistency of Van Til's Methodology" *Westminster Theological Journal* 52 (1990): 49.

34. CVT to Henry Van Til, November 15, 1941, Family Letters from Reinder Van Til.

35. CVT to Henry Van Til, April 20, 1950, Family Letters from Reinder Van Til.

36. CVT, "My Credo," in *Jerusalem and Athens: Critical Discussions on the Theology and Apologetics of Cornelius Van Til*, ed. E. R. Geehan (Nutley, NJ: Presbyterian and Reformed, 1971), 8.

37. CVT, sermon preached at Spring Lake CRC, September 23, 1928, CVT Archives, WTS.

38. CVT, interview by Joseph Hall.

39. CVT, "Kuyper en Amerika," *De Reformatie* 18, no. 14 (December 31, 1937): 150.

40. CVT, "Why Westminster Today," unpublished manuscript, ca. 1970, CVT Archives, WTS.

41. J. Gresham Machen to O. T. Allis, telegram, August 2, 1929, Machen Archives, WTS.

42. J. Gresham Machen to CVT, telegram, August 2, 1929, Machen Archives, WTS.

43. CVT to J. Gresham Machen, telegram, August 12, 1929, Machen Archives, WTS.

44. J. Gresham Machen to O. T. Allis, telegram, August 14, 1929, Machen Archives, WTS.

45. Ned B. Stonehouse to Machen, August 13, 1929, Machen Archives, WTS.

46. "Seminary Loses Fourth Teacher," *New York Times*, September 5, 1929, 14.

47. CVT, "Why Westminster Today."

Chapter 3: From Dutch Reformed to American Presbyterian

1. J. Gresham Machen, "Westminster Seminary: Its Purpose and Plan," in *What Is Christianity and Other Addresses*, ed. Ned B. Stonehouse (Grand Rapids: Eerdmans, 1951), 229.

2. J. Gresham Machen, quoted by Ned B. Stonehouse in "Cooperation among Calvinists," *Presbyterian Guardian*, July 16, 1951, 134.

3. J. Gresham Machen, "A Future for Calvinism in the Presbyterian Church?" *Banner*, April 14, 1930, 333.

4. "To Philadelphia," editorial in *Banner,* September 20, 1929, 645.

5. CVT, "The Story of Westminster Theological Seminary," *Banner,* July 11, 1930, 657–58.

6. J. Gresham Machen to his mother, September 28, 1928, Machen Archives, WTS.

7. Allan MacRae, interview by Charles G. Dennison, October 24, 1991, OPC Archives.

8. As previously noted, Van Til's stress on the importance of methodological consistency led him to praise the work of A. A. Bowman, his unbelieving professor of philosophy at Princeton University. "It is difficult to accord too high a tribute," Van Til wrote in a 1938 review of Bowman's *Studies in the Philosophy of Religion*, "as a piece of philosophical writing," mainly because "in all this Bowman is perfectly consistent." CVT, review of *Studies in the Philosophy of Religion*, by A. A. Bowman, *Westminster Theological Journal* 2 (1939): 62.

9. Quoted in Ned B. Stonehouse, *J. Gresham Machen: A Biographical Memoir* (Grand Rapids: Eerdmans, 1954), 411.

10. Quoted in Stonehouse, *J. Gresham Machen*, 428.

11. Stonehouse, *J. Gresham Machen*, 178.

12. CVT, "The Story of Westminster Theological Seminary," 657.

13. J. Gresham Machen to CVT, May 21, 1930, Machen Archives, WTS.

14. Ibid.

15. CVT to J. Gresham Machen, June 19, 1930, Machen Archives, WTS.

16. CVT to McKendree Langley, April 28, 1975, CVT Archives, WTS.

17. D. G. Hart, "'Machen on Barth': Introduction to a Recently Uncovered Paper," *Westminster Theological Journal* 53 (1991): 189–96.

18. Edmund P. Clowney, quoted by John M. Frame, "Systematic Theology and Apologetics at the Westminster Seminaries," in *The Pattern of Sound Doctrine*, ed. D. VanDrunen (Phillipsburg, NJ: P&R, 2004), 77.

19. CVT, "A Tribute to My Colleagues" *Presbyterian Guardian*, May 1969, 67.

20. Frame, "Systematic Theology and Apologetics at the Westminster Seminaries," 86. For other examples of Van Til's close collaboration with Murray, see also Edmund Clowney, "Professor John Murray at Westminster Theological Seminary," in *The Pattern of Sound Doctrine*, 27–40.

21. Quoted in *Christianity Today*, April 1938, 247.

22. CVT, "A New Princeton Apologetic," *Christianity Today,* January 1933, 5, 12; February 1933, 5–6.

23. CVT, "Christianity—The Paradox of God," *Christianity Today*, February 1934, 11.

24. Donald Mackenzie, "Dr. Mackenzie Replies: An Open Letter to Dr. Van Til," *Christianity Today*, March 1934, 8.

25. "Mackenzie v. Van Til (Conclusion)," *Christianity Today*, May 1934, 13.

26. The *Presbyterian Guardian* was formed in 1935 after Samuel Craig, the editor of *Christianity Today*, parted ways with Machen over the founding of the Independent Board and the Presbyterian Constitutional Covenant Union.

27. CVT, review of *The Karl Barth Theology*, by Alvin Sylvester Zerbe, *Christianity Today,* February 1931, 13–14.

28. CVT, "Princeton's President and Pagan Philosophy," *Presbyterian Guardian*, January 25, 1940, 19. (See also CVT, "More Barthianism at Princeton," *Presbyterian Guardian*, February 1938, 26).

29. Clarence Bouma, *Calvin Forum* (February 1942), quoted by Thomas R. Birch, "Whither Princeton?" *Presbyterian Guardian*, January 25, 1943, 25.

30. CVT, "A Substitute for Christianity," *Presbyterian Guardian,* February 10, 1943, 35–37.

31. William Childs Robinson, "God, the Foundation of Knowledge," *Christianity Today,* March 1936, 237.

32. Samuel G. Craig, "The Disruption of Westminster Seminary," *Christianity Today,* February 1936, 195.

33. CVT to John DeWaard, January 8, 1936, and February 14, 1936, CVT Archives, WTS.

34. CVT to John DeWaard, March 11, 1935, CVT Archives, WTS.

35. CVT to John DeWaard, undated, 1936, CVT Archives, WTS.

36. CVT to John DeWaard, April 8, 1933, CVT Archives, WTS.

37. CVT and R. B. Kuiper to Synod of the CRC, telegram, quoted in *Acts of Synod 1936 of the Christian Reformed Church* (Grand Rapids: Office of the Stated Clerk, 1936), 20.

38. Address by CVT to Synod of the CRC, *Acts of Synod 1936*, 274.

39. Ibid.

40. Ibid.

41. Ibid.

42. William Kok, quoted in Henry J. Kuiper, "Report on Synod," *Banner*, July 17, 1936, 676.

43. I thank Danny E. Olinger for this observation. See his *Geerhardus Vos Anthology* (Phillipsburg, NJ: P&R, 2005).

44. CVT, "Nature and Scripture," in *The Infallible Word*, ed. Ned B. Stonehouse and Paul Woolley, 255–93 (Grand Rapids: Eerdmans, 1946).

45. "Where Do We Go From Here in Theology?" *Religion in Life* 25 (Winter 1955–56): 5–34; Van Til's contribution is found on pages 20–26.

46. CVT, "How Shall We Feed Our Children?" *Presbyterian Guardian,* October 24, 1936, 23.

47. Ibid.

48. Ibid.

49. CVT to John DeWaard, October 9, 1936, CVT Archives, WTS.

50. J. Gresham Machen, "Constraining Love," *Presbyterian Guardian*, December 12, 1936, 102.

51. "Heads New Group of Presbyterians: Dr. Buswell of Wheaton, Ill. Is Named at Philadelphia by Fundamentalists," *New York Times*, November 13, 1936, 8.

52. Quoted by Charles G. Dennison, *History for a Pilgrim People: The Historical Writings of Charles G. Dennison*, ed. Danny E. Olinger and David K. Thompson (Willow Grove, PA: Committee for the Historian of the OPC, 2002), 117.

53. "The Second General Assembly of the Presbyterian Church of America" *Presbyterian Guardian*, November 28, 1939, 82–83. See also "News of the Church: The Second General Assembly of the Presbyterian Church of America," *Christianity Today,* December 1936, 189.

54. CVT to John DeWaard, January 2, 1937, and January 7, 1937, CVT Archives, WTS.

55. CVT, "J. Gresham Machen, 1881–1937," *De Reformatie* 17, no. 19 (February 5, 1937): 150–51. *De Reformatie* was a Dutch newspaper edited by Klaas Schilder from 1920 to 1940. Beginning in 1935, Van Til wrote twenty-four "Letters from America" for the newspaper in Dutch. I am grateful to Simon J. Kistemaker for his translation.

56. CVT, "Why Westminster Today," unpublished manuscript, ca. 1970, CVT Archives, WTS.

57. Ibid.

58. J. Oliver Buswell to CVT, January 30, 1937, CVT Archives, WTS.

59. CVT to J. Oliver Buswell, February 1, 1937, CVT Archives, WTS.

60. Paul Woolley to Harold Laird, undated, CVT Archives, WTS. Woolley's comment paralleled John Murray's condemnation of Buswell's treatment of Geerhardus Vos: "Dr. Buswell is guilty of pitiable distortion and misrepresentation of a scholar who has done more than perhaps any other now living in defense of the essential Deity of our Lord, and that upon the basis of the most exact and penetrating exegesis and apologetic. We do not accuse Dr. Buswell of deliberate distortion. He has, however, shown himself seriously incompetent to deal carefully and fairly with his opponent." John Murray, "Dr. Buswell's Premillennialism," *Presbyterian Guardian*, February 27, 1937, 207.

61. CVT to Henry J. Kuiper, November 2, 1949, CVT Archives, WTS.

62. CVT to Henry Van Til, May 6, 1937, Family Letters from Reinder Van Til.

63. Allan MacRae, interview by Charles Dennison, October 24, 1991, OPC Archives.

64. CVT to Henry Van Til, May 6, 1937, Family Letters from Reinder Van Til.

65. Edwin H. Rian, "A High Honor for Dr. Van Til and Westminster Seminary," *Presbyterian Guardian*, September 1938, 163.

66. Ibid.

67. Edward Heerema, *R.B., a Prophet in the Land: Rienk Bouke Kuiper, Preacher, Theologian, Churchman* (Jordan Station, ON: Paideia, 1986), 124.

68. *Minutes of the Sixth General Assembly of the Orthodox Presbyterian Church* (Philadelphia: OPC, 1939), 16.

69. Charles G. Dennison, "Cornelius Van Til and the Identity of the Orthodox Presbyterian Church," in *Perspectives: A Pre-Assembly Conference Commemorating the 60th Anniversary of the OPC* (n.p.: Committee for the Historian of the OPC, 1997), 30.

Chapter 4: Reformed or Evangelical?

1. CVT, review of *Calvinism: An Interpretation of Its Basic Ideas*, by Henry Meeter, *Presbyterian Guardian*, January 10, 1940, 10.

2. Moisés Silva, "A Half-Century of Reformed Scholarship," *Westminster Theological Journal* 50 (1988): 248–49. Silva adds that the *Westminster Theological Journal* "owes much of its influence and distinctiveness to [Van Til's] remarkably original mind." Van Til's debates on common grace are found in chapter 6 of the present work.

3. CVT to Henry Van Til, October 26, 1941, Family Letters from Reinder Van Til.

4. Leona DeWaard Klooster, interview by the author, June 30, 2004.

5. CVT to John DeWaard, October 26, 1939, CVT Archives, WTS.

6. CVT to Henry Van Til, November 11, 1948, Family Letters from Reinder Van Til.

7. William Edgar, introduction to CVT, *Christian Apologetics*, 2nd ed., ed. William Edgar (Phillipsburg, NJ: P&R, 2003), 11.

8. Lester DeKoster, review of *By What Standard?* by R. J. Rushdoony, *Reformed Journal* 9 (July/August 1959): 21.

9. CVT to Charles Stanton, December 27, 1945, CVT Archives, WTS.

10. CVT to Henry Van Til, June 1, 1945, Family Letters from Reinder Van Til.

11. Case Van Til, interview by the author, February 9, 2005.

12. CVT to Henry Van Til, August 24, 1945, Family Letters from Reinder Van Til.

13. Henry Coray, interview by Charles G. Dennison, February 16, 1991, OPC Archives.

14. William White Jr., *Van Til, Defender of the Faith* (Nashville: Thomas Nelson, 1979), 102.

15. Henry Coray, interview by Charlie Dennison, Dortzbach letter to CVT, ca. April 1970, Van Til Archives.

16. John Gerstner, interview by David F. Coffin, June 15, 1992, PCA Historical Center, St. Louis, MO.

17. Robert D. Knudsen,, interview by Charles G. Dennison, January 30, 1991, OPC Archives.

18. Paul Woolley, "In Gratitude for Seventy Years," *Presbyterian Guardian*, April 1965, 53.

19. *Minutes of the Eighth General Assembly of the Orthodox Presbyterian Church* (Philadelphia: OPC, 1941), 24.

20. *Minutes of the Ninth General Assembly of the Orthodox Presbyterian Church* (Philadelphia: OPC, 1942), 30–33.

21. Ibid., 32.

22. Thomas R. Birch, "The Ninth General Assembly of the Orthodox Presbyterian Church," *Presbyterian Guardian*, June 25, 1942, 191.

23. James Daane, *The Theology of Grace: An Inquiry into and Evaluation of Dr. C. Van Til's Doctrine of Common Grace* (Grand Rapids: Eerdmans, 1954), 147.

24. CVT to John DeWaard, February 14, 1936, CVT Archives, WTS.

25. Peter Eldersveld to CVT, June 19, 1943; Louis Berkhof to CVT, undated, CVT Archives, WTS.

26. John C. Hills to CVT, June 22, 1943, CVT Archives, WTS.

27. CVT, *Why I Believe in God* (Philadelphia: Committee on Christian Education of the OPC, 1948).

28. Ibid.

29. Edmund P. Clowney, interview by Charles G. Dennison, February 19, 1991, OPC Archives.

30. CVT to Charles Stanton, December 27, 1945, CVT Archives, WTS.

31. Edwin H. Rian, "Wheaton College Today," *Presbyterian Guardian*, April 25, 1943, 115–16.

32. *Minutes of the Fourteenth General Assembly of the Orthodox Presbyterian Church* (Philadelphia: OPC, 1947), 9.

33. *The Text of a Complaint Against Actions of the Presbytery of Philadelphia in the Matter of the Licensure and Ordination of Dr. Gordon H. Clark* (Philadelphia: n.p., 1944), 5.

34. *The Answer to a Complaint Against Several Actions and Decisions of the Presbytery of Philadelphia Taken in a Special Meeting Held on July 7, 1944* (Philadelphia: n.p. 1944), 22.

35. Arthur W. Kuschke, interview by the author, October 4, 2004.

36. Robert Strong, "The Gordon Clark Case," lecture delivered at Reformed Theological Seminary, Jackson, Mississippi, 1977, 12.

37. Ibid.

38. Ibid., 5.

39. Ibid.

40. Quoted in Michael Hakkenberg, "The Battle over the Ordination of Gordon H. Clark, 1943–1948," in *Pressing Toward the Mark: Essays Commemorating Fifty Years of the Orthodox Presbyterian Church,* ed. Charles G. Dennison and Richard C. Gamble (Philadelphia: Committee for the Historian of the OPC, 1986), 349–50.

41. John M. Frame, *Cornelius Van Til: An Analysis of His Thought* (Phillipsburg, NJ: P&R, 1995), 113.

42. Edward Heerema, *Whither the Orthodox Presbyterian Church* (privately printed by the author, 1947), 16.

43. Gordon H. Clark, "Blest River of Salvation," *Presbyterian Guardian,* January 10, 1945, 10, 16.

44. *Minutes of the Fifteenth General Assembly of the Orthodox Presbyterian Church* (Philadelphia: OPC, 1948), 17 (appendix).

45. Fred H. Klooster, *The Incomprehensibility of God in the Orthodox Presbyterian Conflict* (Franeker: T. Wever, 1951), 136.

46. Gordon Clark, "The Bible as Truth," *Bibliotheca Sacra* 114, no. 454 (April 1957): 163.

47. Robert L. Reymond, *The Justification of Knowledge: An Introductory Study in Christian Apologetic Methodology* (Nutley, NJ: Presbyterian and Reformed, 1976), 105, 104, 101.

48. These words begin Bavinck's *Reformed Dogmatics,* vol. 2, *God and Creation,* ed. John Bolt, trans. John Vriend (Grand Rapids: Baker, 2004), 29.

49. CVT, *Common Grace* (Philadelphia: Presbyterian and Reformed, 1947), 46.

50. Bavinck, *Reformed Dogmatics,* 2:28. Further on, Bavinck defined analogical knowledge in this way: "a knowledge of a being who is unknowable in himself and yet able to make something of himself known in the being he created" (48).

51. Klooster, *The Incomprehensibility of God,* 12.

52. R. Scott Clark, "Janus, the Well-Meant Offer of the Gospel, and Westminster Theology," in *The Pattern of Sound Doctrine: Systematic Theology at*

the Westminster Seminaries, ed. David VanDrunen (Phillipsburg, NJ: P&R, 2004), 157–60. Clark refers to Van Til's treatment of the terminology in CVT, *Introduction to Systematic Theology* (Nutley, NJ: Presbyterian and Reformed, 1974), 203.

53. CVT, *Common Grace*, 73.

54. CVT to Ronald H. Nash, January 31, 1966, CVT Archives, WTS.

55. Many years later, Van Til and Clark both expressed suspicion toward the Presbyterian Church in America (PCA) and discouraged their churches (the OPC and the RPCES, respectively) from the "joining and receiving" mergers of the 1980s. Van Til prevailed in the OPC, but Clark refused to join the PCA after the merger of 1982, and he spent the last years of his life in Presbyterian independency. Ironically, then, Clark refused to be part of the church whose roots were partially established by his OPC supporters.

56. Arthur W. Kuschke, interview by the author, October 4, 2004.

57. CVT to William Hendriksen, July 7, 1947, CVT Archives, WTS.

58. J. Oliver Buswell, "The Fountainhead of Presuppositionalism: A Review of Common Grace," *The Bible Today* 42, no. 2 (November 1948): 41–64. Van Til replied in *The Bible Today* 42, no. 7 (April 1949): 219–28, and 42, no. 9 (June/September 1949): 278–90. Buswell added some final remarks at the end of Van Til's response.

59. CVT, *The Defense of the Faith* (Philadelphia: Presbyterian and Reformed, 1955), 396.

60. CVT to Henry Van Til, June 1, 1945, Family Letters from Reinder Van Til.

61. "Presuppositionalism," *The Bible Today* 42, no. 8 (May 1949): 261.

62. CVT, review of *Therefore, Stand*, by Wilber M. Smith, *Westminster Theological Journal* 8 (1946): 68–72.

63. Herman Bavinck, *Reformed Dogmatics*, vol. 1, *Prolegomena*, ed. John Bolt, trans. John Vriend (Grand Rapids: Baker, 2003), 515.

64. Ibid., 516.

65. CVT to Douglas Johnson, November 30, 1949, CVT Archives, WTS.

66. CVT to Henry Van Til, November 14, 1942, Family Letters from Reinder Van Til.

67. CVT to Henry Van Til, June 1, 1945, Family Letters from Reinder Van Til.

68. CVT to Henry J. Kuiper, February 19, 1949, CVT Archives, WTS.

69. CVT, "We Are Not Ashamed of Calvinism! An Open Letter to the Editor of *Time* and *Life* Magazines," *Presbyterian Guardian*, September 10, 1947, 245.

70. Ibid., 246.

Chapter 5: The New Machen against the New Modernism

1. CVT, "Kuyper en Amerika," *De Reformatie* 18, no. 14 (December 31, 1937): 150. Thanks to Simon J. Kistemaker for his translation.

2. Ibid.

3. Karl Adam, "Die Theologie der Krisis," *Hochland* 23 (1925–26): 271; quoted by John McConnachie, "The Teaching of Karl Barth: A New Positive Movement in German Theology," *Hibbert Journal* 25 (1927): 385–86.

4. D. G. Hart, "'Machen on Barth': Introduction to a Recently Uncovered Paper," *Westminster Theological Journal* 53 (1991): 189–96.

5. Albert C. Knudson, "German Fundamentalism," *Christian Century* 45 (June 14, 1928): 762–65.

6. CVT, "Reflections on Dr. A. Kuyper, Sr." *Banner*, December 16, 1937, 1187.

7. Karl Barth, *Church Dogmatics* 2.1 (Edinburgh: T. &. T. Clark, 1957), 173.

8. See CVT, *The New Modernism: An Appraisal of the Theology of Barth and Brunner* (Philadelphia: Presbyterian and Reformed, 1946), 364–65.

9. Elmer Homrighausen, "Calm after the Storm," *Christian Century* 56 (April 12, 1939): 447–78.

10. CVT, "New Modernism at Old Princeton," *Presbyterian Guardian*, September 1949, 166–67, and "Reading, Hearing and Keeping the Word of God," *Presbyterian Guardian*, October 16, 1950, 185–86.

11. John A. Mackay, *The Presbyterian Way of Life* (Englewood Cliffs, NJ: Prentice-Hall, 1960), 43.

12. CVT, "Karl Barth on Scripture," *Presbyterian Guardian*, January 9, 1937, 137–38.

13. CVT, "Karl Barth on Creation," *Presbyterian Guardian*, February 27, 1937, 204–5.

14. CVT, "Karl Barth and Historic Christianity," *Presbyterian Guardian*, July 1937, 108–9.

15. CVT, *The New Modernism*, 3, xv.

16. Ibid., 376. Van Til made the Machen connection even more explicit in the title of his 1962 book *Christianity and Barthianism*.

17. Louis Berkhof, review of *The New Modernism*, by CVT, *Banner*, November 14, 1947, 1264.

18. James Daane, review of *The New Modernism*, by CVT, in *Calvin Forum* 13 (February 1948): 147.

19. H. Evan Runner, review of *The New Modernism*, by CVT, *Presbyterian Guardian*, April 10, 1946, 101.

20. Francis A. Schaeffer to CVT, April 13, 1970, CVT Archives, WTS.

21. Bernard Ramm, *After Fundamentalism: The Future of Evangelical Theology* (San Francisco: Harper and Row, 1983), 23; George Marsden, *Reforming Fundamentalism: Fuller Seminary and the New Evangelicalism* (Grand Rapids: Eerdmans, 1987), 101.

22. CVT, *The New Modernism*, 3.

23. CVT, "A False View of the Trinity," *Presbyterian Guardian*, December 1937, 209.

24. A. Donald MacLeod, *W. Stanford Reid: An Evangelical Calvinist in the Academy* (Montreal: McGill-Queen's University Press, 2004), 61–62.

25. Robert L. Reymond, *The Justification of Knowledge* (Nutley, NJ: Presbyterian and Reformed, 1976), 105.

26. CVT heard that Gordon Clark made these remarks to students in Willow Grove in 1948, and CVT reported this to Henry Van Til in a November 1948 letter. For Clark on Barth, see "Special Report: Encountering Barth in Chicago," *Christianity Today*, May 11, 1962, 36.

27. CVT, "Seeking for Similarities in Theology," *Banner*, January 22, 1937, 75.

28. Norman Geisler, *Christian Apologetics* (Grand Rapids: Baker, 1976), 79; Ronald Nash, "Gordon Clark's Theory of Knowledge," in *The Philosophy of Gordon Clark*, ed. R. H. Nash (Philadelphia: Presbyterian and Reformed, 1968), 167; R. C. Sproul, John Gerstner, and Arthur Lindsley, *Classical Apologetics: A Defense of the Christian Faith and a Critique of Presuppositional Apologetics* (Grand Rapids: Zondervan, 1984), 245.

29. CVT, *The New Modernism*, 7.

30. CVT to Henry Van Til, November 14, 1942, and December 20, 1949, Family Letters from Reinder Van Til.

31. CVT, *The New Modernism*, 287.

32. CVT, *The Sovereignty of Grace: An Appraisal of G. C. Berkouwer's View of Dordt* (Philadelphia: Presbyterian and Reformed, 1969), 107n1.

33. CVT, *The New Modernism*, 362, 369.

34. CVT, "Kant or Christ?" *Calvin Forum* 7 (February 1942): 133–35.

35. CVT to Geerhardus Vos Jr., December 10, 1971, and to John F. Jansen, January 23, 1975, CVT Archives, WTS.

36. R. B. Gaffin Jr., "Geerhardus Vos and the Interpretation of Paul," in *Jerusalem and Athens: Critical Discussions on the Theology and Apologetics of Cornelius Van Til*, ed. E. R. Geehan (Nutley, NJ: Presbyterian and Reformed, 1971), 228.

37. CVT, *The Intellectual Challenge of the Gospel* (London: Tyndale House, 1950), 10–11.

38. Ibid., 13.

39. Ibid., 40.

40. Meredith G. Kline credited Van Til for his perception of the "covenant-creature identification," which John Murray "strangely missed in spite of his specific role as theologian and his more directly exegetical method." Kline to CVT, March 30, 1976, CVT Archives, WTS.

41. G. W. Bromiley, review of *The Intellectual Challenge of the Gospel*, by CVT, *Evangelical Quarterly* 23 (1951): 297–98; and T. F. Torrance, review of *The New Modernism*, by CVT, *Evangelical Quarterly* 19 (1947): 144–49.

42. Geoffrey W. Bromiley, "The Karl Barth Experience," in *How Karl Barth Changed My Mind*, ed. Donald K. McKim (Grand Rapids: Eerdmans, 1986), 69.

43. Quoted in David W. Bailey, *Speaking the Truth in Love: The Life and Legacy of Roger Nicole* (Birmingham, AL: Solid Ground Christian Books, 2006), 185.

44. MacLeod, *W. Stanford Reid*, 61. MacLeod went on to blame Van Til for the overstatement and generalization that characterized Reid's own scholarship (61).

45. M. E. Osterhaven, review of *The Sovereignty of Grace*, by CVT, *Reformed Review* 23 (Fall 1969): 37.

46. Carl F. H. Henry, *Fifty Years of Protestant Theology* (Boston: W. A. Wilde, 1950), 96.

47. CVT, *The New Modernism*, viii.

48. Richard B. Gaffin Jr., interview by Charles G. Dennison, January 30, 1991, OPC Archives.

49. Hans Urs von Balthasar, *The Theology of Karl Barth: Exposition and Interpretation,* trans. Edward T. Oakes (San Francisco: Ignatius Press, 1992), 45.

50. CVT, "Has Karl Barth Become Orthodox?" *Westminster Theological Journal* 16 (1954): 181.

51. Karl Barth to Geoffrey Bromiley, June 1, 1961, quoted in Eberhard Busch, *Karl Barth: His Life from Letters and Autobiographical Texts* (Grand Rapids: Eerdmans, 1994), 380.

52. Karl Barth, *Church Dogmatics* 4.2 (Edinburgh: T. &. T. Clark, 1958), xii.

53. Sydney E. Ahlstrom, *A Religious History of the American People* (New Haven: Yale, 1972), 947.

54. Charles Clayton Morrison, "The Liberalism of Neo-Orthodoxy, Part I," *Christian Century* 67 (June 7): 697.

55. CVT, "Wanted—A Reformed Testimony," *Presbyterian Guardian,* July 16, 1951, 125–26, 136–37.

56. CVT to Henry Van Til, August 24, 1955, Family Letters from Reinder Van Til.

57. CVT to Theodore J. Jansma, April 30, 1948, CVT Archives, WTS.

58. CVT, autobiographical comments, from 1953 notebook, CVT Archives, WTS.

59. C. S. Lewis to Douglas Johnson, December 16, 1947, CVT Archives, WTS.

60. E. J. Carnell to CVT, January 26, 1948, CVT Archives, WTS.

61. CVT to Theodore J. Jansma, April 30, 1948, CVT Archives, WTS.

62. Rudolph Nelson, *The Making and Unmaking of an Evangelical Mind: The Case of Edward Carnell* (Cambridge: Cambridge University Press, 1987), 45.

63. CVT, quoted in William B. Eerdmans to CVT, August 6, 1948, CVT Archives, WTS.

64. E. J. Carnell to CVT, September 17, 1948, CVT Archives, WTS.

65. E. J. Carnell to CVT, August 14, 1948, CVT Archives, WTS.

66. Ibid.

67. E. J. Carnell to CVT, January 11, 1949, CVT Archives, WTS.

68. E. J. Carnell to CVT, June 9, 1952, CVT Archives, WTS.

69. E. J. Carnell to CVT, June 27, 1952, CVT Archives, WTS.

70. Carl F. H. Henry, *The Protestant Dilemma: An Analysis of the Current Impasse in Theology* (Grand Rapids: Eerdmans, 1940), 83.

71. Henry, *Fifty Years of Protestant Theology*, 96.

72. Carl F. H. Henry to CVT, August 12, 1948, and April 4, 1949, CVT Archives, WTS.

73. CVT to Peter De Visser of Eerdmans, July 1, 1948, CVT Archives, WTS.

74. CVT to Henry Van Til, February 16, 1948, Family Letters from Reinder Van Til.

75. CVT to Henry Van Til, January 2, 1947, Family Letters from Reinder Van Til.

76. CVT to Henry Van Til, undated, ca. 1945, Family Letters from Reinder Van Til.

77. CVT to Jack Rinsema, July 24, 1967, CVT Archives, WTS.

78. Ramm, *After Fundamentalism*, 78.

79. William M. Shea, *The Lion and the Lamb: Evangelicals and Catholics in America* (New York: Oxford, 2004), 153.

80. CVT, *The New Modernism*, 377.

81. J. G. Machen, "Karl Barth and 'The Theology of Crisis,'" *Westminster Theological Journal* 53 (1991): 197–207.

82. I. A. Diepenhorst, review of *The Intellectual Challenge of the Gospel*, by CVT, *Free University Quarterly* 2 (1952–53): 139.

83. CVT to Henry Van Til, February 25, 1953, and April 13, 1953, Family Letters from Reinder Van Til.

84. CVT, review of *De Triomf der Genade in de Theologie van Karl Barth*, by G. C. Berkouwer. *Westminster Theological Journal* 18 (1955): 58–59.

85. CVT, *Christianity and Barthianism* (Philadelphia: Presbyterian and Reformed, 1962), 113.

86. CVT to G. Vander Stelt, December 13, 1968, CVT Archives, WTS. (The letter addresses "Professor G. Vander Stelt," but Van Til meant John A. Vander Stelt.)

87. G. C. Berkouwer, *The Triumph of Grace in the Theology of Karl Barth*, trans. Harry R. Boer (Grand Rapids: Eerdmans, 1956), 385, 386, 388.

88. CVT, *The Defense of the Faith* (Philadelphia: Presbyterian and Reformed, 1955), 235.

89. CVT, "Professor Vollenhoven's Significance for Reformed Apologetics," in *Wetenschappelijke Bijdragen: Door Leeringen van Dr. D. H. Th. Vollenhoven Aangeboden ter Gelegenheid van Zijn 25-Jarig Hoogleraarschap aan de Vrije Universiteit*, ed. S. U. Zuidema (Franeker: T. Wever, 1951), 71.

90. CVT, "Herman Dooyeweerd (A Personal Tribute)," *Westminster Theological Journal* 39 (1977): 319.

Chapter 6: Through the Fires of Criticism

1. CVT to J. K. Van Baalen, February 19, 1949, CVT Archives, WTS.

2. *Acts of Synod 1946 of the Christian Reformed Church* (Grand Rapids: Christian Reformed Publishing House, 1946), 13. See also "Christian Reformed Church Sends Fraternal Greetings," *Presbyterian Guardian,* June 25, 1947, 184.

3. *Acts of Synod 1946 of the Christian Reformed Church,* 13.

4. CVT to Henry Van Til, April 14, 1950, Family Letters from Reinder Van Til.

5. CVT to Nicholas J. Monsma, February 16, 1950, CVT Archives, WTS.

6. Ibid.

7. John Bolt, "From Princeton to Wheaton," in *Vicissitudes of Reformed Theology in the Twentieth Century,* ed. George Harinck and Dirk van Keulen (Zoetermeer: Meinema, 2004), 172.

8. CVT, "Common Grace," *Twentieth Century Encyclopedia of Religious Knowledge,* ed. Lefferts A. Loetscher (Grand Rapids: Baker, 1955), 272.

9. CVT to Nicholas J. Monsma, February 14, 1950, CVT Archives, WTS.

10. Robert K. Churchill, review of *Common Grace,* by CVT, *Presbyterian Guardian,* February 25, 1948, 52.

11. CVT, "Calvinism and Art: Common Grace Does Not Solve All the Problems," *Presbyterian Guardian,* December 1948, 272–74. Letters from Paul Woolley and John Murray appeared in the *Presbyterian Guardian,* February 1949, 27, 28–29.

12. Henry R. Van Til, *The Calvinistic Concept of Culture* (Philadelphia: Presbyterian and Reformed, 1959), 141.

13. Ibid., 187.

14. CVT to Henry Van Til, December 20, 1954, Family Letters from Reinder Van Til.

15. "The Reformed Journal," *Reformed Journal* 1 (March 1, 1951): 1.

16. "Why," *Torch and Trumpet,* April–May 1951, 1.

17. Henry Stob, *Summoning up Remembrance* (Grand Rapids: Eerdmans, 1995), 299.

18. CVT to Clarence Bouma, June 14, 1951, CVT Archives, WTS.

19. Paul Woolley to CVT, September 24, 1951, CVT Archives, WTS.

20. Robert Marsden to CVT, October 15, 1951, CVT Archives, WTS.

21. Ned B. Stonehouse to CVT, April 6, 1952, CVT Archives, WTS.

22. George Gritter to CVT, May 2, 1952, CVT Archives, WTS.

23. E. J. Young to CVT, April 6, 1952, CVT Archives, WTS.

24. CVT to Nicholas J. Monsma, February 16, 1950, CVT Archives, WTS.

25. The gift from the Calvin students is found in the CVT Archives, WTS.

26. Thelma Van Til, interview by the author, October 5, 2004.

27. Quoted by Arthur W. Kuschke, interview by the author, October 4, 2004.

28. Stob, *Summoning up Remembrance,* 318.

29. George Stob, "The Christian Reformed Church and Her Schools" (ThD diss., Princeton Theological Seminary, 1955), 439.

30. James D. Bratt, *Dutch Calvinism in Modern America: A History of a Conservative Subculture* (Grand Rapids: Eerdmans, 1984), 191.

31. CVT, *Letter on Common Grace* (Phillipsburg, NJ: L. Grotenhuis, 1952), 64.

32. Edwin H. Palmer, "Caricature," *Calvin Forum* 20 (November 1954): 62–65.

33. CVT to Henry Van Til, September 25, 1952, Family Letters from Reinder Van Til.

34. Robert Churchill, "Largeness of Faith: The Church in Transition," *Presbyterian Guardian*, January 15, 1954, 12.

35. Jesse De Boer, "Professor Van Til's Apologetics, Part 1," *Calvin Forum* 19 (August–September 1953): 12.

36. Jesse De Boer, "Professor Van Til's Apologetics, Part 3," *Calvin Forum* 19 (November 1953): 57.

37. John H. Bratt to CVT, October 22, 1953, CVT Archives, WTS.

38. Nicholas J. Monsma to CVT, October 19, 1953, CVT Archives, WTS.

39. Philip Edgcumbe Hughes to CVT, February 12, 1954, and July 27, 1956, CVT Archives, WTS.

40. Jesse De Boer to CVT, October 22, 1953, CVT Archives, WTS.

41. Henry Stob to the editor of the *Calvin Forum*, March 8, 1954, Calvin College Archives. (Handwritten on the typed letter were the words "not submitted for publication.")

42. Leonard Verduin, "Daane's *Theology of Grace*: A Symposium," *Calvin Forum* 20 (April 1955): 181.

43. James Daane, "An Inherited Epistemology: I," *Calvin Forum* 20 (April 1955): 186.

44. CVT to Henry Van Til, October 4, 1952, Family Letters from Reinder Van Til.

45. Thedford Dirkse, "The Extent of the Antithesis," *Calvin Forum* 19 (March 1954): 147–49.

46. CVT, "Antitheses in Education," in *Fundamentals of Christian Education: Theory and Practice*, ed. Cornelius Jaarsma (Grand Rapids: Eerdmans, 1953), 437.

47. CVT to Henry Van Til, October 22, 1953, Family Letters from Reinder Van Til.

48. CVT, "Antitheses in Education," 451.

49. Ibid., 441.

50. CVT to Henry Van Til, October 4, 1953, Family Letters from Reinder Van Til.

51. CVT to Henry Van Til, May 5, 1955, Family Letters from Reinder Van Til.

52. CVT, "You Are My Witnesses," commencement charge, Westminster Theological Seminary, May 13, 1953.

53. CVT to Henry Van Til, February 14, 1954, Family Letters from Reinder Van Til.

54. CVT journal entry, September 27, 1953, CVT Archives, WTS.

55. John H. Ramsey to CVT, February 24, 1951, and March 10, 1951, CVT Archives, WTS.

56. CVT journal entry, March 16, 1956, CVT Archives, WTS.

57. CVT journal entry, November 24, 1953, CVT Archives, WTS.

58. CVT, *Paul at Athens* (Phillipsburg, NJ: L. Grotenhuis, 1956).

59. CVT, *The Defense of the Faith* (Philadelphia: Presbyterian and Reformed, 1955), 355.

60. CVT, *An Introduction to Systematic Theology* (Nutley, NJ: Presbyterian and Reformed, 1974), 229–30.

61. Robert Letham has argued that Van Til's "one person, three persons" formula was confusing although he affirms Van Til's orthodox intention: "There is no question of God being less than personal." Robert Letham, *The Holy Trinity: In Scripture, History, Theology, and Worship* (Phillipsburg, NJ: P&R, 2004), 181, 462. Lane Tipton has come to Van Til's defense in "The Function of *Perichoresis* and the Divine Incomprehensibility," *Westminster Theological Journal* 64 (2002): 289–306.

62. CVT to Emo F. J. Van Halsema, January 3, 1957, CVT Archives, WTS.

63. CVT, *Christianity and Idealism* (Philadelphia: Presbyterian and Reformed, 1955), 3.

64. CVT journal entry, December 29, 1955, CVT Archives, WTS.

65. James D. Bratt, *Dutch Calvinism in Modern America: A History of a Conservative Subculture* (Grand Rapids: Eerdmans, 1984), 192.

66. CVT journal entry, December 2, 1955, CVT Archives, WTS.

67. Elton M. Eenigenburg, review of *The Defense of the Faith*, by CVT, *Reformed Review* 10 (October 1956): 53–54, and quoted in *Torch and Trumpet*, November 1956, 23.

68. James Daane, to the editor of the *Calvin Forum* 14 (October 1948): 49.

69. Henry Stob, "Observations on the Concept of the Antithesis," in *Perspectives on the Christian Reformed Church: Studies in Its History, Theology, and Ecumenicity,* ed. Peter De Klerk and Richard R. De Ridder (Grand Rapids: Baker, 1983), 245.

70. Herman Hoeksema, quoted by James Daane, "An Inherited Epistemology—I," *Calvin Forum* 20 (April 1955): 187n.

71. William Young, "Daane's 'A Theology of Grace,'" *Calvin Forum* 20 (April 1955): 179; John H. Stek, review of *The Theology of James Daane*, by CVT, *Banner*, October 16, 1959, 28; and S. J. Ridderbos, "Daane on Van Til," *Reformed Journal* 5 (February 1955): 9–12.

72. CVT, *The Defense of the Faith*, 214.

73. Norman Shepherd to CVT, September 27, 1960, CVT Archives, WTS; CVT, *Equal Ultimacy* (Philadelphia: privately printed, 1960 or 1961).

74. CVT, "Herman Dooyeweerd (A Personal Tribute)," *Westminster Theological Journal* 39 (1978): 327.

75. CVT to Alexander C. DeJong, September 28, 1962, CVT Archives, WTS.

76. CVT to H. J. Kuiper, December 9, 1958, CVT Archives, WTS.

77. CVT to Henry Van Til, September 5, 1951, Family Letters from Reinder Van Til.

78. CVT, *The Triumph of Grace: The Heidelberg Catechism* (Philadelphia: Westminster Theological Seminary, 1962).

79. CVT to William Hendriksen, January 18, 1956, CVT Archives, WTS.

80. CVT to unknown addressee, October 22, 1953, CVT Archives, WTS.

81. *Torch and Trumpet,* May–April 1953, 27.

Chapter 7: Presbyterian Patriarch

1. "John J. DeWaard Dies Suddenly," *Presbyterian Guardian,* August 25, 1959, 214–15, 222.

2. CVT to R. J. Rushdoony, February 26, 1967, CVT Archives, WTS. The reference here is to Bishop Joseph Butler (1693–1752), whose work *The Analogy of Religion* (1736) was Van Til's favorite example of the bankruptcy of classical apologetics.

3. CVT to Robert M. Nuermberger, November 22, 1967, CVT Archives, WTS.

4. CVT, "The New Evangelicalism," *Presbyterian Guardian,* October 15, 1957, 131–32.

5. Harold Ockenga, quoted in "New Evangelism," *Presbyterian Guardian,* December 16, 1957, 175.

6. John Mackay, quoted in Monroe Parker, *Frontline,* July–August 1991, 25.

7. CVT, *The New Evangelicalism* (Philadelphia: Westminster Theological Seminary, 1960), 47.

8. Ibid., 34, 29–30.

9. Ibid., 40.

10. Ronald Nash to D. A. Wait, November 30, 1962, CVT Archives, WTS.

11. CVT, *The Defense of the Faith* (Philadelphia: Presbyterian and Reformed, 1955), 316.

12. "Van Til Honored by Wheaton Philosophers," *Presbyterian Guardian,* November 16, 1959, 299.

13. Carl F. H. Henry to CVT, September 11, 1961, CVT Archives, WTS.

14. "The Evangelical Undertow," *Time,* December 20, 1963, 57.

15. CVT to Ronald Nash, October 4, 1963, CVT Archives, WTS.

16. CVT, *A Christian Theory of Knowledge* (Nutley, NJ: Presbyterian and Reformed, 1969), 5.

17. CVT, "The Reformation Today," in *The God of Hope: Sermons and Addresses* (Phillipsburg, NJ: Presbyterian and Reformed, 1978), 181.

18. "Editor's Note" that accompanied Walter R. Martin, "More About Karl Barth," *Eternity,* November 1959, 21. The reaction of Van Til's students to this piece is described in a letter from CVT to Gilbert and Jessie den Dulk, November 1, 1959, CVT Archives, WTS.

19. Donald Grey Barnhouse to CVT, September 27, 1954, CVT Archives, WTS.

20. CVT to Karl Barth, December 21, 1965, CVT Archives, WTS.

21. Karl Barth to Geoffrey Bromiley, June 1, 1961, quoted in Eberhard Busch, *Karl Barth: His Life from Letters and Autobiographical Texts* (Grand Rapids: Eerdmans, 1994), 380; CVT, "Has Karl Barth Become Orthodox?" *Westminster Theological Journal* 16 (1954): 181.

22. CVT, *Christianity and Barthianism* (Philadelphia: Presbyterian and Reformed, 1962), 446.

23. Ibid., vii.

24. Carl F. H. Henry, review of *Christianity and Liberalism,* by CVT, *Christianity Today,* December 21, 1962, 303.

25. James Daane, review of *Christianity and Barthianism,* by CVT, *Reformed Journal* 13 (January 1963): 29.

26. Van Til, *Christianity and Liberalism* (Philadelphia: Presbyterian and Reformed, 1962), 445–46.

27. Karl Barth, quoted by Martin, "More About Karl Barth," 22.

28. "Witness to an Ancient Truth," *Time,* April 20, 1962, 59.

29. Arthur W. Kuschke, interview by the author, October 4, 2004.

30. Karl Barth to Edward Geehan, November 14, 1965, CVT Archives, WTS.

31. CVT to Karl Barth, December 21, 1965, CVT Archives, WTS.

32. CVT to Fred Klooster, November 19, 1968, CVT Archives, WTS.

33. Edward John Carnell, "Barth as Inconsistent Evangelical," *Christian Century* 79 (June 6, 1962): 713–14.

34. CVT to William Gray, August 13, 1962, CVT Archives, WTS.

35. E. J. Carnell, *An Introduction to Christian Apologetics* (Grand Rapids: Eerdmans, 1948), 178.

36. Another factor not to be overlooked in Van Til's reaction to Carnell was his displeasure for the way in which Carnell had turned on J. Gresham Machen in *The Case for Orthodox Theology.*

37. R. B. Kuiper to CVT, May 7, 1965, CVT Archives, WTS.

38. CVT, "Report on the Reformed-Lutheran Conversations," in *Minutes of the Thirty-first General Assembly of the Orthodox Presbyterian Church* (Philadelphia: OPC, 1964), 103.

39. Herman Otten to CVT, August 13, 1964, CVT Archives, WTS. See also CVT, "Martin E. Marty," *Lutheran News,* May 18,1964, 9–11.

40. CVT, cover letter accompanying distribution of *The Confession of 1967,* May 1967, CVT Archives, WTS.

41. CVT, *The Confession of 1967: Its Theological Background and Ecumenical Significance* (Philadelphia: Presbyterian and Reformed, 1967), 88.

42. Edmund P. Clowney, *Another Foundation: The Presbyterian Confessional Crisis* (Philadelphia: Presbyterian and Reformed, 1965), 4.

43. CVT, *The Confession of 1967,* 84.

44. Francis A. Schaeffer, *The God Who Is There: Speaking Historic Christianity into the Twentieth Century* (Downers Grove, IL: InterVarsity Press, 1968), 17.

45. Francis A. Schaeffer, *Death in the City* (Downers Grove, IL: InterVarsity Press, 1969), 130; Van Til's criticism can be found in a letter from CVT to David Dean, April 23, 1969, CVT Archives, WTS.

46. CVT, preface to "The Apologetic Methodology of Francis A. Schaeffer" (privately printed, 1972 or 1973).

47. William Edgar, "No News Is Good News," *Westminster Theological Journal* 57 (1995): 359–82.

48. John Gerstner to CVT, February 20, 1960; CVT to Gerstner, February 26, 1960, CVT Archives, WTS.

49. *The Book of Church Order of the Orthodox Presbyterian Church,* rev. ed. (Philadelphia: Great Commission Publications, 1988), 299.

50. CVT, *Christianity in Conflict,* vol. 2, pt. 3, "Biblical Dimensionalism" (Philadelphia: Westminster Theological Seminary, 1966), 10, 49.

51. CVT to Fred Klooster, January 9, 1970, CVT Archives, WTS.

52. CVT to Henry Van Andel, August 16, 1962, CVT Archives, WTS.

53. CVT to Nick Van Til, May 19, 1966, Family Letters from Reinder Van Til.

54. Fred Klooster to CVT, January 28, 1973, CVT Archives, WTS. The draft report was commonly referred to as "Report 36," and the final report as "Report 44."

55. CVT to R. J. Rushdoony, May 22, 1961, CVT Archives, WTS.

56. T. Grady Spires, "A Tribute to Cornelius Van Til," *Christianity Today*, December 30, 1977, 20.

57. CVT to Harold Lindsell, December 17, 1968, CVT Archives, WTS.

58. "Response by C. Van Til" to Paul K. Jewett, in *Jerusalem and Athens: Critical Discussions on the Theology and Apologetics of Cornelius Van Til,* ed. E. R. Geehan (Nutley, NJ: Presbyterian and Reformed, 1971), 226–27.

59. CVT to E. R. Geehan, May 28, 1970, CVT Archives, WTS.

60. Fred Klooster to CVT, January 30, 1972, CVT Archives, WTS.

61. CVT to Meredith G. Kline, March 20, 1968, CVT Archives, WTS.

62. CVT to Paul Woolley, May 15, 1966, CVT Archives, WTS.

63. Ibid.

64. CVT to T. Grady Spires, January 6, 1972, CVT Archives, WTS.

65. Edmund P. Clowney, "Molded by the Gospel," *Presbyterian Guardian,* May 1969, 57.

66. CVT to Fred Klooster, January 12, 1968, CVT Archives, WTS. See also John M. Frame, *Cornelius Van Til: An Analysis of His Thought* (Phillipsburg, NJ: P&R, 1995).

67. Quoted in the *Presbyterian Guardian,* May 1969, 69.

68. Richard B. Gaffin Jr., "The Scandal of the Cross," sermon from 1 Corinthians 1:18–25 preached in a memorial service for CVT, Westminster Theological Seminary, May 27, 1987.

Chapter 8: Steadfast, Unmovable, and Abounding

1. CVT, "Joshua's Appeal to Covenant Consciousness," in *The God of Hope: Sermons and Addresses* (Phillipsburg, NJ: Presbyterian and Reformed, 1978), 47, 48, 49.

2. Ibid., 50, 52.

3. Meredith G. Kline to CVT, May 1970, CVT Archives, WTS. A year later, Kline dedicated his *Structure of Biblical Authority* to Van Til, acknowledging that Van Til had "by far the most profound impact on my thinking of all my teachers."

4. Lewis Smedes to CVT, April 23, 1970, CVT Archives, WTS.

5. Lawrence Eyres to CVT, April 17, 1970, CVT Archives, WTS.

6. CVT, "The Certainty of Our Faith," *Presbyterian Guardian,* August/September 1973, 102–6.

7. "In the Beginning, God: An Interview with Cornelius Van Til," *Christianity Today,* December 30, 1977, 21.

8. J. Van Bruggen, "An Interview with Prof. C. Van Til," *Outlook* 28 (July 1978): 14–17.

9. CVT, *Toward a Reformed Apologetics* (Philadelphia: privately printed, 1972), 3.

10. CVT to unknown addressee, March 21, 1974, CVT Archives, WTS.

11. Scott Oliphint, "The Consistency of Van Til's Methodology," *Westminster Theological Journal* 52 (1990): 48, 49.

12. CVT, quoted in Ian Murray, *Life of John Murray* (Edinburgh: Banner of Truth, 1984), 153, 158.

13. CVT, undated journal entry, probably January 1979, on the anniversary of Rena's death, CVT Archives, WTS.

14. Paul Woolley to CVT, January 12, 1978, CVT Archives, WTS.

15. CVT to John Huizenga, September 9, 1983, Calvin College Archives.

16. CVT, "J. Oliver Buswell: Valiant for Truth," *Presbyterion* 2 (1976): 135–37.

17. Robert G. den Dulk, "Cornelius Van Til," from Banner of Truth Trust West Coast Conference; found at: https://www.banneroftruth.org/pages/articles/article_detail.php?234.

18. CVT, "Herman Dooyeweerd (A Personal Tribute)," *Westminster Theological Journal* 39 (1978): 327.

19. CVT, "A Tribute to My Colleagues," *Presbyterian Guardian,* May 1969, 68.

20. Jonathan Male, "Dr. Van Til, a Good and Faithful Servant," *New Horizons in the Orthodox Presbyterian Church* 16 (May 1995), 15.

21. Henry W. Coray, "After Fifty Years," *New Horizons in the Orthodox Presbyterian Church,* June–July 1986, 2.

22. Described in CVT to Gilbert den Dulk, April 14, 1959, CVT Archives.

23. CVT to Robert Drake, November 7, 1972, CVT Archives, WTS.

24. R. J. Rushdoony to CVT, February 27, 1967, CVT Archives, WTS.

25. R. J. Rushdoony to CVT, January 17, 1970, CVT Archives, WTS.

26. Gary North to CVT, February 12, 1971, CVT Archives, WTS.

27. CVT to Gregg Singer, May 11, 1972, CVT Archives, WTS.

28. Ibid.

29. Gary North, quoted in Anson Shupe, "The Reconstructionist Movement on the Christian Right," *Christian Century* 106 (October 4, 1989): 881.

30. Greg L. Bahnsen, *Theonomy in Christian Ethics* (Nutley, NJ: Craig Press, 1977), iii; CVT, *Christian Theistic Ethics* (Philadelphia: den Dulk Christian Foundation, 1971), 134.

31. Meredith G. Kline, "Comments on an Old-New Error," *Westminster Theological Journal* 41 (1978): 188.

32. T. David Gordon, email to the author, July 24, 2003. See also his "Van Til and Theonomic Ethics," in *Creator, Redeemer, Consummator: A Festschrift for Meredith G. Kline*, ed. Howard Griffith and John R. Muether, 271–78 (Greenville, SC: Reformed Academic Press, 2000).

33. Kline, "Comments on an Old-New Error," 178.

34. R. J. Rushdoony, *Institutes of Biblical Law* (Nutley, NJ: Craig Press, 1973), 687.

35. Gary North, *Dominion and Common Grace* (Tyler, TX: Institute for Christian Economics, 1987), 9.

36. CVT to Charles McIlhenny, February 24, 1967, CVT Archives, WTS.

37. Greg L. Bahnsen, *Van Til's Apologetic: Readings and Analysis* (Phillipsburg, NJ: P&R, 1988), 22n65.

38. Robert P. Swieringa, *Dutch Chicago: A History of the Hollanders in the Windy City* (Grand Rapids: Eerdmans, 2002), 676.

39. John M. Frame, "Toward a Theology of the State," *Westminster Theological Journal* 51 (1989): 199–226; Edmund P. Clowney, "The Politics of the Kingdom," *Westminster Theological Journal* 41 (1979): 291–310.

40. See William Edgar, "Francis Schaeffer and the Public Square," in *Evangelicals in the Public Square*, ed. J. Budziszewski (Grand Rapids: Baker, 2006), 169.

41. J. Van Bruggen, "An Interview with Prof. C. Van Til," *Outlook* 28 (July 1978): 16.

42. CVT to Jim West, March 29, 1974, CVT Archives, WTS.

43. Robert B. Strimple, email to the author, January 10, 2005.

44. One account of the controversy by a former member of the Westminster faculty is O. Palmer Robertson, *The Current Justification Controversy* (Unicoi, TN: Trinity Foundation, 2003).

45. Harvie M. Conn, *Eternal Word and Changing Worlds: Theology, Anthropology, and Mission in Trialogue* (1984; reprint, Phillipsburg, NJ: P&R, 1992), 255.

46. CVT, "Why Westminster Today," unpublished manuscript, ca. 1970, CVT Archives, WTS.

47. Jack Sawyer, personal correspondence to the author, February 7, 2006.

48. CVT, "More Catechism Needed," *Presbyterian Guardian*, November 1976, 2.

49. CVT, "Westminster Divine Notes Editorial Weakness," *Banner*, November 7, 1975, 20; "Bill Bright Is Not Right," *Banner*, June 3, 1977, 24.

50. Quoted in Swierenga, *Dutch Chicago*, 66.

51. Steven F. Miller, email to the author, January 17, 2005; see also *WTS Bulletin* 1987, number 4.

52. *Minutes of the Fifty-fourth General Assembly of the Orthodox Presbyterian Church* (Philadelphia: OPC, 1987), 40.

53. Robert D. Knudsen, "In Memoriam: Cornelius Van Til," *New Horizons in the Orthodox Presbyterian Church,* June–July 1987, 19.

54. Richard B. Gaffin Jr., "The Scandal of the Cross," sermon from 1 Corinthians 1:18–25 preached in a memorial service for CVT, Westminster Theological Seminary, May 27, 1987.

55. Ibid.

56. John M. Frame, *Cornelius Van Til: An Analysis of His Thought* (Phillipsburg, NJ: P&R, 1995), 389. The changing character of the WTS curriculum was evident in a study of alumni by the author in 1989. Among the findings: whereas Van Til and Murray were by far the most influential faculty among graduates in the 1950s and 1960s, by the 1980s professors of biblical studies (Dillard, Poythress, and Gaffin—then professor of New Testament) had eclipsed systematicians and apologists in their impact on students.

Conclusion: Against the World, for the Church

1. CVT to John DeWaard, February 27, 1940, CVT Archives, WTS.

2. CVT, "Why Westminster Today," unpublished manuscript, ca. 1970, CVT Archives, WTS.

3. John W. Stewart, "Introducing Charles Hodge to Postmoderns," in *Charles Hodge Revisited*, ed. John W. Stewart and James H. Moorhead (Grand Rapids: Eerdmans, 2002), 1.

4. CVT to Bouma (first name unclear), June 14, 1951, CVT Archives, WTS.

5. William Shea, *The Lion and the Lamb: Evangelicals and Catholics in America* (New York: Oxford University Press, 2004), 151.

6. John M. Frame, *Cornelius Van Til: An Analysis of His Thought* (Phillipsburg, NJ: P&R, 1995), 397.

7. Gary North, *Dominion and Common Grace: The Biblical Basis of Progress* (Tyler, TX.: Institute for Christian Economics, 1987), 9–10.

8. CVT, "Calvin as a Controversialist," *Torch and Trumpet*, July–August 1959, 5. The subsequent article by Van Til with the same title was published in R. C. Sproul, ed., *Soli Deo Gloria: Essays in Reformed Theology, Festschrift for John H. Gerstner* (Nutley, NJ: Presbyterian and Reformed, 1976), 1–10.

9. John Stackhouse, *Humble Apologetics: Defending the Faith Today* (Oxford: Oxford University Press, 2002).

10. Carl Raschke, *The Next Reformation: Why Evangelicals Must Embrace Postmodernity* (Grand Rapids: Baker, 2004), 100–101.

11. CVT, "Calvin as a Controversialist," in Sproul, ed. *Soli Deo Gloria*, 8.

12. William Edgar, introduction to CVT, *Christian Apologetics*, 2nd ed., ed. William Edgar (Phillipsburg, NJ: P&R, 2003), 8, 10.

13. CVT, *The Triumph of Grace: The Heidelberg Catechism*, vol. 1, "Introduction" (Philadelphia: Westminster Theological Seminary, 1962)

Bibliographic Essay

*L*ester DeKoster might not have despaired about Van Til's "scattered writings" had he had access to *The Works of Cornelius Van Til, 1895–1987,* a CD-ROM edited by Eric H. Sigward and produced by the Logos Library System. The searchable CD includes full texts of 30 books, 11 pamphlets, 22 manuscripts, 136 articles (in English and Dutch), and 75 book reviews, as well as 52 hours of audio recordings. The CD includes some important obscure material, such as Van Til's "Letter from America" that he wrote in Dutch for *De Reformatie* and the commencement charges he delivered to Westminster Seminary graduates in the 1950s.

The CD-ROM also includes a bibliography compiled by Eric D. Bristley, *A Guide to the Writings of Cornelius Van Til, 1895–1987* (Chicago: Olive Tree Publications, 1995). Bristley's comprehensive work is chronologically arranged and carefully annotated in ways that account for Van Til's frequent recycling of material in subsequent publications.

Van Til's papers and correspondence are housed in the library of Westminster Seminary in Philadelphia. Westminster's archives also include among the J. Gresham Machen papers some correspondence between Van Til and Machen. Reinder Van Til graciously made available to me additional letters from Van Til to his nephew Henry Van Til (Reinder's father).

265

According to John Frame, Van Til's best-known works are these: *The New Modernism* (1946), *Common Grace* (1947), *The Defense of the Faith* (1955), *Christianity and Barthianism* (1979), and *A Christian Theology of Knowledge* (1979), all published by Presbyterian and Reformed. (As noted in chapter 7, the second edition of *The Defense of the Faith* is considerably abridged. Also, P&R's forthcoming annotated version of the first edition restores Van Til's polemics against his Christian Reformed adversaries. This revision is a part of P&R's current project to reissue several of Van Til's syllabi in attractive new editions.)

New readers looking for an entry into Van Til's thought would best begin with Van Til's two pamphlets, *Why I Believe in God* (Philadelphia: Committee on Christian Education of the OPC, 1948), *The Intellectual Challenge of the Gospel* (London: Tyndale House, 1950), as well as his essay, "My Credo" (which first appeared in the Festschrift, *Jerusalem and Athens*). Van Til's own assessment of his literary output is found in *Toward a Reformed Apologetics* (Philadelphia: privately printed, 1972). Generally underappreciated and often ignored in assessments of Van Til's corpus is his *Confession of 1967: Its Theological Background and Ecumenical Significance* (Philadelphia: Presbyterian and Reformed, 1967).

Rousas J. Rushdoony was the first to popularize Van Til's writings in two books: *By What Standard? An Analysis of the Philosophy of Cornelius Van Til* (Fairfax, VA: Thoburn Press, 1958) and *Van Til* (Philadelphia: Presbyterian and Reformed, 1960). The latter, a booklet, was part of the publisher's Modern Thinkers Series in its International Library of Philosophy and Theology. Other popularizations include John Frame, *Van Til, the Theologian* (Phillipsburg, NJ: Pilgrim, 1976); Jim S. Halsey, *For a Time Such as This: An Introduction to the Reformed Apologetic of Cornelius Van Til* (Nutley, NJ: Presbyterian and Reformed, 1976); Thom Notaro, *Van Til and the Use of Evidence* (Phillipsburg, NJ: Presbyterian and Reformed, 1980); and Richard L. Pratt Jr., *Every Thought Captive: A Study Manual for the Defense of Christian Truth* (Phillipsburg, NJ: Presbyterian and Reformed, 1979).

After Van Til's death, John M. Frame and Greg L. Bahnsen undertook more ambitious efforts. Frame's *Cornelius Van Til: An Analysis of His Thought* (Phillipsburg, NJ: P&R, 1995) is a thorough exploration of Van Til's teaching, though the author uses an idiosyncratic "multi-perspectival" hermeneutic through which to interpret Van Til's presuppositionalism, producing more of a creative expansion of Van Til's thought than a historical expression. A particularly helpful feature of Frame's book is its annotated bibliography (pp. 445–52). Bahnsen's *Van Til's Apologetic: Readings and Analysis* (Phillipsburg, NJ: P&R, 1998) is a solid systematization of Van Til's work, although it lacks sufficient attention to the redemptive-historical elements in Van Til's thought. Bahnsen organizes selections from Van Til's writings into nine chapters, each with helpful introductory essays and extensive interpretive notes.

The first major critical assessment of Van Til's thought is the 1971 Festschrift, *Jerusalem and Athens: Critical Discussion on the Philosophy and Apologetics of Cornelius Van Til*, edited by E. R. Geehan (Nutley, NJ: Presbyterian and Reformed). This remarkably diverse anthology includes works by interlocutors from Europe (G. C. Berkouwer, H. Dooyeweerd, and H. Ridderbos) and South Africa (H. G. Stoker), along with some former students (R. B. Gaffin Jr., R. D. Knudsen, and W. S. Reid) and critics (P. K. Jewett, J. W. Montgomery, and an early Clark Pinnock). Most of the contributions include a response by Van Til. A generally theonomic interpretation of Van Til's thought is advanced in a second Festschrift, *Foundations of Christian Scholarship: Essays in the Van Til Perspective*, edited by Gary North (Vallecito, CA: Ross House, 1976). This work applies Van Til's thought to academic disciplines such as psychology, economics, political science, and mathematics. (Bibliographic references on Van Til's relationship with the theonomic movement follow below.) The *Westminster Theological Journal* issued a third Festschrift, of sorts, on the centennial of Van Til's birth. The Spring 1995 issue (vol. 57, no. 1) featured reflections on Van Til's work by William Dennison, William Edgar, John Frame, Richard Gaffin, and Scott Oliphint. A more recent anthology on Van Til's apologetics is *Revelation and Reason: New Essays in Reformed Apologetics*, edited by K. Scott Oliphint and Lane G. Tipton (Phillipsburg, NJ: P&R, 2007).

Several Westminster Seminary professors have contributed analyses of Van Til's thought and works. Edmund P. Clowney underscores the importance of Van Til's preaching in his article, "Preaching the Word of the Lord: Cornelius Van Til, V.D.M.," *Westminster Theological Journal* (hereafter *WTJ*) 46 (1984): 233–53. William Edgar assesses the impact of Van Til's work in his introductions to new editions of Van Til's *Christian Apologetics* (Phillipsburg, NJ: P&R, 2003) and *An Introduction to Systematic Theology* (Phillipsburg, NJ: P&R, 2007). Also, see K. Scott Oliphint's "The Consistency of Van Til's Methodology," *WTJ* 52 (1990): 27–49.

In his *Paul's Two-Age Construction and Apologetics* (Lanham, MD: University Press of America, 1986), William D. Dennison stands out among Van Tilian interpreters by underscoring the central (though at times latent) eschatological aspects of Van Til's Reformed apologetics.

On applying Van Til's presuppositional thinking to Christian education, see Gregory Maffet, "The Educational Thought of Cornelius Van Til: An Analysis of the Ideological Foundations of his Thought" (EdD diss., University of Akron, 1984).

As noted in the introduction, William White's *Van Til: Defender of the Faith* (Nashville: Thomas Nelson, 1979) is the first book-length biography of Van Til. This "authorized biography" is rich with many personal anecdotes of a longtime close friend. Wesley A. Roberts contributes a chapter on Van Til in the 1985 anthology edited by David F. Wells, *Reformed Theology in America* (Grand Rapids: Eerdmans, 1985). John Robbins's long-standing animus finds expression in his vitriolic pamphlet, *Cornelius Van Til: The Man and the Myth* (Jefferson, MD: Trinity Foundation, 1986).

A valuable source of biographical information on Van Til is the *Presbyterian Guardian,* an independent magazine whose publication life (1935–79) was virtually coterminous with Van Til's professional career. In addition to publishing more than sixty of Van Til's articles and reviews, the *Guardian* chronicled much of his seminary activities and pastoral labors. An indispensable aid in accessing the *Guardian* is James T. Dennison's *Cumulative Index to the Presbyterian Guardian* (Escondido, CA: privately published, 1985). Researchers should also note the predecessor to the *Guardian, Christianity Today* (1930–41), which published some of Van Til's very early work.

Like the works of his colleagues at Westminster Seminary, many of Van Til's books first appeared as articles in the *Westminster Theological Journal,* to which he contributed a dozen articles and over fifty reviews. Van Til also authored fourteen articles in the *Torch and Trumpet* from 1951 to 1961. And for accessing Van Til's writing in the Dutch Reformed community, The Christian Reformed Church Periodical Index (available at: http://www.calvin.edu/library/database/crcpi/) is a helpful tool.

Several historical studies of the Dutch immigration experience in America are valuable for exploring Van Til's sociological background. Two massive works that well describe the context of Van Til's Dutch-American upbringing are Robert P. Swierenga's *Dutch Chicago: A History of Hollanders in the Windy City* (Grand Rapids: Eerdmans, 2002) and Jacob Van Hinte's *Netherlanders in America: A Study of Emigration and Settlement in the Nineteenth and Twentieth Centuries in the United States of America* (Grand Rapids: Baker, 1985). Some of the titles in the Historical Series of the Reformed Church in America (edited by Donald J. Bruggink) help to piece together the different factions of Dutch-American life, especially *Family Quarrels in the Dutch Reformed Churches in the Nineteenth Century,* by Elton Bruins and Robert P. Swieringa (Grand Rapids: Eerdmans, 1999). Above all, readers should take note of James D. Bratt's masterful *Dutch Calvinism in America: A History of a Conservative Subculture* (Grand Rapids: Eerdmans, 1984). Abraham Kuyper's particular impact in America is described in John Bolt's study, *A Free Church, a Holy Nation: Abraham Kuyper's American Public Theology* (Grand Rapids: Eerdmans, 2001). The English-speaking Reformed world is finally able to begin assessing Herman Bavinck's deep influence on Van Til as Bavinck's four-volume *Gereformeerde Dogmatiek* is translated into English: *Reformed Dogmatics,* edited by John Bolt, translated by John Vriend (Grand Rapids, Baker, 2003–8).

Broader interpretations of the religious experience of American ethnic immigrants can be found in Sydney Allstrom's *A Religious*

History of the American People (New Haven: Yale, 1972) and Mark A. Noll's *The Old Religion in the New World* (Grand Rapids: Eerdmans, 2002).

The Hekman Library of Calvin College and Seminary contains a wealth of information about the school during Van Til's college days, including a complete set of the student newspaper, *The Chimes*, and college yearbooks. Its Heritage Hall archives house church records and other resources about the Christian Reformed congregations within which Van Til grew up, as well as the Spring Lake, Michigan, church that he briefly pastored. Calvin College histories include Harry Boonstra's *Our School: Calvin College and the Christian Reformed Church* (Grand Rapids: Eerdmans, 2001) and John J. Timmerman's *Promises to Keep: A Centennial History of Calvin College* (Grand Rapids: Calvin College and Seminary, 1975).

Princeton Seminary's history has been well chronicled. Particularly rich in detail is David B. Calhoun's two-volume history, *Princeton Seminary* (Edinburgh: Banner of Truth, 1994–96). For an overview of Princeton University during Van Til's student days, readers should consult *The Princeton Graduate School: A History*, by Willard Thorp, Minor Myers Jr., and Jeremiah Stanton Finch (Princeton NJ: Princeton University, 1978).

Several studies on the history of the Orthodox Presbyterian Church include various references to Van Til's role in the OPC. Two standard biographies of the denomination's founding leader are by Ned B. Stonehouse, *J. Gresham Machen: A Biographical Memoir* (Grand Rapids: Eerdmans, 1954; reprinted, Willow Grove, PA: Committee for the Historian of the OPC, 2004), and D. G. Hart, *Defending the Faith: J. Gresham Machen and the Crisis of Conservative Protestantism in Modern America* (Baltimore: Johns Hopkins University Press, 1994). The Committee for the Historian of the Orthodox Presbyterian Church has published additional resources on the denomination's history, including *Fighting the Good Fight: A Brief History of the Orthodox Presbyterian Church,* by D. G. Hart and John R. Muether (Philadelphia: Committee for the Historian of the OPC, 1995). Van Til's role in the emerging identity of the OPC is a prominent feature in Charles G. Dennison's *History for a Pilgrim People: The Historical*

Writings of Charles G. Dennison, edited by Danny Olinger and David K. Thompson (Willow Grove, PA: Committee for the Historian of the OPC, 2002). Dennison also conducted many oral history interviews of key figures in the Orthodox Presbyterian Church, including Van Til himself (on Dec. 15, 1982) and many of his contemporaries. These interviews are stored in the archives of the Orthodox Presbyterian Church (currently housed in the library of Westminster Theological Seminary in Philadelphia).

Other studies of the so-called fundamentalist-modernist controversy of the 1920s and 1930s include *The Presbyterian Conflict*, by Edwin Rian (Grand Rapids: Eerdmans, 1940; reprinted, Philadelphia: Committee for the Historian of the OPC, 1992), *The Broadening Church: A Study of Theological Issues in the Presbyterian Church since 1869*, by Lefferts A. Loetscher (Philadelphia: University of Pennsylvania Press, 1954), and *The Presbyterian Controversy*, by Bradley J. Longfield (New York: Oxford University Press, 1991).

Sources on the 1937 disruption in the OPC and at Westminster Theological Seminary include George P. Hutchison, *The History Behind the Reformed Presbyterian Church, Evangelical Synod* (Cherry Hill, NJ: Mack, 1974) and George Marsden, "Perspective on the Division of 1937," in *Pressing Toward the Mark: Essays Commemorating Fifty Years of the Orthodox Presbyterian Church*, edited by Charles G. Dennison and Richard C. Gamble, 295–328 (Philadelphia: Committee for the Historian of the OPC, 1986). The PCA Historical Center Archives in St. Louis contains additional resources on this disruption, including the papers of J. Oliver Buswell and Allan MacRae.

A definitive history of Westminster Theological Seminary has yet to be composed. Several perspectives by present and former faculty members are collected in the Festschrift for Robert B. Strimple edited by David VanDrunen, *The Pattern of Sound Doctrine: Systematic Theology at the Westminster Seminaries* (Phillipsburg, NJ: P&R, 2004). O. Palmer Robertson discusses recent controversies at Westminster Seminary and the Orthodox Presbyterian Church in his booklet, *The Current Justification Controversy* (Unicoi, TN: Trinity Foundation, 2003). Sinclair Ferguson surveys the early years of the *Westminster*

Theological Journal in "'The Whole Counsel of God': Fifty Years of Theological Studies," *WTJ* 50 (1988): 257–81.

The Gordon Clark controversy has generated its own paper trail. Much of the debate can be traced through the minutes of the twelfth General Assembly of the OPC (1945, pp. 5–30), thirteenth General Assembly (1946, pp. 38–83), and fifteenth General Assembly (1948, appendix, 1–96). Herman Hoeksema's *The Clark–Van Til Controversy* (Hobbs, NM: Trinity Forum, 1995), originally a series of articles that Hoeksema composed for the *Standard Bearer*, reveal his sympathies for Clark's hyper-Calvinistic leanings. John Frame devotes a chapter to the controversy in his *Van Til: An Analysis of his Thought*. Remarkably, Frame goes on to describe himself as appalled at the way other interpreters included the larger evangelical struggle. Similarly, Robert Strong dismisses Van Til's involvement in a lecture he delivered at Reformed Theological Seminary in 1977, "The Gordon H. Clark Case" (a copy of which is housed in the Reformed Theological Seminary [Jackson] library). Both Strong and Frame wrote about the controversy after leaving the OPC themselves, and their accounts are marred by their disillusionment with their former church. Similarly, John Robbins denies the broader evangelical coalition that used Clark for the pursuit of its agenda in the OPC. See his *Can the Orthodox Presbyterian Church be Saved?* (Unicoi, TN: Trinity Foundation, 2004). On the epistemological differences between Van Til and Clark, Robert L. Reymond seeks middle ground in *The Justification of Knowledge: An Introductory Study in Christian Apologetic Methodology* (Nutley, NJ: Presbyterian and Reformed, 1976).

The broader ecclesiastical dimensions of the controversy are described in Edward Heerema's *Whither the Orthodox Presbyterian Church?* (Wyckoff, NJ: privately published, 1947). Michael Hakkenburg's article, "The Battle over the Ordination of Gordon H. Clark," pp. 329–50 in *Pressing Toward the Mark*, remains the most definitive account of the debate. Also important is Fred H. Klooster's doctoral dissertation at the Free University of Amsterdam, *The Incomprehensibility of God in the Orthodox Presbyterian Conflict* (Franeker: T. Wever, 1951).

For discussions of Van Til's formulations of the Trinity, one should consult Lane G. Tipton, "The Triune Personal God: Trinitarian Theology in the Thought of Cornelius Van Til" (PhD diss., Westminster Theological Seminary, 2004), and Ralph A. Smith, *Paradox and Truth: Rethinking Van Til on the Trinity by Comparing Van Til, Plantinga, Kuyper* (Moscow, ID: Canon, 2002). Robert Letham locates Van Til among other modern Trinitarian developments in *The Holy Trinity: In Scripture, History, Theology, and Worship* (Phillipsburg, NJ: P&R, 2004).

Gregory C. Bolich notes the role that Van Til played in early evaluations of Barth and the transition in American thinking in his *Karl Barth and Evangelicalism* (Downers Grove IL: InterVarsity Press, 1980). See also the extensive treatment of Van Til in Phillip R. Thorne, *Evangelicalism and Karl Barth: His Reception and Influence in North American Evangelical Theology* (Allison Park, PA: Pickwick Publications, 1995). Evangelical reappraisal of Barth began with G. C. Berkouwer's *The Triumph of Grace in the Theology of Karl Barth*, translated by Harry R. Boer (Grand Rapids: Eerdmans, 1956). In the appendix (pp. 384–93) Berkouwer challenges Van Til's interpretation of Barth. Recently, Kevin Vanhoozer takes Van Til to task for his "hermeneutic of epistemological suspicion" in "A Person of the Book? Barth on Biblical Authority and Interpretation," Van Hoozer's contribution to *Karl Barth and Evangelical Theology: Convergences and Divergences*, edited by Sung Wook Chung (Grand Rapids: Baker, 2006).

On Van Til's formulation of common grace, Sinclair Ferguson's aforementioned article, "The Whole Counsel of God," provides a helpful summary. For Van Til's debates in the Christian Reformed church, consult the extensive interactions in the *Calvin Forum*. For a lively account of the Calvin Seminary during Van Til's semester as visiting professor, see George Stob's doctoral dissertation, "The Christian Reformed Church and Her School" (ThD diss., Princeton Theological Seminary, 1955). Later skirmishes are described in Henry Stob's autobiographical *Summoning up Remembrance* (Grand Rapids: Eerdmans, 1995). Stob also examines Van Til's influence within the CRC in his "Observations on the Concept of the Antithesis," in *Perspectives on the Christian Reformed Church: Studies in Its History, Theology, and Ecumenicity*, edited by Peter De Klerk and Richard R. De Ridder, 241–58 (Grand Rapids: Baker, 1983). By connecting Van Til's view on the antithesis to Herman Hoeksema's, Stob follows James Daane's charge that Van Til, Hoeksema, and Louis Berkhof all represented the "static" strand in Dutch-American theology against which progressives were fighting. See Daane's *A Theology of Grace: An Inquiry into and Evaluation of Dr. C. Van Til's Doctrine of Common Grace* (Grand Rapids: Eerdmans, 1954).

Several biographies on Van Til's contemporaries shed helpful light on his life and times. In addition to the aforementioned works on Machen, see R. B., *A Prophet in the Land: Rienk Bouke Kuiper, Preacher, Theologian, Churchman* (Jordan Station, ON: Paideia, 1986). Rudolph Nelson argues that E. J. Carnell carved apologetic territory between Gordon Clark and Van Til in *The Making and Unmaking of an Evangelical Mind: The Case of Edward Carnell* (Cambridge: Cambridge University Press, 1987). Carl F. H. Henry includes passing references to Van Til in his *Confessions of a Theologian: An Autobiography* (Waco, TX: Word, 1986). In *W. Stanford Reid: An Evangelical Calvinist in the Academy* (Montreal: McGill-Queen's University Press, 2004), A. Donald MacLeod examines the influence that Van Til had (for good and ill) on Reid's life and work. Furthermore, MacLeod includes an extensive treatment of the Norman Shepherd controversy at Westminster Seminary. Readers should also take note of a new biography of Herman Hoeksema by Patrick Baskwell, *Herman Hoeksema: A Theological Biography* (Longwood, FL: Lulu Press, 2007).

Historical studies about the renaissance of American evangelicalism in the late twentieth century generally observe Van Til's leadership role, despite his personal reservations about the "New Evangelicalism." George Marsden records Van Til's influence in *Reforming Fundamentalism: Fuller Seminary and the New Evangelicalism* (Grand Rapids: Eerdmans, 1987). Mark Noll's 1984 survey of the Evangelical Theological Society reveals Van Til's shadow over members of that organization. See the appendix to his *Between Faith and Criticism: Evangelicals, Scholarship, and the Bible in America* (San Francisco: Harper & Row, 1986). Perhaps the greatest symbol of Van Til's role in shaping evangelical thought is his appearance on the cover of *Christianity Today* on December 30, 1977. Among the features in that issue is a warm tribute by his former student T. Grady Spires of Gordon College.

Van Til's relation to Roman Catholic biblical scholarship is recorded in William Shea, *The Lion and the Lamb: Evangelicals and Catholics in America* (New York: Oxford University Press, 2004), and Leonardo De Chirico, *Evangelical Theological Perspectives on Post-Vatican II Roman Catholicism* (New York: P. Lang, 2003).

As noted in chapter 7, Van Til was reluctant to publish reservations about Francis Schaeffer. He finally relented to many requests and produced *The Apologetic Methodology of Francis A. Schaeffer* (1970). A student of both men, William Edgar provides an analysis in "Two Christian Warriors: Cornelius Van Til and Francis A. Schaeffer Compared," *WTJ* 57 (1995): 57–80. Edgar engages in further comparison in his "Francis Schaeffer in the Public Square," found in J. Budziszewski, ed., *Evangelicals in the Public Square* (Grand Rapids: Baker, 2006).

Van Til's break with Dooyeweerd became public with Van Til's lengthy response to Dooyeweerd in *Jerusalem and Athens* (pp. 89–127). He later memorialized Dooyeweerd in "Herman Dooyeweerd (A Personal Tribute)," *WTJ* 39 (1977): 319–27. Analyses of the differences between these two philosophers are found in Robert D. Knudsen, "The Transcendental Perspective of Westminster's Apologetic," *WTJ* 48 (1986): 223–39, and K. Scott Oliphint, "Jerusalem and Athens Revisited," *WTJ* 49 (1987): 65–90.

Many works have studied Van Til's relationship with the theonomic movement. Van Til is prominently cited in R. J. Rushdoony's *Institutes of Biblical Law* (Nutley, NJ: Craig Press, 1973) and Greg L. Bahnsen's *Theonomy in Christian Ethics* (Nutley, NJ: Craig Press, 1977). Meredith G. Kline's review of Bahnsen's book was an effort to dislodge Van Til from theonomic conclusions, "Comments on an Old-New Error," *WTJ* 41 (1978): 172–89. A dispensational-based analysis of the differences between Van Til and theonomy is found in *Dominion Theology: Blessing or Curse? An Analysis of Christian Reconstruction*, by H. Wayne House and Thomas Ice (Portland: Multnomah, 1988). The faculties of Westminster Seminary, east and west, produced an anthology in which Van Til's relationship to theonomy was considered in *Theonomy: A Reformed Critique*, edited by Will Barker and W. Robert Godfrey (Grand Rapids: Zondervan, 1990). Gary North's colorful rejoinder,

Westminster's Confession: The Abandonment of Van Til's Legacy (Tyler, TX: Institute for Christian Economics, 1991), featured a portrait of Van Til torn in half on the cover. North himself took issue with Van Til's views of common grace in *Dominion and Common Grace: The Biblical Basis of Progress* (Tyler, TX: Institute for Christian Economics, 1987). In his article, "Van Til and Theonomic Ethics," in *Creator, Redeemer, and Consummator: A Festschrift for Meredith G. Kline*, edited by H. Griffith and J. R. Muether (Greenville, SC: Reformed Academic Press, 2000), T. David Gordon argues that the influence of Geerhardus Vos separates Van Til from theonomy.

Surveys of Christian apologetics in America differ on how to classify Van Til's work, and commentators construct a variety of taxonomies. Bernard Ramm places Van Til in the "revelational" camp, along with Augustine and E. J. Carnell, in his *Types of Apologetic Systems: An Introductory Study to the Christian Philosophy of Religion* (Wheaton: Van Kampen, 1953). In his second edition, Ramm replaces Van Til and Carnell with chapters on John Calvin and Abraham Kuyper in *Variety of Christian Apologetics* (Grand Rapids: Baker, 1961), acceding to reviewers who recommended that he focus on "classic examples of apologetics." In *Testing Christianity's Truth Claims: Approaches to Christian Apologetics* (Chicago: Moody, 1976), Gordon R. Lewis describes Van Til's position as "Biblical Authoritarianism," while Norman Geisler, in *Christian Apologetics* (Grand Rapids: Baker, 1976), classifies Van Til under "Fideism," along with Pascal, Kierkegaard, and Barth. James Emery White compares Van Til's approach to the approaches of Francis Schaeffer, Carl Henry, Donald Bloesch, and Millard Erickson in *What Is Truth?* (Nashville: Broadman & Holman, 1994). John Frame defends Van Til's presuppositional approach in *Five Views on Apologetics*, edited by Steven B. Gowan (Grand Rapids: Zondervan, 2000). Most recently Kenneth D. Boa and Robert M. Bowman Jr. identify Van Til in the "Reformed Apologetics" camp, along with Calvin, Dooyeweerd, Gordon Clark, and Alvin Plantinga, in *Faith Has Its Reasons: An Integrative Approach to Defending Christianity*, 2nd ed. (Colorado Springs: NavPress, 2005).

Among self-styled "friendly critics" of Van Til are American evangelical apologists such as Ronald Nash, who describes Van Til's apologetics as "pious nonsense" in *The Word of God and the Mind of Man* (Grand Rapids: Zondervan, 1982). In *Classical Apologetics: A Rational Defense of the Christian Faith and a Critique of Presuppositional Apologetics*, authors R. C. Sproul, John Gerstner, and Arthur Lindsley lament the rise of Van Til's thought as the majority opinion even while ironically dedicating the book to Van Til.

Curiously, Van Til is absent from many studies of postmodernism despite his anticipation of the postmodern turn and the emerging culture of interpretation. One exception is Calvin College philosopher James K. A. Smith, who suggests affinities between Van Til's apologetics and the emergence of radical orthodoxy in *Introducing Radical Orthodoxy: Mapping Out Post-Secular Theology* (Grand Rapids: Baker, 2004). See also Smith's *Who's Afraid of Postmodernism? Taking Derrida, Lyotard, and Foucault to Church* (Grand Rapids: Baker, 2006). In contrast, William Edgar sounds a note of Van Tilian skepticism toward postmodernism in his essay, "Turn! Turn! Turn!" in the aforementioned anthology, *Revelation and Reason*.

Index

Adams, Jay, 223
Afscheiding, 23–24, 26, 27, 28, 37, 45, 78, 87
Ahlstrom, Sydney E., 136
alcohol, 38, 106
Allis, O. T., 61, 75–76, 82, 87, 208
American Calvinism, Van Til on, 46, 119
American Council of Christian Churches, 106
Americanization, of Dutch-Reformed, 36–39
amillennialism, 218
analogical knowledge, 110–12, 116, 126, 178
antithesis
  and common grace, 25, 224
  in the Christian Reformed Church, 177
  Henry Van Til on, 155
  Hoeksema on, 174
  Kuyper on, 25–26, 187
  Schaeffer on, 199
  Van Til on, 55, 162, 166–68, 174
apologetic methodology, 16–17, 44, 113–14, 200, 235
archtypal and ectypal knowledge, 111–12
Aristotle, 120, 129, 130

Arminianism, 81, 86, 125, 138, 147, 184, 185, 234
Armstrong, William Park, 61
art, 154
"atom bomb" statement, 160–61, 170
Auburn Affirmation, 60, 62, 68, 70, 73, 123
Augustine, 53, 154, 232
autonomy, 129–30, 176, 183, 198–99, 217, 219, 237

Bahnsen, Greg, 217–19
Balthasar, Hans Urs von, 135
Barnhouse, Donald Grey, 188
Barthianism. *See* neo-orthodoxy
Barth, Karl, 19, 71, 109
  activism of, 125, 189
  American tour, 188–92
  as anti-Calvinist, 118
  Carl Henry on, 141
  Christology of, 123
  and Confession of 1967, 194–95
  on creation, 123
  death of, 191
  influence on Berkouwer, 145
  influence on Christian Reformed Church, 79, 172–73, 177

279

influence on Princeton Seminary, 74,
120, 121–22
response to Van Til, 135–36, 188,
190–91
on Scripture, 123
Bavinck, Herman, 27
on common grace, 152–53
influence on Berkouwer, 145
influence on Van Til, 44, 45, 56,
110–11, 115–16
Bavinck, J. H., 152
Beets, Henry, 38, 77, 119, 147
Belgic Confession, 21
Berkhof, Louis, 44, 51, 86, 98–99, 124,
142, 152, 153, 160, 173
Berkouwer, G. C., 129, 144–45, 172,
175, 177, 189, 202–3
Bible
authority of, 201
inerrancy of, 176
infallibility of, 183, 193–94
Bible Presbyterian Church, 108, 197,
219
biblical counseling, 223
biblical theology, 72, 215
Boer, Harry, 156, 159
Bolt, John, 152
Bonhoeffer, Dietrich, 196
Boonstra, Harry, 42
Borgman, William, 34
Boston University, 11, 170, 202
Bouma, Clarence, 74, 138, 150–51,
156–57, 159, 162
Bowman, A. A., 57, 172, 245n8
Bratt, James, 26, 161, 173
Bratt, John, 164
Bright, Bill, 225
Bromiley, Geoffrey W., 133–34
Brown, Harold O. J., 203
Brunner, Emil, 71, 74, 120, 122, 123–
24, 129, 141
Buber, Martin, 202
Bultmann, Rudolf, 196

Buswell, J. Oliver, 56, 82–83, 85–88,
101, 113, 141, 205, 213, 220, 222
on Vos, 248n60
Butler, Bishop Joseph, 56, 180, 198,
259n2
Butler University, 108

Calumet region (Indiana), 33, 36
Calvary Orthodox Presbyterian Church
(Glenside, PA), 215–16, 226
Calvin College and Seminary, 65, 79,
149, 151, 155, 182, 210, 231
during Van Til's student years, 42–46
Janssen controversy, 46–49
recognition of Van Til, 210–11
recruitment of Van Til, 98–99,
156–60
"Seminary situation," 155–60, 161
Calvin College Chimes, 42–44, 48–49, 51
Calvin Forum, 93, 150, 163–70, 173,
177
Calvin, John, 16, 18, 44, 53, 122, 154,
174, 178, 193, 232, 235–36
Calvin Preparatory School, 39
Campus Crusade for Christ, 225
Carnell, E. J., 126, 133, 138–40, 142,
183, 191–92, 260n36
Case for Calvinism, The (Van Til), 192
catechetical instruction, 58, 224–25
Chicago, 26, 28, 30–33, 36, 218
Christian Century, 120, 135, 136,
191–92, 194
Christian education, 80–81, 97–98,
117, 151, 166
Christianity and Barthianism (Van Til),
161, 188–90, 216, 230
Christianity and Idealism (Van Til),
171–72
Christianity and Liberalism (Machen),
52, 70, 124–25, 172, 189–90
Christianity Today (1930–49), 246n26
Christianity Today (1956–), 184, 186,
202, 210

Christian Reconstruction. *See* theonomy
Christian Reformed Church, 28, 210
  Americanization of, 36–39
  and biblical authority, 201
  fiftieth anniversary, 225
  and founding of Westminster, 65–67
  and Princeton Seminary, 67, 122,
    174, 178
  Van Til addresses Synod, 117
  Van Til's departure from, 77–79
  Van Til's ties to, 62, 65, 149, 177,
    187–88
Christian Theory of Knowledge (Van
  Til), 187
Christian University Association, 97
Christology, 123
Churchill, Robert, 153, 163
Clark, Gordon H., 16, 19, 56, 126,
    141, 177, 210
  criticism of Van Til, 109–12
  departure from OPC, 108
  influence on Carnell, 139
  ordination of, 98, 100–108
  presuppositionalism of, 113
  rationalism of, 112, 113, 127–28
  refusal to join Presbyterian Church in
    America, 251n55
  separatism of, 187, 201
Clark, R. Scott, 111–12
classical apologetics, 130, 132, 235
classical education, 98, 151
Cleveringa, A., 35
Clowney, Edmund, 72, 100, 195, 198,
    204, 219, 220, 221–23, 224
Columbia Theological Seminary, 75
"Committee of Nine," 96–97
Common Grace (Van Til), 50, 152–53
common grace. *See also* Kalamazoo
    Synod of 1924 (CRC)
  and antithesis, 224
  Daane on, 174
  Hoeksema on, 47, 49–50, 112
  Kuyper on, 25–26, 45

Rushdoony and North on, 218
  Van Til on, 92, 152–53, 162, 173–74
Confession of 1967, 194–96, 209
Conn, Harvie, 204, 223
consistency, 69–70, 200, 205, 234, 240,
    245n8
Consultation on Church Union, 196
controversy, 70, 234–36
Coray, Henry, 95, 215
corporate witness of the church, 238
cosmonomic philosophy, 147
covenant, 54, 80, 110, 202
  and creation, 55, 116, 128, 133
  and philosophy of history, 172
Covenant College, 83, 108, 182
Covenant Theological Seminary, 83
Craig, Samuel, 75
creation, 104, 123, 127–28, 132
  and covenant, 55, 116, 128, 133
Creator-creature distinction, 17, 101,
    102, 104, 110, 128, 132, 151, 171
Creator-creature relation, 110, 128
crisis theology, 120, 122. *See also*
    neo-orthodoxy
cultural analysis, 154–55, 197, 223
cultural transformation, 151, 199, 219

Daane, James, 98, 124, 156, 165, 170,
    173–75, 189, 201, 214, 237
Danhof, Henry, 47, 49–50
De Boer, Cecil, 163–65, 169, 170, 173,
    178
De Boer, Jesse, 163–65, 170, 178
Debrecan, 88–89
de Cock, Hendrik, 22–23, 28
Defense of the Faith, The (Van Til),
    113, 170–71, 187–88
DeKoster, Lester, 225
den Dulk, Gilbert, 161, 168, 179, 181
den Dulk, Jessie, 161, 179
den Dulk, Robert, 161
Dennison, Charles G., 15, 90, 230
De Reformatie, 153

determinism, 174, 175, 189
DeVelde, Everett, 89
DeWaard, John J., 49, 50, 57, 76, 131, 168, 179
Dewey, John, 81
DeWitt, John R., 46, 180
DeWolf, L. Harold, 192
dialectical theology, 120. *See also* neo-orthodoxy
Diepenhorst, I. A., 144
Dirkse, Theodore, 166
dispensationalism, 81–82, 87
Doleantie, 25–26, 27, 28, 37, 45, 78
Dooyeweerd, Herman, 114, 153, 197, 200, 216
   death of, 214
   Van Til's appreciation of, 146–47
   Van Til's concerns about, 175–77, 200, 202, 203, 205
Dordt College, 79, 182
Dortzbach, Elmer, 95
Dutch-American immigration, 23–24, 30–33, 36–39

Ebeling, Gerhard, 196
ecumenical movement, 183, 196
ecumenism, of Van Til, 187, 237–38
Edgar, William, 93, 199, 237
Edman, V. Raymond, 101
Eenigenburg, Elton M., 173
Eerdmans, William, 139
Eldersveld, Peter, 98–99
election, 174, 175
Enlightenment, 22, 24, 198, 203, 219, 234, 236–37
epistemology, 55
equal ultimacy, of election and reprobation, 174, 175
Erdman, Charles, 82
Ericson, Edward, 25
eschatological liberty, 87
eschatology, 131, 218
Eternity magazine, 188

evangelicalism
   and the OPC, 106–8
   reaction to Barth, 143–44
   Van Til on, 125, 136–44, 182–87
Evangelical Presbyterian Church (1956–65), 197
"Evangelicals and Catholics Together," 196
evidential apologetics, 16, 68, 181, 235
existentialism, 174
Eyres, Lawrence, 209

Faith Theological Seminary, 87, 197
Falwell, Jerry, 219
family visitation, 58
Ferber, Edna, 32
Ferré, Nels, 80
fideism, 127, 237
foundationalism, 181
Frame, John, 19, 72, 106–7, 191, 204, 219, 223, 228
Freeman, David, 77
freemasonry, 150, 163
free offer of the gospel, 103
Free University of Amsterdam, 27, 47, 109, 144, 146, 175, 214, 231
French Revolution, 22, 25
Fuchs, Ernst, 196
Fuller Theological Seminary, 139, 140, 141, 144, 182, 184, 202, 209
fundamentalism, 125, 126, 143–44, 182, 219
fundamentalist-modernist controversy, 120, 183

Gaffin, Richard B., Jr., 131, 135, 191, 205, 227–28
Galbraith, John, 225–26
gardening, 29, 93, 168
Geehan, E. R., 191, 202, 216
Geisler, Norman, 127
Gereformeerde Kerken in Nederland, 28, 153

Gereformeerde Kerken (Vrijgemaakt), 153
Gerstner, John H., 95, 126, 127, 195, 199–200, 235
Gilson, Étienne, 130
Gordon College, 98, 204
Gordon, T. David, 217
Graham, Billy, 184
Greek philosophy, 102, 127–28, 209
Greene, William Brenton, 59–60, 73
Griffiths, H. McAllister, 76, 77
Gritter, George, 158
Groningen, 22–23, 28, 31, 94
ground motives (Dooyeweerd), 146, 176
Guinness, Os, 180

Haitjema, Th. L., 135
Hakkenburg, Michael, 107
Hammond, Indiana, 32, 33, 36
Heerema, Edward, 89, 107
Hegel, G. W. F., 198
Heidegger, Martin, 196
Heidelberg Catechism, 22, 30, 177, 209, 238
Hendriksen, William, 112, 159, 160
Hendry, George S., 122, 191
Henry, Carl F. H., 125, 134, 138, 141–42, 186, 189, 205
Hepp, Valentine, 121, 152, 162
Hesselink, I. John, 225
Heyns, William, 44
Highland, Indiana, 34
Hills, John C., 99
Historie and *Geschichte*, 123
Hodge, Caspar Wister, 52, 55, 61, 72
Hodge, Charles, 55, 56, 86, 122, 233
Hoeksema, Herman, 42, 47, 49–50, 173–74, 177, 189
   on common grace, 152–53
   on Clark, 112
Homrighausen, E. G., 74, 122, 191
Hordern, William, 192
hospital visitations, 168, 215

Hughes, Philip Edgecumbe, 133, 164

idealism, 54, 57, 151, 164, 171–72
image of God, 128, 129
incomprehensibility of God, 102, 103–4, 109, 110–11, 125
Independent Board for Presbyterian Foreign Missions, 75, 82, 246n26
indifferentism, 68–69, 184
intellect, primacy of, 101–2
Intellectual Challenge of the Gospel, The (Van Til), 113, 132–34, 140, 144
International Council of Christian Churches, 137
InterVarsity, 180
irrationalism, 113, 127–28, 237
isolation, 36–37, 178, 187, 211, 225, 227

Jaarsma, Cornelius, 166
Jansma, Theodore, 99
Janssen, Ralph, 44, 46–47
Japan, 181
Jellema, William Henry, 45, 57, 141, 151, 159, 176, 213
Jerusalem and Athens (Van Til Festschrift), 202, 214, 216
Jewett, Paul King, 126, 202
Johnson, Douglas, 138
Johnson, Lyndon, 218
"Joint Declaration on the Doctrine of Justification," 196
justification controversy (Westminster Seminary), 221–23

Kalamazoo Synod of 1924 (CRC), 49–50, 112, 152, 174, 178
Kampen Theological School, 27, 45
Kant, Immanuel, 16, 129–30, 132, 143, 189, 193, 209
Kantzer, Kenneth, 186
Kelly, Alden, 80
Kierkegaard, Søren, 140, 189

Kirchliche Dogmatik (Barth), 121, 134, 172
kleine luyden, 23, 24
Kline, Meredith G., 203, 208, 217–18, 253n40
Klooster, Fred H., 92, 94, 109, 111, 155, 160, 201, 203
Klooster, Leona, 92, 93
Knudsen, Robert, 95, 203–4, 227
Kok, William, 78
Korea, 181
Kromminga, D. H., 112
Kucharsky, David, 210
Kuiper, B. K., 37
Kuiper, Henry J., 47, 86
Kuiper, R. B., 42, 76, 77, 161, 193
    on Janssen controversy, 48
    presidency of Calvin College, 71
    presidency of Calvin Seminary, 160
    retirement from Westminster Seminary, 156
    study at Princeton, 51
    at Westminster Seminary, 66, 67, 89, 169
Kuizenga, John E., 73, 74
Kuyper, Abraham
    on antithesis, 18, 151, 152, 187, 224
    on common grace, 152–53, 224
    and the Christian Reformed Church, 119–20, 178
    on culture, 154–55
    influence on Van Til, 44–46, 56, 235
    leadership in Netherlands, 23, 24–25
    and Machen, 78
    neo-Calvinism of, 25–26, 38, 131
    on Reformed boundaries, 37
    visit to North America, 26

law of contradiction, 140
Letham, Robert, 258n61
Lewis, C. S., 138, 238
liberalism. *See* modernism

Life magazine, 117
Lindsell, Harold, 202
Lindsley, Arthur, 127
Lutheran Church, Missouri Synod, 193–94
Lutheran News, 194
Luther, Martin, 193, 209

Macartney, Clarence, 75
Machen, J. Gresham, 169, 229–32
    on Barth, 120, 144, 231
    confessionalism of, 18
    death of, 84–85, 88, 89, 91, 230–31
    evidential apologetics of, 16, 68–71
    and founding of the Orthodox Presbyterian Church, 83
    and founding of Westminster Seminary, 61–63, 65–66
    as Kuyper of American Presbyterianism, 78
    on liberalism, 124–25, 189–90
    at Princeton Seminary, 52, 59–60
    trial and suspension of, 76–77
    Van Til on, 208, 209
Mackay, John A., 74, 122, 183
Mackenzie, Donald, 73–74
MacLeod, A. Donald, 126
MacRae, Allan, 68, 76, 86–88, 113, 138, 222
Maritain, Jacques, 130
Marsden, George, 125
Marsden, Robert, 158, 179, 208
Marty, Martin, 194
Masselink, William, 160, 162–63, 170
McCord, James, 193
McCosh, James, 57
McIntire, Carl, 86, 88, 108, 197, 219
Meeter, Henry, 91
Meeter, John, 62
mere Christianity, 238–39, 240
metanarrative, 237
Methodism, 37, 143, 170, 243n33
Mexico, 181

militance, 18, 43, 108, 117, 144, 196, 199, 201, 219, 228, 238–39
Miller, C. John, 198
Miller, Steven, 226
missionaries, 181
modernism, 130, 177
  and neo-orthodoxy, 122, 136, 192
Moes, Herman, 39, 42, 51
Monsma, Nicholas, 164
Montgomery, J. W., 216
Mouw, Richard, 180
multi-perspectivalism, 223
Munster, Indiana, 33, 36, 56, 59, 94, 169, 213, 240
Murray, John, 72, 85, 87, 94–95, 99, 100, 154
  on Buswell, 248n60
  on common grace, 152, 162
  death of, 212
  on Clark, 105, 106, 109
mystery, 110, 116
myth, 126

Nash, Ronald H., 113, 127, 180, 185, 201
National Association of Evangelicals, 137, 182
National Union of Christian Schools, 166
natural theology, 153
Nederlandse Hervormde Kerk, 22, 78
Nelson, Rudolph, 139
neo-Calvinism, 25–26, 38, 122, 131
neo-evangelicalism, 136–44, 182–83
neo-orthodoxy
  and evangelicalism, 183–85
  as liberalism, 136, 144
  and modernism, 143, 192
  in the Northern Presbyterian Church, 194–96
  in Van Til, 109–10, 126–27
Netherlands, 21–28, 201
neutrality, 130, 153, 155, 183

"New Evangelicalism" (Van Til), 182–86
new hermeneutic, 196
New Modernism, The (Van Til), 124–25, 127, 130, 131, 134, 135, 141, 144, 172, 188–89
New York Times, 62, 83, 93
Nicene Creed, 171
Nicole, Roger, 134
Niebuhr, Reinhold, 190
Northern Presbyterian Church, 108, 194, 230
North, Gary, 216–18, 235
nouthetic counseling, 223

Ockenga, Harold, 138, 182–83, 185, 209
old Princeton, 67–68, 117, 232–34
Oliphint, K. Scott, 57, 212
ontological Trinity, 54, 55
orange analogy (Schaeffer), 198
Orlebeke, Clifton J., 178
Orthodox Presbyterian Church, 76–79
  Book of Church Order, 216
  discontent within, 96, 103
  and evangelicalism, 106–8
  fiftieth anniversary, 225–26
  founding of, 83–84
  General Assembly, 89–90, 207–8
  merger talks, 199, 220–22, 225, 233
  non-American direction, 87, 230
  "Recommended Curriculum" for ministerial candidates, 200
  Reformed identity of, 97, 137
Otten, Herman, 194

Palmer, Edwin, 163
pantheism, 127–28
paradox, 126–27
Patton, Francis L., 68
Paul at Athens (Van Til), 133, 170
phenomenology, 202
Philadelphia Presbytery (OPC), 102–4

Phil-Mont Christian Academy, 117
Philosophia Reformata, 146, 227
Pighius, 174
Pinnock, Clark, 180, 216
Plantinga, Alvin, 55, 151
Plato, 129, 178
Plymouth Conference for the
    Advancement of Evangelical
    Scholarship, 138
politics, 154, 218–19
post-denominationalism, 240
postmillennialism, 218
postmodernism, 236–37
Potchefstroom University, South Africa,
    210
pragmatism, 54, 151
preaching, 42, 59, 214, 215, 236
predication, 132
premillennialism, 81–82, 87
Presbyterian Church in America, 221,
    222, 224, 251n55
Presbyterian Church in the USA, 76, 78
Presbyterian Church of America. *See*
    Orthodox Presbyterian Church
Presbyterian Constitutional Covenant
    Union, 75, 246n26
Presbyterian Guardian, 73–74, 84, 97,
    106, 123, 198, 224, 246n26
Presbyterian Lay Committee, 194
presuppositionalism, 113–14, 115, 140
    of Clark, 113
    of Frame, 223
    of Schaeffer, 197–98
Princeton Theological Seminary. *See
    also* old Princeton
    Barth's visit to, 190
    and the Christian Reformed Church,
        67, 122, 174, 178
    decline of, 231
    neo-orthodoxy at, 121–22
    Van Til's polemic against, 73–74, 120,
        209
    Van Til's studies at, 50–56

Van Til's teaching, 58–60, 66
Princeton University, 56–58
Prinsterer, Groen Van, 22
Protestantism, 238
Protestant Reformed Church, 50

Radius, Marian, 131
Ramm, Bernard, 125, 143, 183
Ramsey, John H., 169–70
Raschke, Carl, 236
rationalism, 112, 113, 127–28, 237
redemptive history, 129–30, 209, 218, 237
Reformed apologetics, 17, 113–14,
    200, 230
Reformed Church in America, 24, 28,
    48, 120
Reformed Church in the U.S., 177
Reformed Episcopal Church, 210
Reformed epistemology, 55, 80
Reformed Fellowship, 156
Reformed Journal, 155–56, 227
Reformed Presbyterian Church, Evan-
    gelical Synod, 86, 108, 197, 199,
    220–21
Reformed Presbyterian Church (General
    Synod), 108
Reformed scholasticism, 111
Reformed Theological Seminary, 182
Reid, William Stanford, 126
relativism, 199
reprobation, 174, 175
Republican Party, 154, 218
resurrection, 131
revelation, 129
Reymond, Robert, 109–10, 126
Rian, Edwin, 88–89, 96–97, 101, 103,
    108, 117
Ridderbos, S. J., 174
Ripon, California, 161, 168
Robinson, William Childs, 75
Roman Catholicism, Van Til on, 143,
    169–70, 234
Roosevelt, Franklin Delano, 130, 218

Runner, H. Evan, 99, 124–25
Rushdoony, Rousas J., 175, 216–18
Rutgers, William, 159, 160

Schaeffer, Francis, 113, 125, 197–99,
    205, 209, 219, 220–21, 227
Schilder, Klaas, 153, 155, 174, 177
Schleiermacher, Friedrich, 190
scholasticism, 44, 56, 130, 147
Scripture, Barth on, 123
secularism, 199, 203, 219
separatism, 183, 184, 187
Shea, William M., 143, 234
Shepherd, Norman, 175, 191, 221–23
skepticism, 111, 129
Skilton, John, 212, 226
Smedes, Lewis, 209
Smith, Wilbur, 115
Southern Presbyterian Church, 79, 108,
    120, 221
Speer, Robert, 76, 77
Spires, T. Grady, 202, 204
Spring Lake, Michigan, 58–59, 60–61,
    163
Sproul, R. C., 127
Stek, John H., 174
Stevenson, J. Ross, 59, 60
Stevenson, Mrs. Frank, 84
Stewart, John, 233
Stob, George, 49, 156, 159, 161
Stob, Henry, 153, 156, 160, 161, 165, 173
Stoker, Hendrik, 146–47, 214
Stonehouse, Ned B., 52, 62, 66, 69,
    102, 137, 142, 158, 160, 180
Stone Lectures (Kuyper), 26
Strimple, Robert, 222
Strong, Robert, 105–8, 116–17
Swierenga, Robert P., 23, 38
syllabi, of Van Til, 92, 93, 94
Synod of Dort, 22, 175

Taiwan, 181
Tanaka, Goji, 181

Ten Hoor, Foppe, 44, 45–46, 243n33
theodicy, 52–53
theonomy, 217–19
Thomas Aquinas, 56, 110, 130, 198
Thompson, Murray Forst, 96–97
Three Forms of Unity, 22
Tillich, Paul, 80, 193
Time magazine, 117, 186, 190, 192
Timmerman, John J., 42–43
Tipton, Lane, 258n61
tobacco, 38, 94
Torch and Trumpet, 156, 161, 163,
    176, 178, 201
Torrance, T. F., 133
Toward a Reformed Apologetics (Van
    Til), 211
transcendental apologetics, 114, 146,
    199, 200
Trinity, Van Til on, 171, 258n61
Trinity Christian College, 79, 182
truck farming, 33
two circles diagram, 116
Tyndale Lectures, 132, 169

unbelief, dialectical character of, 237
United Presbyterian Church in the
    U.S.A., 194–96
United Presbyterian Church of North
    America, 108, 187
University of Chicago, 46, 191, 194
University of Leiden, 24, 27
University of Pennsylvania, 176
Ursinus, Zachary, 177

Van Baalen, Jan Karel, 56
Van Til, Cornelius
    birth and childhood of, 28–30, 32–36
    education at Calvin College, 41–49
    education at Princeton Seminary,
        50–56
    wedding of, 56
    as pastor, 58–59, 214

as instructor at Princeton Seminary, 58–60
at Westminster Seminary, 65–76, 94–96
as visiting professor at Calvin Seminary, 156–61
retirement from Westminster, 203–4, 209, 220–24
death of, 226–28
on antithesis, 55, 162, 166–68, 174
as churchman, 185–86, 195, 214
on common grace, 92, 152–53, 162, 173–74
ecumenism of, 187, 237–38
Van Til, Earl (son), 61, 149, 159, 213
Van Til Hall (Westminster Seminary), 220
Van Til, Hendrik (brother), 31, 94
Van Til, Henry (nephew), 41, 94, 142, 154–55, 156, 180, 201
Van Til, Ite (father), 28–29, 30, 33, 34, 84–85, 94, 130
Van Til, Klazina (mother), 28, 94
Van Til, Nick (nephew), 128, 142, 182
Van Til, Reinder (brother), 31, 32, 34, 35, 49–50, 142–43
Van Til, Rena (wife), 35, 56, 58–59, 92, 94, 159, 169, 212–13, 216, 226
Van Til, Thelma (daughter-in-law), 92, 213
Verduin, Leonard, 165
Volbeda, Samuel, 44, 97, 159
Vollenhoven, D. H. Th., 146–47, 153, 214
Vos, Geerhardus, 72, 73, 215
  Buswell on, 248n60
  on covenant of works, 80
  death of, 131
  influence on Van Til, 18, 128, 129–30, 162, 172, 218
  at Princeton Seminary, 50, 52, 61

Warfield, B. B., 55, 132
  apologetics of, 68, 69–70, 71, 232
  on Calvinism, 26, 132, 185
  influence on Van Til, 56
Wells, David, 180
West, Alexander Fleming, 57
Western Theological Seminary (Holland, MI), 173, 225
Westminster Confession of Faith and Catechisms, 55, 80, 83–84, 171, 195, 215, 224
Westminster Seminary California, 161, 220
Westminster Theological Journal, 91–92, 101
Westminster Theological Seminary
  expansion of, 220
  founding of, 61–63
  influence on OPC, 103, 106
  and international Calvinism, 117, 224
  jubilee celebration, 223–24
  Van Til's estrangement from, 220–24
Wheaton College, 82, 100, 101, 107, 139, 186
White, William, 19, 95
Why I Believe in God (Van Til), 29, 99–100, 113, 126
Wilson, Robert Dick, 49, 51
Winona Lake School of Theology, 169
Wolterstorff, Nicholas, 151
Woodbridge, Charles J., 76, 81, 184, 185
Woolley, Paul, 75, 86, 95, 154, 156, 203, 209, 213, 214, 232
World Council of Churches, 196
worldview, 236

Young, E. J., 142, 159, 169, 203
Young, William, 174

Zylstra, Henry, 156